Peoples of a Sonoran Desert Oasis

Public Lands History

GENERAL EDITORS

Ruth M. Alexander
Adrian Howkins
Jared Orsi
Sarah Payne

Peoples of a Sonoran Desert Oasis

JARED ORSI

Recovering the Lost History and Culture of Quitobaquito

UNIVERSITY OF OKLAHOMA PRESS : NORMAN

Publication of this book is made possible through the generosity of Edith Kinney Gaylord.

Library of Congress Cataloging-in-Publication Data

Names: Orsi, Jared, 1970– author.
Title: Peoples of a Sonoran Desert oasis : recovering the lost history and culture of Quitobaquito / Jared Orsi.
Other titles: Recovering the lost history and culture of Quitobaquito | Public lands history ; . 6.
Description: Norman : University of Oklahoma Press [2023] | Series: Public lands history ; volume 6 | Includes bibliographical references and index. | Summary: "Tells the human history Quitobaquito, the second-largest oasis in the Sonoran Desert, which lies in the southwestern part of Organ Pipe Cactus National Monument, close to the US-Mexico border. Remnants of landscapes ancient and recent testify to Quitobaquito's once thriving communities, the expulsion of O'odham people, the erasure of their pasts, the remembering of their stories, and the role of the National Park Service in all of this"— Provided by publisher.
Identifiers: LCCN 2023005953 | ISBN 978-0-8061-9294-9 (hardcover) | ISBN 978-0-8061-9295-6 (paperback)
Subjects: LCSH: United States. National Park Service--Public relations. | Tohono O'odham Indians—History. | Quitobaquito Springs (Ariz.)—Ethnic relations. | Organ Pipe Cactus National Monument (Ariz.)—History. | BISAC: NATURE / Environmental Conservation & Protection | HISTORY / Indigenous Peoples in the Americas
Classification: LCC F817.O7 O75 2023 | DDC 979.177—dc23/eng/04/07/2023
LC record available at https://lccn.loc.gov/2023005953

Peoples of a Sonoran Desert Oasis: Recovering the Lost History and Culture of Quitobaquito is Volume 6 in the Public Lands History series.

The paper in this book meets the guidelines for permanence and durability of the Committee on Production Guidelines for Book Longevity of the Council on Library Resources, Inc. ∞

For Dad
with love and gratitude

CONTENTS

MAPS

ACKNOWLEDGMENTS

HISTORY IS A COLLABORATIVE ENTERPRISE, public history all the more so. In completing this project, I have benefited immensely from the support of family, friends, and colleagues—as well as generous people I barely know. Without them this book would have been impossible.

No one has played a bigger role in it than Ruth Alexander. We have met every two weeks or so since the summer of 2019 to discuss our book manuscripts, which were in process simultaneously. With her sharp mind and generous spirit, Ruth made our exchanges provocative, intellectually safe, and lots of fun. I came to rely on those conversations for constructive writing criticism, solutions to thorny research challenges, and accountability for deadlines. Her unflagging enthusiasm for this project saw me through the times when working on it was at its hardest. I could not ask for a better writing buddy.

I am also tremendously grateful to Mark Fiege for that conversation in my office in 2011 that planted the seed of this book; to Maren Bzdek, who encouraged me to take it on; to Lauren Kingston and Rijk Moräwe, who went far beyond their Park Service jobs to advise me along the way; to Richard Orsi, who read multiple drafts of chapters; to Ariel Schnee, my main partner at the Public Lands History Center, a mentor in doing oral history, and a congenial research travel companion; to Clarissa Trapp and Margaret Gentry, talented and dedicated graduate research assistants and now colleagues; to Amanda Hastings, mapmaker extraordinaire at Colorado State University's Geospatial Centroid; and to O'odham friends who shared with me their memories and stories, Lorraine Marquez Eiler, Jefford Francisco, Verlon Jose, and Marlene Vazquez.

Thank you to the many other folks who contributed to this project as well—archivists, museum professionals, current and former students, National Park Service staff, and all who provided a kindness, sent me a document, introduced me to someone, gave me an opportunity, suggested an idea, or otherwise helped this project along: Eric Bitner, Jim Bradford, Sean Buffington, Rachel Campbell,

Caitlyn Carrillo, Erika Castaño, Tyler Coleman, T. J. Ferguson, Connie Thompson Gibson, Kyle Greene, Sallie Hejl, Barbara Hoddy, Laura Hoff, Peter Holm, Maren Hopkins, Brenna Lissoway, Brandon Luedtke, Carrie Mardorf, Krista Muddle, Gary Nabhan, Steve Nash, Pat O'Brien, Jeff Pappas, Ami Pate, Graham Peck, Margaret Regan, Steven Rossi, Susan Ruff, Sue Rutman, Khaleel Saba, Seth Schermerhorn, Aidan Smith, Yufna Soldier Wolf, Bob Spude, Sardius Stalker, Scott Stonum, Sam Tamburro, Randy Thompson, Tim Tibbitts, Brenda Todd, Matt Vandzura, Sue Walter, Cory White, Mike Wilson, Emily Yost, and the students of History 492 Capstone Seminar, Colorado State University Fort Collins, Spring 2012.

I stand on the strong shoulders of scholars who have waded into this subject before me, including Donald Bahr, Peter Bennett, Bill Broyles, Jerome Greene, J. Brett Hill, Wilton Hoy, Brenna Lissoway, Gary Nabhan, Adrianne Rankin, Laura Alice Watt, Ofelia Zepeda, the authors of *Dry Borders*, and the authors of *A Natural History of the Sonoran Desert.* I am a beneficiary of their hard work and excellence.

Special thanks to Colorado State University Fort Collins colleagues, especially Tracy Brady, Leisl Carr Childers, Mike Childers, Derek Everett, Stephanie G'Schwind, Jessica Jackson, Sophia Linn, Ann Little, Sarah Payne, Ariel Schnee, Doug Sheflin, Dimitris Stevis, Adam Thomas, and Mary Van Buren, as well as still-valued former colleagues Thomas Cauvin, Mark Fiege, Judy Gaughan, Adrian Howkins, Prakash Kumar, and Janet Ore. During the course of this project, I have worked under three excellent department chairs, all of whom have supported this research; thank you to Robert Gudmestad, Diane Margolf, and Doug Yarrington.

Universities don't run without the hard work and talent of administrative professionals. Thank you to the many who have assisted me with communications, finance, travel, grant management, and numerous other services: Lisa Anaya, Catherine Coleman Cane, Jeff Dodge, Catherine Douras, Lorraine Dunn, Beth Etter, Lauren Lucio, Sherry McElwain, Jenna Milliman, Stacy Nick, Allison Pine, Nancy Rehe, Wes Scharf, Eden Trujillo, and Sharon Van Gorder.

In addition to Clarissa and Margaret, numerous students invested many hours on the project. They transcribed oral histories, conducted research, provided constructive criticism on drafts, and compiled bibliographies. I am grateful for the good work put in by Nolan Dahm, Logan Haas, Lauren Hennessey, Dillon Maxwell, Alex Miller, Corinne Neustadter, and Amber Scott.

This book was immensely improved by copyediting by Laurel Anderton and feedback from two expert reviewers, Lary Dilsaver and Thomas Sheridan, as well as by the staff at the University of Oklahoma Press, especially my editors, first Adam Kane and then Alessandra Jacobi Tamulevich.

Attending conferences and conducting research in Ajo, Arizona, was one of the great joys of the project. Thank you to Jay Brady of the Sonoran Desert Inn and Conference Center for hospitality, and to Aaron Cooper, director of the

International Sonoran Desert Alliance, for speaking invitations, use of ISDA facilities, and interviews with me about this book. And thanks to all of the ISDA staff and volunteers for making Ajo such a vibrant community.

Generous financial support came from the National Park Service and the CSU Department of History, College of Liberal Arts, and Office of the Vice President for Research. Large grants from the Henry Luce Foundation and the National Park Service's Southwest Border Resource Protection Program also supported related research. This book began with a research contract from the National Park Service. Thank you to the NPS for allowing me to use that research and to publish portions of the resulting book here. That permission does not imply an endorsement of this book by the National Park Service.

I am deeply grateful to my Fort Collins family, Jim and Nadine Hunt, Richard and Dolores Orsi, Peter Orsi, Rain and CJ Orsi, and, especially, Rebecca Orsi-Hunt, for support of this book and of me along the way. Thanks also to my Arizona family, Don and Suzie Orsi and Bertie Charboneau, for delightful visits on my research trips.

Finally, I wish to acknowledge an unpayable debt to the people who have lived and labored at Quitobaquito and in its vicinity. I am in particularly deep admiration and appreciation of the generations of indigenous peoples for whom the area has been, is, and always will be home. As I write this from my office at the Public Lands History Center on the campus of Colorado State University Fort Collins, I am keenly aware that I sit on land that the Arapaho, Cheyenne, and Ute peoples call home. And this book is about the Arizona and Sonora lands of the Akimel O'odham, Cocopah, Hia C'ed O'odham, Hopi, Maricopa, Quechan, Tohono O'odham, Yaqui, and Zuni peoples. For me, Quitobaquito's history has stimulated a fascinating intellectual journey, but for them it was life. They made the story. I hope to have honored them by attempting to tell a part of it.

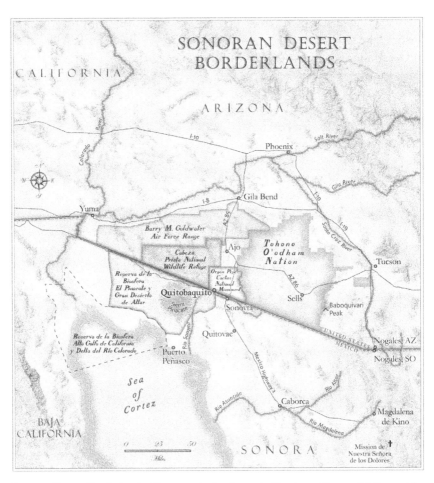

Sonoran Desert Borderlands. Cartography by Amanda Hastings, Geospatial Centroid, Colorado State University.

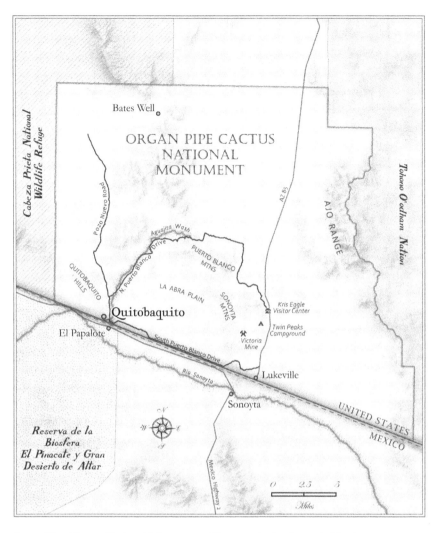

Organ Pipe Cactus National Monument. Cartography by Amanda Hastings, Geospatial Centroid, Colorado State University.

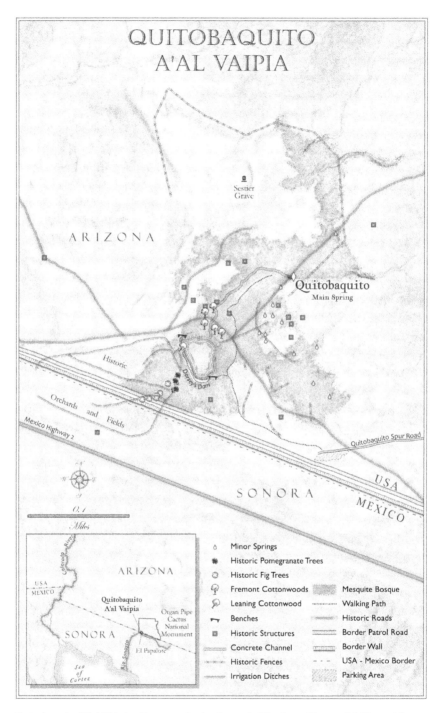

Quitobaquito/A'al Vaipia. Cartography by Amanda Hastings, Geospatial Centroid, Colorado State University.

INTRODUCTION | # Excluding, Erasing, and Persisting
The Making of Quitobaquito

A BUMPY FORTY-FIVE-MINUTE drive through the southern Arizona desert in Organ Pipe Cactus National Monument brings you to Quitobaquito, a small place with a bouncy name and big implications. Natural springs seep from the nearby hillside into a small pond, and greenery sprouts along its edges. Quitobaquito (*KEY-toe-bah-KEY-toe*) is rich both ecologically and historically, but from the dusty parking lot where you stand, that is not immediately obvious. No interpretive exhibits greet you, only a yellow and black sign warning, "Smuggling and/or illegal immigration are common in this area. . . . Please be aware of your surroundings at all times. . . . Dial 911 to report suspicious activity." A few hundred feet away, big rigs roar along Mexico's Carretera Federal Número 2 past shabby restaurants, truck stops, and shanties.

In 2019, when I began this book, US president Donald Trump started building a border wall. As I continued writing, the thirty-foot-high barrier to block people from entering the country from the south inched its way along the international boundary toward Quitobaquito, one panel of steel bollards at a time. By the time I finished, the structure had severed Quitobaquito from its historical regional connections and industrialized its ambience. Although not very evident beneath the towering wall, remnants of landscapes ancient and recent testify to Quitobaquito's once thriving communities, the expulsion of its people, the erasure of their pasts, the remembering of their stories, and the role of the National Park Service in all of this.

In skies far away and in the ground under your feet, something has been happening for millennia that makes Quitobaquito a spot of remarkable human activity and connectivity. Moisture rides air masses rising off the Pacific Ocean, and, if conditions are right, rain falls over La Abra Plain, across which you just drove. Located about half a mile east of Quitobaquito, the plain is an approximately one-hundred-square-mile alluvium-filled basin surrounded by hills and

Quitobaquito Pond, 2019. Photo by Jared Orsi.

abutting the Mexican border. For perhaps twelve to fifteen million years, water and wind have carried bits of rock from the mountains and deposited them on the plain, whose original floor now lies as much as a thousand feet beneath millennia of eroded sediment. For the last several thousand years, the rains have not come often, but when they do, they fall in torrents, filling Aguajita Wash, which runs along the west side of the basin. Almost as soon as the water arrives though, it is gone. The wash drains quickly to the Sonoyta River, in Mexico. Long ago in places like this, Sonoran Desert inhabitants diverted the precious floodwaters onto fields. The infrequent rains made agriculture chancy, but sometimes there was just enough moisture to coax a crop from the desert.

Quitobaquito, however, provided a little more opportunity. Whatever water does not run off La Abra Plain, the thirsty ground gulps up. Down through sand, silt, and gravel it seeps into saturated zones anywhere from twenty to one hundred feet below the surface, where it flows, only inches per year, along the southwestward tilt of the plain. Impermeable subterranean granite bedrock on the downhill side of the basin near the international border impedes the flow. Hydrologists are not certain whether the granite forestalls groundwater movement entirely or merely greatly delays it. Either way, most of the flow that has not been tapped by plants and transpired back into the atmosphere percolates through the permeable sediments and highly conductive fractured bedrock of the Quitobaquito Hills.[1]

Because of this combination of precipitation, topography, and subsurface geology, something very unusual occurs at the southern toe of the Quitobaquito

Quitobaquito Pond with border wall in background, 2022. Photo by Ariel Schnee. Used with permission.

Hills. There is year-round surface water. The groundwater gurgles to the surface through two perennial springs and several intermittent ones. Although their flow rate fluctuates, they are sufficient to fill a lagoon a little larger than half a football field. Because ancient rainfall seeps out there, Quitobaquito Springs—though not an otherwise notable spot—has been a botanical and zoological haven and a thoroughfare of human movement through the area for at least twelve thousand years. You are not the first one to walk here.

A Human Landscape

To explore Quitobaquito's lost landscapes, leave the unpaved parking lot. Stroll past the rectangular brown Park Service sign that reads simply "Quitobaquito" and head for that green bosque to the northwest. Impenetrable as it looks, you'll find a path that wends into the thicket and comes out on a miraculous scene. Emerald bulrushes and stately cottonwoods ring a blue pond. Waterfowl paddle and dive. With a little luck, you might glimpse a mud turtle or two in the shallows. If you know what to look for, there's a lot going on here, as well as some clues to interesting things that used to be present.

Take a seat on the wooden bench in front of you, a manifestation of the Park Service's desire to lure birders and other nature enthusiasts to the site. If you suspect that the southwest side of the pond looks a little too straight for nature to have made, however, you're right. Step over to it, and you'll discover that it's a human-made berm. A newcomer from Georgia named Dorsey mounded it up

Overlooking Quitobaquito, 2019. The pond sits within the densely vegetated area at the center of the photograph. A truck rumbles by behind it on Mexican Highway 2. Photo by Jared Orsi.

in the early 1860s to impound the flow of the springs. To your left, the stand of mesquite and other desert brush have choked out the remnants of an orchard once irrigated by pond water. To your right, you won't see a cottonwood leaning out over the pond, though in the decade before 2016, it gave park staff headaches as it threatened to collapse and rupture the dam, destroying a historical artifact and draining the pond where endangered Sonoran pupfish and mud turtles swim. In removing the cottonwood—after cutting shoots to preserve its genetic material—the park managed to preserve both natural and cultural resources.

Straight ahead, at the northwest end of the dam, you'll be standing in front of something else you can no longer see, the buildings, stone grinding mills, and automobiles of the Orozco homestead. From the 1880s to the 1950s, Luis Orozco and his descendants homesteaded at Quitobaquito on both sides of the border, digging wells, hunting game, cutting down trees, and irrigating crops. Although of Native descent, specifically Hia C'ed O'odham, the family has a Spanish surname that attests to the centuries of cultural mixing that took place around the region after the 1690s. In the late nineteenth and early twentieth centuries, many of Quitobaquito's Hia C'ed O'odham residents left to work for railroads and mines, but the Orozcos stayed, even after Organ Pipe Cactus National Monument was established around them in 1937. Hunting, farming, and other activities they had been engaging in for generations were now illegal inside the borders of the national monument and a source of irritation to Park

Orozco adobes. Stone grinding mill and ramadas nestled among cottonwoods and buildings belonging to the Orozco family. Burros were hitched to the millstone to grind wheat and other grains. When the buildings were razed by the Park Service in 1962, the millstone was saved and now sits outside the monument's visitor center. Courtesy of Western Archeological and Conservation Center, National Park Service, Organ Pipe Cactus National Monument, Catalog 15919.

Service officials, who tried to push the family out. The Orozco patriarch Jim appealed to a white old-timer friend, Tom Childs, who wrote to Arizona senator Carl Hayden. The senator brokered a compromise, and the government bought out the Orozco interests in 1959. Believing the old buildings of the Orozco compound to be incompatible with nature preservation, the Park Service bull-dozed them. Orozco family members and some of their relatives and neighbors are buried near the pond, and Hia C'ed O'odham who remember them live in Ajo, Gila Bend, Phoenix, and elsewhere, still seeking federal recognition of their existence as a people.

Sestier grave, 2022. The grave of French-born José Lorenzo Sestier, a Quitobaquito resident and shopkeeper, overlooks the pond. One of the few extant pieces of physical evidence testifying to the human occupation of the site, it has become an informal shrine, where visitors leave offerings of stones, coins, and other small objects. Photo by Ariel Schnee. Used with permission.

Continue north, away from the pond, up a small incline to a lone tombstone overlooking the oasis. It marks the grave of José Lorenzo Sestier, a French shopkeeper for miner and merchant Mikul Levy. Son of Jewish immigrants and university educated in Germany, Levy exported crops and ore from the region and imported tools, food, and other manufactured items from Mexico and the United States around the turn of the twentieth century. Sestier and Levy sold their wares to Hia C'ed O'odham, Tohono O'odham, Americans, Mexicans, and even to Chinese and Japanese migrants who evaded US Asian exclusion laws by entering Arizona through Sonora. At various points in the first half of the twentieth century, border inspectors also lived at the oasis, their job being to roust out the Asian wayfarers as well as to interdict the smuggling of cattle and alcohol across the border. Today's racial diversity and transborder violations are nothing new to these parts.

Head back toward the north side of the pond. As you get close, you'll have to make your way through a thicket. It's overgrown now, but this is the site of additional disappeared Orozco-era structures. The Hia C'ed O'odham who lived here built houses of sticks and grass. Early Euro-American visitors described a village at Quitobaquito, so it's also likely that at some points in history there was a cluster of such thatch houses. These would have included small huts set apart from the village, where women would seclude themselves during menstruation. There were probably playgrounds and places where men would gather to smoke and gamble. There may even have been a racetrack, for the O'odham were enthusiastic runners. Another type of traditional structure that Quitobaquito featured was the ramada. Made from cactus ribs, mesquite branches, and grass, ramadas resembled outdoor rooms with four corner posts and a roof, but no walls. Women such as Victoria León, for whom Levy named his Victoria Mine, sat under these simple structures while making baskets or grinding corn or cholla seeds. Under the shade of the ramada, women also enforced cultural norms by recalling the tragedies that befell young women who failed to isolate themselves during menstruation, thought too much about boys, or transgressed other O'odham taboos. Densely overgrown today, the area surrounding Quitobaquito was not a wilderness but actually an old garden. Here, for a long period, human beings tended their environment, using its abundance to construct spaces hospitable for their culture to flourish. Part human artifice and part natural bounty, sometimes segregated by gender, and always changing, the place you can no longer see here remains a primer for learning about indigenous cultures.

Your bushwhacking will bring you to a rivulet burbling through a concrete trench a few inches deep and several inches wide. In it swim thousands of tiny pupfish, officially designated as endangered by the US Fish and Wildlife Service. The Park Service has built them a home, carefully calibrated for size,

Victoria León. Mikul Levy named the lucrative Victoria Mine after this woman, who was part Mexican and part O'odham. Courtesy of Western Archeological and Conservation Center, National Park Service, Organ Pipe Cactus National Monument, Catalog 15919.

Historical artifacts, 2013. Trash scatters dating to the turn of the twentieth century, relics of a time when Quitobaquito was a populated place, can be seen in some areas near the pond. Photo by Clarissa Trapp. Used with permission.

temperature, and flow, to allow them to live and breed in their artificial habitat. From its mouth at the pond, follow the ditch upstream, pushing branches out of your face and falling nearly to your knees as you duck under others and come out onto a path. A few hundred feet up, there's a bog on the side of a hill, northeast of the pond. Mucky, overgrown, and hard to get a good visual angle on, though you'll try from different sides, this is the main spring that feeds the pond. The O'odham hold springs like this, as passages between the earth and the underworld and as sources of life-giving water, to be filled with living spirits. Quitobaquito Springs is one of the most sacred.[2] From this small orifice bubbles the water that makes the oasis and all its human stories possible.

You can circle back to your car along the east side of the oasis. As you step here and elsewhere at Quitobaquito, sense the depth of human time. Keep an eye out for rusted cans, wagon and ranch implement parts, and other items that date to the time of the Orozcos, Levy, León, and Sestier. Also know that scattered under the ground, perhaps even right beneath your feet, lie relics testifying to even older human presence. Near the northwest corner of the pond, archaeologist Bernard Fontana found objects as old as twelve thousand years.[3] Other archaeologists have found artifacts hundreds, even thousands of years old. Some originated as far away as Mesoamerica and hint at an ancient, far-flung commerce that linked Quitobaquito to cultures in Mexico. It is possible that some of the maize that seeded the first agriculture in what is now the US Southwest passed by here in the hands of traders, and that local elites displayed their wealth with imported copper bells and macaw feathers. The earth under the path, under the parking lot, under the steel bollards contains the evidence of those worlds. Even if you can't see it, know it is there.

Quitobaquito, then, is a lasagna of landscapes, one layered atop another. Landscapes like this entail not only the shape and features of the land but also their meanings. Landscapes are works of both nature and people. Inspired and constrained by their environmental context, people modify land in response to their values to make it more hospitable for their dreams. Landscapes, therefore, physically manifest a society's culture. Because culture and nature are both dynamic, so, too, are the landscapes they inspire, taking on new forms over time as people's aspirations and the environment each change. A landscape, then, is an artifact that expresses past interactions among what people made, what they thought, and their ever-changing environmental contexts. Landscapes also reflect contestation and power inequalities because some people have greater ability than others to turn their ideas into reality on the land.[4]

Over and over at Quitobaquito, for twelve thousand years, people have made landscapes. This has been true of indigenous peoples who lived in grass huts, homesteaded, irrigated, mined, and built railroads. It is also true of the Park Service, whose ideas about pupfish, cottonwoods, and birders can still be seen at the oasis, along with the agency's traditional partiality to places that appear peopleless. The border wall is yet another landscape feature built according to a particular set of hopes and fears. Quitobaquito, then, is an artifact that evolved from an ancient but ongoing social process of different people making landscape according to their aspirations and within the limits of what society and the environment allow them to accomplish. For a long time, however, the National Park Service managed the oasis's landscape as if it were devoid of people, as if the layers of landscapes did not exist. That is why Organ Pipe had to chase away the Orozcos in the 1950s and bulldoze their homestead. Quitobaquito therefore reveals not only the historical making of landscapes but their erasure as well.

Exclusion

On September 9, 2020, a Hia C'ed O'odham woman climbed into the bucket of a backhoe not far from Quitobaquito. Both the construction equipment and Amber Ortega were there because of the border wall—the backhoe to build it, Ortega to stop it. The wall, Ortega later said, "felt violent. It felt degrading. It felt like a continuation of the violence done to our people." She believed she had to defend her people and their land. She was also violating a legal safety closure order. Border Patrol agents and Park Service law enforcement asked her to leave. As an indigenous person on ancestral tribal land, she suggested they should leave. In a video taken of the incident, someone shouts, "This is

O'odham land, this is sacred area, this is where our ancestors are from. You do not have permission to be here. . . . We need you to cease and desist. Take your machines with you." The rangers arrested Ortega and a fellow protester, Nellie Jo David, also Hia C'ed, and drove them three hours to an Immigration and Customs Enforcement detention center. The two women endured shackles, strip searches, and verbal invective. They got no bed to sleep in that night and no phone until the next morning. Even after release, they were required to check in frequently, give video tours of their homes, and submit regular urine samples. They were prohibited from leaving the state. To escape this "living hell," David pled guilty and paid her $200 fine. But Ortega fought it. She was not a trespasser, she insisted. Rather, invoking the 1993 Religious Freedom Restoration Act, she maintained that she had acted under sincere religious conviction in defense of her people's sacred space. Her hearing took place in November 2021, and in January, she was acquitted.[5] So thoroughly invisible had Quitobaquito's past landscapes become that when remnants of them, such as the daughter of people who had lived there for thousands of years, showed up, they appeared to be interlopers. Quitobaquito, a rich palimpsest of landscapes, had become a place of erasure and exclusion.

The border wall has become the most visible manifestation of exclusion. Its objectives were partly to prevent people from crossing the border but also partly to enthuse Trump's most ardent supporters by signaling that poor, desperate people of color are not welcome in the United States. To expedite construction, the administration waived the 1990 Native American Graves Protection and Repatriation Act and other laws designed to protect the heritage of Ortega's ancestors and other indigenous peoples. This action evinced a national lack of concern for indigenous pasts and a long-standing comfort with erasing them. By extension, then, the wall is also a grand monument to define who belongs in the United States of America and who does not, and implicitly to mark the nation as white. To achieve these goals, the administration was willing to mow down saguaros, destroy subterranean archaeological treasures, disrupt the serenity of the pond, and desecrate places O'odham peoples hold sacred. And it arrested Amber Ortega, whose ancestors belonged at Quitobaquito, and jailed her in a facility intended for noncitizens who enter the country illegally. Troubling as this all is, it is not new. Exclusion is decades old at the park, and stories have excluded just as surely as walls. Here is one example.

About fifteen miles across the monument, on North Puerto Blanco Drive, after the visitor center, campground, and park administration buildings recede from your rearview mirror, a roadside interpretive marker commemorates the fiftieth anniversary of the 1964 Wilderness Act and notes that 97 percent of Organ Pipe is designated wilderness. "Wilderness: The Place of Our Past," it reads. With its invitation to hike, reconnect with nature, experience wonder, and enjoy beauty, the sign speaks to twenty-first-century visitors, mostly white and comparatively well off, who come to the park primarily seeking leisure. Against a backdrop of

Ramada. Picnic area on North Puerto Blanco Drive, 2013. The sign celebrates the fiftieth anniversary of the Wilderness Act, and the ramada that shades the picnic table resembles those built by O'odham people at Quitobaquito and throughout their homelands (also see fig. 4). The park has since replaced this ramada with a metal one. Photo by Jared Orsi.

a panoramic photo of vast, empty desert, the sign describes wilderness as "where the wild things live," an area "less traveled and uncultivated . . . away from the intrusions of human activity . . . a place to escape the civilized world." Although not its intent, the sign's effect is to encourage visitors to imagine "the Sonoran Desert wilderness as if you were the first to walk in this special place." The picnic site behind the sign has transformed the traditional O'odham structure of the ramada from an object that recalls where women like Victoria León worked into an amenity where picnickers sit in the shade, enjoy the view, and imagine themselves to be the first people ever to come there or ever to sit under a ramada.

Subtly, the sign tells a story. The story is about places of the past being wilderness, empty of people. Or if people were there, they were barely there—few in number, making no impact, leaving no trace of their existence long ago in the distant time. It is for the best that they are gone, the story implies, because human presence would spoil the nature, wonder, and beauty. It would shatter the illusion of fancying oneself to be the first to take in that view. The Wilderness Act and the sign sustain this narrative deception. They let you come, temporarily, to enjoy a place without people. The sign's story has no room for Sestier, Levy, José Juan Orozco, or Victoria León, no room for Amber Ortega or twenty-first-century Hia C'ed O'odham residents of Ajo and their childhood memories of visiting Quitobaquito with its cemetery, thatched huts, adobes, grinding mills, automobiles, and ramadas. Although preservation of human history, including modifications to the landscape, is not legally incompatible with the Wilderness Act, in this sign, people have been erased from the landscape to transform it to match modern ideas of a wilderness.

That is a problem. National parks are supposed to preserve history, not erase it. The Park Service's 1916 founding legislation included "historic objects" among the items it directed the new agency to conserve, and the executive order establishing Organ Pipe in 1937 declared a "public interest" in preserving the monument's "artifacts of historic and scientific interest."[6] Given this, there should be signs at Quitobaquito revealing its peopled past. Instead, the narrative of emptiness and peoplelessness of wilderness has swallowed the evidence that once marked human presence. Eventually, erasure and exclusion came to appear natural, so that today O'odham individuals pay fines for trespassing and white visitors imagine they are the first to set foot there. By erasing past peoples to facilitate exclusion, national park wilderness stories and the nation's desire to wall itself off from outsiders have reinforced the legitimacy of the removal of people in the first place.

Recovering Lost Landscapes

Therefore, this book casts national parks not only as places where people have engaged in recreation and preserved land but also as places where they have obscured and forgotten America's heritage as a colonial power. For many Americans, colonialism calls to mind images of patriots battling redcoats for liberty. If they dig a little deeper, Americans sometimes realize that the United States, too, has been a colonizer. They might think of corporations extracting natural resources overseas, the military suppressing independence in Cuba and the Philippines, or settlers taking land from American Indians. Historians have firmly linked colonialism to national parks, chronicling the expulsion of tribes and non-Native working people from protected areas and the criminalization of hunting and other subsistence activities.[7] But at Quitobaquito and many other places, a third phase of colonialism proceeded after the appropriation of land and resources, and it continues into the present. This form of colonialism exercises its power through cultural interpretation and by naturalizing exclusion. It expunges past stories and encourages visitors to think of themselves as the first people to have walked in the Sonoran Desert. It casts Amber Ortega as an intruder in her ancestors' home. This colonialism follows appropriation with erasure. It distorts evidence of past landscape making and relegates previous inhabitants to a distant, primitive past with minimal relevance to the present except as ancient curiosities. Sometimes, as in the case of the Orozcos, this lingering colonialism completely obliterates previous presence. By framing the oasis as a place to be preserved without people, the

Park Service also limited visitors' awareness of past occupants, the landscapes they made, and the legitimacy of their claims to those landscapes. It naturalized the absence of people from a landscape that had not been without inhabitants for many thousands of years. Though only a postage-stamp-sized bit of land, Quitobaquito reveals in one place the process of forgetting the nation's colonial residue. It historicizes how excluding and erasing—and, significantly, resistance to those things—played out on the landscape and in people's lives, and it illustrates the ways that the National Park Service has participated in denying the United States' role as a colonizing power.

This book, then, seeks first simply to recover those lost landscapes, to make them visible again and thus to demonstrate the distortion of history that came with their erasure (chapters 1–2). Second (chapters 3–5), the book illuminates the processes by which the mid-twentieth-century Park Service, embodying larger forces in American history, simplified those landscapes by removing their inhabitants and promulgating a narrative in which Quitobaquito had little past, but rather only an eternal present, frozen in time at an imaginary moment at which it had no inhabitants. Drawing borders on the land, the Park Service, sometimes in cooperation with other federal agencies, established a space within which it attempted to protect that bit of frozen time in perpetuity from external influences. Finally (chapter 6), the book examines the last quarter century, in which the nation as a whole and O'odham people specifically have reckoned with America's colonial heritage. Once again reflecting the aspirations of American society, Organ Pipe Cactus National Monument staff have embraced that process, working with the Tohono O'odham, Hia C'ed O'odham, and other indigenous peoples to enhance access and involve them in preservation. Recovering lost landscapes at Quitobaquito, then, reveals the process by which colonial legacies became embedded in national park landscapes and points to the possibility of remaking them to extinguish some of those legacies.

ONE | Becoming and Persisting in
an Impermanent World

The O'odham and Their Landscapes,
from the Beginning to 1821

UNDERSTANDING WHY AND HOW MUCH the National Park Service (NPS) transformed the landscape at Quitobaquito requires snapshots of the oasis before the
arrival of park rangers. This chapter provides part of that picture by retrieving
the oasis's indigenous landscapes from about twelve thousand years ago to the
early nineteenth century. The Hia C'ed O'odham term for Quitobaquito is A'al
Vaipia, meaning "little springs" or "little water." The Tohono O'odham have
named it similarly, A'al Waipia. Under any name, its early landscapes contrast
with the NPS's and bring into relief the changes that came later. They also exhibit
attributes of previous cultures that the park can strive to recover as it remakes
Quitobaquito today into a landscape that preserves and conveys the oasis's human
history.

It is, however, hard to know much about A'al Vaipia/Quitobaquito before the
nineteenth century. Written sources first appeared with the Spanish arrival in the
1690s but remained scant for another century and a half after that. To recover
prior landscapes, we need to conjecture from evidence from similar places that we
know more about. Additionally, we can employ a variety of disciplinary lenses.
For example, oral traditions of modern O'odham provide clues about the values
of their ancestors. Because people embed their aspirations in the landscapes they
build, these stories, which express their values, can help us conjecture the modifications they might have made to the environment at the oasis. The chapter
also employs the natural sciences, including geology, hydrology, climatology,
and dendrochronology, to capture the environment of the O'odham homelands
as it has changed over the long term. Anthropology, archaeology, and linguistics
provide insights into how various peoples lived in the Sonoran Desert and what

kinds of landscapes they might have built in response to their aspirations and their environment. Finally, the observations of Spanish colonizers offer the first written references to A'al Vaipia itself. Together, oral traditions, science, and historical documents sketch the landscapes the O'odham designed at A'al Vaipia to persist as a people over time despite the impermanence of history and nature.

A Brief History of the People

The first maker of landscapes at A'al Vaipia was Earth Doctor. Long ago, O'odham stories say, darkness lay on top of the water. As they rubbed each other in the first act of cosmic procreation, it sounded like ripples lapping at the edge of a pond. From this union was born Earth Doctor, the first being. He made the earth, but it was unstable. He formed it into a ball, stretched the darkness east, west, north, and south, and made a sky, but still the earth shook. Earth Doctor caused the sky and the earth to create Elder Brother, or I'itoi, and Coyote. I'itoi placed his hands on the earth to quiet it, but it would not be still. He became a mockingbird who spoke all the world's languages, but the earth still moved. Finally, I'itoi became a spider and spun a web, tying the earth to the sky. At last the earth remained still.[1]

Earth Doctor also made the sun and the moon, and all the plants and animals. He made the light, water, and stars, and the first woman and man. He changed Black Beetle and Rattlesnake and other animals, who were dissatisfied with their original forms. He determined which creatures would live in the forests, the mountains, and the desert. The People danced and sang to remake the world and ensure its stability, to make the corn grow, and to celebrate the metamorphosis of puberty when children turned into adults.[2]

I'itoi sang especially well. From far and wide, people called him to sing the songs to usher their daughters into adulthood. One day, he rolled up his sleeping mat and left his metate and sallied from his cave on Baboquivari Peak. He went north to the great river, to the land of an influential man, Siwani, to sing for the man's daughter, who was coming of age. The ceremony was to take place at a big pond. But Siwani became enraged with I'itoi and killed him. Later, some women fetching water found I'itoi's body and watched as he came back to life and sang his way into the east. This happened four times. After the fourth time, he remained dead for a long while. The people grew afraid of Siwani and did whatever he told them. One day, some children went to the pond to play. They met an old man. I'itoi had come back to life. After many travels, I'itoi came to a large village in the south. The chief sent two gopher boys into the earth to ask the People below to aid I'itoi. The earth opened and the People came forth. Siwani sent Coyote to find out how many people had come from below. Now Coyote had a special talent. Whenever he laughed at something, it changed. Seeing people streaming out of the earth, he laughed. In response, the earth closed, and no more came out. Already, though, there were many. I'itoi led them to the walled towns where Siwani lived. In an epic battle, Siwani and his allies were killed by I'itoi's army or driven far to the north or west. I'itoi's victorious followers, conquerors of Siwani, were the first O'odham. In gratitude, I'itoi gave them land. The People scattered and settled where it suited them. And Coyote, ashamed of having served Siwani, forever after feared that people would not like him and therefore always went around alone.[3]

This brief history is a composite of the many creation myths of the O'odham peoples. O'odham origin stories vary from village to village and teller to teller. Although they narrate consistent themes and roughly similar sequences, there is no single canonical telling, and the versions differ, sometimes substantially, in details, a testament to the general decentralization of O'odham culture. Archaeologists trace O'odham ancestral presence in Arizona and Sonora to at least early in the first century CE, though the O'odham evolved considerably through interactions with other groups over the next millennium and a half. Lack of corroborating sources and archaeological data prevents us from knowing exactly when they became a distinct people, but it happened sometime before the Spanish arrival in the late seventeenth century. The cultural coalescence these stories chronicle loosely describes events that probably took place in the fifteenth century. They have been recited for generations by skilled storytellers.

The foregoing rendition draws mostly from linguists Dean and Lucille Saxton, who relied primarily on the narration of native O'odham speaker and accomplished early twentieth-century anthropologist Juan Dolores, though I also borrow occasional elements from anthropologist Ruth Underhill and her anonymous O'odham informants, as well as from Pima storytellers of the 1920s, including William Blackwater and Thomas Vanyiko, and others from around the same period. Anthropologist Donald Bahr also synthesized O'odham stories in *The Short, Swift Time of Gods on Earth* based on the 1935 Pima (Akimel O'odham) rendition of Juan Smith and William Allison. Because of the stories' archaic language and their absence of words borrowed from the tongues of peoples with whom the O'odham have more recently come into contact, the Saxtons concluded that O'odham narratives have been told for at least several centuries. Moreover, the consistency of the accounts indicates a stable body of collective memory, whose details may vary but whose broad sequences and themes endure across generations. According to Bahr, the O'odham describe the act of narrating their origins with the phrase "to haul the rafter." The story is the rafter, the roof beam. To narrate it is to bring up an essential piece of the edifice of their culture, one that holds everything else together.[4] Old and durable, and linking storytelling with physical construction, oral traditions reveal much about what has mattered most to the O'odham past and present and the values with which they have built landscapes, including at A'al Vaipia.

In particular, the O'odham understood the world to be inherently unstable. It would not be still unless I'itoi as a spider ensnared it in his web. Corn would not grow unless people sang the proper songs. Dramatic transfigurations occurred at a mere laugh from Coyote. The world worked out well only when beings modified it and made it suitable for human life. In addition, boundaries of imagined categories were fluid. I'itoi became a spider; his sister was impregnated by a gopher and gave birth to human twins; a woman grew claws; a man became an eagle and married a woman who gave birth to human children. In O'odham stories the borders between deities, people, and animals were transmutable. So was the boundary between life and death. The People understood themselves as historical, as beings who first became and then evolved in response to momentous occurrences—floods, migrations, battles, and other events. Between an unstable earth, permeable boundaries, and the dynamic character of history, their world was one in flux. This contrasts with the worldview of the National Park Service and its historical intent to draw boundaries within which to preserve stasis in landscapes. In short, the People had little expectation of permanence. They understood all things, in the words of archaeologist J. Brett Hill, as being "in the process of becoming something else."[5] The landscapes they built at the edges of ponds like A'al Vaipia must have accommodated that.

Given the prevalence of water in the origin stories, the springs likely meant A'al Vaipia was inhabited, or at least frequented. Perhaps there was a large village there, like the southern chief's. Or perhaps it was simply a place from which women who lived elsewhere fetched water or where children came to play and sometimes encountered I'itoi. It would, of course, have been an excellent place to grow corn and sing the songs that made the stalks reach skyward. The people would have ground their corn with metates—everybody, including I'itoi, had these flat stones for mashing grain. A'al Vaipia might have been one of the places that suited the people who scattered in the aftermath of I'itoi's epic battle with Siwani, a piece of land they claimed as their reward for supporting the victorious creator. In ancient times, A'al Vaipia could have been a place where these dispersed people might have sung the puberty songs I'itoi taught them, thereby ensuring the propagation of their descendants spiritually, just as the water ensured it physically. Whatever temporary or permanent settlements they established at or near the oasis, Coyote likely hung around. Evolutionary biologists tell us the species became habituated to living near human beings all over North America.[6] Coyote's previous treachery in siding with Siwani, however, explains why he probably was a loner, lurking on the outskirts of the village, but not welcome inside it. Gophers, beetles, mockingbirds, spiders, and rattlesnakes lived nearby too. If the stories are right, from long ago A'al Vaipia was likely a place where people gathered, established society, intermingled easily with plants and animals, and made a landscape to suit their needs as they both changed and persisted over time. This tolerance for impermanence was highly adaptive in the land I'itoi had granted them.

Oasis in a Difficult Environment

A'al Vaipia is an oasis in a difficult environment. Even though it covers only about eight-tenths of an acre on the surface and averages only five feet deep, the pond is embedded in geologic and climatic systems of global scale. Between twenty million and forty million years ago, the western edge of the North American tectonic plate became attached to the Pacific oceanic plate and started moving to the northwest, stretching the land between what is now Arizona and the Pacific coast and creating a fault zone. The rock underneath the fault zone was superheated to a fluid state, while the material on top was brittle. The pull-apart action continued, and twelve million to fifteen million years ago the brittle crust shattered, with some pieces sinking into the fluid rock and others remaining on top. By about eight million years ago, the present landscape had formed, consisting of narrow parallel ranges of mountains trending northwest–southeast, with wider valleys in between. Since then, the valleys have filled with material eroded from the heights, often to depths of five thousand feet or more. This combination of geologic processes took place nowhere else in the world and resulted in today's unique Basin and Range Province of western North America. A'al Vaipia lies at the southeastern toe of one of the ranges, the Quitobaquito Hills.[7]

The oasis is also nested within global climatic systems. Over the last sixty-five million years or so, the area now occupied by the Sonoran Desert has varied from tropical forest to grasslands to desert thornscrub, sometimes oscillating back and forth among these, as earth's temperatures warmed or cooled or as mountain ranges arose to influence the movement of air masses. Its current climate stabilized about 4,500 years ago. Today, the earth absorbs heat at the equator, where warm air rises and moves away toward the poles. By about 30° north or south latitude, it has cooled enough to begin to sink, warming and drying as it does. On the western edge of continents, this tends to create relatively stable high-pressure systems that keep rain from entering the area except when the system weakens. Thus, on the western edge of every continent at 30° north and south, there is a desert. The Sonoran Desert is one of North America's four deserts, along with the Mojave, Chihuahuan, and Great Basin. The Sonoran Desert lies between approximately 23° and 35° north latitude and encompasses some one hundred thousand square miles spread over five different states (California and Arizona in the United States, and Baja California, Baja California Sur, and Sonora in Mexico). All seven of the world's major biomes, even sea and tundra, are present in or near the edges of the Sonoran Desert. At Organ Pipe and other parts of the northern Sonoran Desert, the global air circulation that desiccates the continents' western edges at 30° is intensified by a rain shadow, by which mountains to the west capture rain from moist Pacific air currents, leaving little to fall on inland regions.[8]

Three features of the Sonoran Desert have made it a difficult place to eke out a life. The most obvious is aridity. The region receives between three and fifteen inches of rain annually, with precipitation declining from east to west and from high to low elevation. Some places can go more than a year with only a trace of rain. But from the perspective of many desert inhabitants, it is the unpredictability of the rains more than the scarcity that distinguishes the desert. Whenever the high-pressure systems caused by sinking air from the equator break down, moist air from the Pacific can enter the desert. This tends to happen in a bimodal seasonal pattern, with torrential thunderstorms pounding the desert in the monsoon months between July and early September, and gentler, longer-lasting winter rains soaking the ground between late December and early March. But there are always exceptions. Monsoon rains might drench one valley and bypass another. In a wet year, precipitation can double, while a dry one can bring rainless days on end. Some places might get more than their annual average of rain in a single storm. Dendrochronology reveals this long-term variability. Severe drought at the end of the thirteenth century forced people to leave the northern Sonoran Desert almost entirely. The following century, however, was the wettest in two thousand years. After a wet seventeenth century, eighteenth-century drought persisted until the 1880s, followed by wet years and flooding. The decades after 1920 saw the driest quarter century in seven hundred years.

On top of all this are the temperature extremes. Since 1944, Organ Pipe Cactus National Monument headquarters has recorded temperatures ranging from 14° to 116° Fahrenheit. Lower temperatures have occurred atop the nearby Ajo Mountains and higher temperatures in the park's lower, western reaches, where Quitobaquito lies.[9] To survive in the Sonoran Desert, then, creatures need to develop ways to conserve water, endure both torrents and dry spells, abide the scorching sun, and tolerate occasional frosts. The law of the minimum, the ecological principle dictating that to survive, an organism must be able to endure its environment's worst circumstances, rules here. Conditions for existence in the Sonoran Desert are impermanent. All creatures must accommodate that.

Life has nevertheless flourished. The Sonoran Desert hosts 350 species of birds, 20 amphibians, 100 reptiles, 30 fish, and some 2,000 native plants, making it the richest desert in North America in biodiversity. Plants and animals take advantage of microclimates. North-facing slopes retain more moisture than south-facing ones. Desert shrubs and small trees shade miniature havens for smaller organisms. Many plant species exploit the riparian areas along the dry washes or the few perennial streams. More than 85 percent of the Sonoran Desert's animals depend on riparian habitats for some part of their life as well. Exposed rock absorbs winter sunlight and provides a frost-free refuge when nights dip below freezing. The ubiquitous thorns and prickles that arm many desert plants shade the parts that store water while minimizing the surface area through which water might transpire from the plant. Rock basins known as tinajas capture rainwater and store it for weeks or months at a time. And the cold, clear springs of oases foster pockets of biological profusion. Quitobaquito, for instance, hosts more than 271 vascular plants from 198 genera and 63 families. Despite constituting only 3.5 percent of the park's area, it is home to 45 percent of its flora.[10]

Staying Put and Moving About: *The First Peoples*

From the beginning, human life in the Sonoran Desert demanded innovation, adaptability, and opportunism to take advantage of abundance where and when it materialized. Based on artifacts identified by archaeologist Julian Hayden, the first women to fetch water at A'al Vaipia and the earliest children to play there may have done so as early as 8000 to 10,000 BCE, long before I'itoi called the O'odham out of the earth. Possibly, Hayden posited, people arrived there seventeen thousand to thirty-five thousand years ago as members of the so-called Malpais tradition, a still controversial theory. Agriculture evolved in southern Arizona perhaps sometime around 2100 BCE and by the first century CE gave rise to the society archaeologists call the Hohokam, which thrived into the fifteenth century. Their descendants (who were also possibly their conquerors) became the people who today call themselves the O'odham. Some of the early O'odham were sedentary and relied on agriculture. Others moved seasonally and supplemented their harvests with hunting and gathering. A final group moved much more frequently, doing very little farming. These first peoples responded to the difficult environment of the Sonoran Desert by building landscapes conducive to their adaptive strategies.[11]

Most peoples who have come to the Sonoran Desert have employed some combination of two basic strategies, staying put and moving about. The land does not provide all of life's necessities in any one place, even at an oasis like A'al Vaipia. To acquire the things they needed, not only to get by but to be well off, some people moved about, using or gathering the resources of one place for a time and then going someplace else to find different supplies. For at least twelve thousand years, mobility has been practiced by many peoples in the area, including but not limited to various precontact peoples, the protohistoric and early historic O'odham, horse-borne Apaches, nineteenth-century gold seekers en route to California mines, modern tourists, and international border crossers in the twenty-first century. Because it offered water, A'al Vaipia was always a good place for stopping, camping, resting, farming, and trading, a key stop on mobile peoples' rounds.

Another way to cope with desert scarcity is to stay put. People who stay put acquire sole control over a piece of land, extract more resources than they can use, and exchange the excess for goods that cannot be procured locally. Sedentary Native American peoples, missionaries, ranchers, farmers, miners, merchants, and the National Park Service are among those who have tried to stay put in the Sonoran Desert. Often people mix the strategies. A society might designate a few people to be mobile so that others might be sedentary. Explorers, for example, seek new places for settlement. Traders carry goods from one place to another. Surveyors or Border Patrol officers move along international lines to enforce the boundaries that facilitate landownership and state control over commerce. Gold seekers follow trails to the mines. Impoverished Central American communities send young males to work in the United States and send cash back home.

The archaeological record indicates that the strategy of staying put in these parts likely began with the advent of the Hohokam people. "Hohokam" is a term archaeologists use to designate a culture that appeared by 300 CE, possibly earlier. The name derives from the O'odham word "Huhugam," which means ancestors who are no longer here but did not disappear, a paradox that expresses the rich O'odham belief that they are the same people as the Huhugam but different from them—the same because they shared a language and culture; different because the O'odham were their conquerors. Near the confluence of the Gila and Salt Rivers and on the banks of their tributaries near modern Phoenix, the Hohokam built great agricultural landscapes. They diverted streams to fields through canals to grow corn and other crops. They erected substantial towns with multistory buildings, most famously the great houses at Casa Grande. In a good year, they could harvest two crops by tapping early-spring snowmelt runoff from rivers and late-summer monsoon rains. They were ruled centrally by the *sivanyi*, a class of priests believed to control the wind and rain, a significant source of power in a hydraulic society. Archaeologists initially conceptualized the Hohokam as a unified ethnic culture, with numerous regional variations resulting from diverse environmental conditions and different degrees of contact with surrounding people. More recently, scholars have considered the Hohokam as a regional system made up of different ethnicities linked through trade and other connections. This model posits a Hohokam hearth in the Salt and Gila River basins and understands places like A'al Vaipia to the south as peripheries. Some settlements show vestiges of mixed ethnic influence.[12] In any case, the hearth cities extended their influence over a far-flung region, over peoples of multiple ethnicities. The Hohokam invested heavily in their agricultural infrastructure and extracted intensively.

To facilitate the persistence of sedentary activities, the Hohokam also excelled in moving things around. Hohokam archaeological remains have been found throughout Organ Pipe Cactus National Monument, including several multi-component sites and segments of old trails at Quitobaquito. Shell debris and evidence of food-processing activity testify to ancient trade routes and indicate that the area now encompassed by Organ Pipe played an important role in regional commerce.[13] A network of travel corridors now called salt trails crisscrossed the monument, connecting A'al Vaipia and other nearby points to the Hohokam settlements to the north and providing conduits that reached far beyond Arizona. Remains near and along the paths suggest that traffic picked up considerably during the Classic Hohokam period around 1150–1450 CE. Passing by several Hohokam sites, one of the trails connected A'al Vaipia with the Bates Mountains to the north via several tinajas and other water sources. Two branches, one leading northeast to the Hohokam cities in the Salt River basin and one heading northwest to the Hohokam-Patayan villages on the Gila River, converged at Tjuni Ka:ak, a prehistoric crossroads near what is now called Bates Well in modern Organ Pipe Cactus National Monument. South from A'al Vaipia, trails ran across the Pinacate lava beds and continued to the Gulf of California.

These regional paths conveyed shells, salt, foodstuffs, and minerals such as obsidian, hematite, and limonite. Regional trails connected to others that led northeast to Chaco and other towns of the Four Corners area and south to Mesoamerica. Group-to-group trade carried maize to the greater Southwest no later than four thousand years ago.[14] Later, during the Classic Hohokam period, trade with Mesoamerica brought luxury items—pyrite mirrors, copper items, macaws, and possibly cacao. And then in the fifteenth century, for reasons that are still not definitively understood, the Hohokam ceased to be archaeologically identifiable.

It is here that the archaeological record intersects with the rafter, the group of creation narratives that hold the O'odham cultural edifice together even through social change. For a long time, archaeologists believed that the end of the ancient material record implied a collapse. In theory, a culture that bent nature to its will and left a substantial imprint on the landscape should have vanished only because it encountered some calamity. Archaeologists have cited the possibility of environmental, political, social, and nutritional upheavals to explain apparent disappearance. More recently, however, scholars have begun to pay greater attention to O'odham oral traditions and have detected more subtle explanations. Some archaeologists now believe that these stories, although metaphorical, may loosely recount history. "Hauling the rafter," the act of telling old stories, derives from an O'odham verb meaning "to make straight" or "to be in a line." Bahr believed this etymology indicates the intent of O'odham stories to relate a linear chronology. Further evincing the O'odham people's keen sense of history, tribal guides in 1775 gave their first recorded Spanish interlocutor a surprisingly accurate age of the great house ruins at Casa Grande, which had been constructed half a millennium before. Or consider the etymological similarities between "Siwani," the name of the strongman whom Elder Brother defeated, and the "sivanyi," the priests who ruled the Hohokam cities. Archaeologist Lynn S. Teague has argued that regional conflict between people the Hohokam tried to dominate and this class of priests who controlled the water might be stories about the causes of the disappearance of the Hohokam from the archaeological record. The epic battle between I'itoi and Siwani may very well be a manifestation of that conflict. If so, the O'odham may be descendants of both the rebels who defeated the centralized Hohokam polity and the Hohokam who adopted different ways of living in the region in the aftermath. Bahr has proposed that the Hohokam experienced internal warfare, sending defeated ones away to the north, per the rafter, while the ones who remained became the O'odham.[15]

Whatever transpired, we do know two things. The core of the precontact Hohokam civilization managed to flourish in the Sonoran Desert for a millennium by staying put and moving trade goods around to supplement what could not be found or farmed along southern Arizona's rivers. In addition, as possible rebels and descendants of the Hohokam, the O'odham peoples never again sought a centralized power structure. They developed a dispersed pattern of living in smaller, more numerous, more egalitarian, less tightly organized groupings than the Hohokam had, which required a different way of life, or, in O'odham parlance, a different *himdag*. And a different himdag implies different kinds of built landscapes. Gone were the large towns, elaborate buildings, and hydraulic engineering. According to several versions of the rafter, after the defeat of the sivanyi, the followers of I'itoi dispersed onto lands he allowed them to select as a reward for their loyalty. "Each village will talk a little differently," I'itoi told them, "but you will all understand one another."[16] The cultural differences among these groups were delineated primarily by geography. Although ethnically similar, they had no central political authority structure beyond the villages. Although modern O'odham and anthropologists divide these ancestors into eight or more groupings, they fit into three rough categories of landscape makers—One-Villagers, Two-Villagers, and No-Villagers, emerging over the next century or so in areas previously dominated by the Hohokam.

One-Villagers stayed put. They lived in small, dispersed villages lining the Gila, Santa Cruz, and other rivers, roughly in the former core areas of the Hohokam. Spaniards would later call them Pimas. They called themselves Akimel O'odham, or River People. They farmed the floodplains but with much more basic irrigation works and smaller towns than the Hohokam engineers had employed. Something as simple as a log thrown across the river was often enough to divert water onto their crops of maize, beans, and squash. In addition to two summer harvests, a winter crop was sometimes possible, but unreliable, because their plants were not resistant to the frosts that occasionally struck between October and April. In all, agriculture accounted for approximately 60 percent of their diet, and close to 100 percent in a good year. The group supplemented this through hunting, fishing, and gathering of mesquite beans, saguaro cactus fruit, and other wild plants, and by trading with neighbors. The abundance of their riparian environment enabled them to rely on a comparatively small number of food plants. In this way, they spread their subsistence among a variety of resources, rotated that dependence seasonally, and placed minimal demands on their environment.[17] This allowed them to meet their basic needs most of the time with a minimum of movement.

Two-Villagers moved about. Spaniards called them Papagos, a rendition of the term for "bean eaters" in their language. They called themselves the Tohono O'odham, or Desert People. They lived away from the rivers, alternating seasonally between mountain villages near permanent springs and the desert lowlands. In the wet summer months of July, August, and September, the Tohono O'odham practiced a type of agriculture known as *ak chin* farming, which entailed capturing floods from summer storms in small reservoirs at the mouths of washes and using the water to irrigate crops. In the version of the O'odham creation story that Juan Dolores told to the Saxtons, when Corn taught people to plant, he instructed them to "look for good ground at the arroyo mouths," where "the land is moist and soft." Plant there, Corn said, just before it is "about to rain." If the people sang the songs correctly, he promised, the maize would "come up and ripen well." In a good year, farming might yield as much as 45 percent of their food, though unpredictable precipitation was more often sufficient to produce only 17 to 25 percent. This required them to travel to acquire wild foods that grew elsewhere. In the winter, the Two-Villagers ascended to mountain villages, where tinajas and other wet spots trapped water. There they hunted game. Because they lived in a sparser environment than the riparian One-Villagers, the Two-Villagers journeyed farther in their hunting and gathering and employed a larger number of plants and animals. In hard times, they sometimes prevailed upon their One-Villager neighbors for assistance. This sometimes took the form of migrant labor—trading wild foods they had gathered in exchange for the right to farm a bit of riparian land, or trading field work for a share of the yield. Other exchange mechanisms involved wagering, in which visitors challenged sedentary villagers to a race or other contest with food being the prize. Gifting was common too, with those who lacked begging from those better off, incurring a reciprocal future obligation.[18] The Tohono O'odham beat the law of the minimum by spreading risk across a variety of strategies on the bet that not all would fail at once.

No-Villagers inhabited the least abundant area of any of the three O'odham peoples, and so they migrated the most. Spaniards called them Sand Papagos or Areneños, and they called themselves Hia C'ed O'odham, or Sand People. Centered in the volcanic Sierra Pinacate in the northwestern part of modern Sonora, their territory stretched from the Gulf of California to the Gila River and from the Ajo Mountains to the Gila Mountains in modern Yuma County. This territory lies at the dry western end of the Sonoran Desert's east–west precipitation gradient and at the low end of its elevation gradient. Most of it receives only five to ten inches of precipitation annually, and it is one of the hottest parts of North America. Much of it is covered by plants that provide little value as foodstuffs for humans. Quitobaquito and the entirety of Organ Pipe Cactus National Monument lie within this territory and the transition zone between the northern and eastern ranges of the Hia C'ed O'odham and the western perimeter of the Tohono O'odham. The Hia C'ed O'odham survived in this meager environment by movement. Investing little in permanent structures, they assembled grass houses, which, according to a later Hia C'ed elder, "could be taken down or taken with them when they moved on." They hunted mountain sheep, deer, pronghorn, small mammals, and lizards. They moved between temporary camps, gathering fish, shellfish, ocean mammals, shorebirds, and sea turtles at the Gulf of California and following the ripening of cactus fruit and

Areneños. Drawing of two Hia C'ed O'odham people by Arthur Schott, 1857. Originally appeared in *United States and Mexican Boundary Survey: Report of William H. Emory.* Courtesy of Wikimedia Commons.

other desert plants inland as they bloomed at different times and places. Some did a bit of farming at oases such as A'al Vaipia, and along the short perennial stretches of the Sonoyta River. They also traded with surrounding groups.[19]

Until the second half of the seventeenth century, this was the decentralized geography of the people who succeeded the Hohokam. Spanish population estimates are likely inaccurate, and in any case inconsistent, but it appears the territory they encountered at the end of the seventeenth century was highly populated, with perhaps around thirty thousand inhabitants. Just as I'itoi had said, the Hia C'ed, Tohono, and Akimel O'odham constituted three distinct peoples with overlapping himdags. Each village retained its full autonomy. The groups generally occupied different spaces, but with all three moving seasonally at least to some degree and responding to longer-term climatic shifts, the physical boundaries were hardly clear-cut. Quitobaquito, less than twenty miles west of the Ajos, which the Two-Villagers used, but not as far as the lava-crusted One-Villager lands to the southwest, may have fallen into one of the blurry borderlands and thus may have been used by both. The territory ranging roughly northeast from the Gulf of California to the Gila and Santa Cruz Rivers would come to be known as the Papaguería, or land of the Papagos, when people with a very different himdag arrived at the end of the century.[20]

A Clash of Himdags:
The Spaniards and the O'odham, 1687–1821

In October 1775, while traveling with the expedition of Spanish explorer Juan Bautista de Anza, Franciscan missionary Father Pedro Font became the first white man known to write down an O'odham rafter. Upon asking about the origins of the ruins of Casa Grande, Font learned from his informant that the great structure had been built some five centuries before by Bitter Man, who controlled rain and wind. Subsequent tellers repeated similar versions of the story into the twentieth century, suggesting their authenticity and endurance. Moreover, the story echoes the sivanyi's centralized authority through control of the weather, as well as references to periods of drought and bounty. The rafter Font heard thus resonates with archaeological, scientific, and folkloric stories of Hohokam rule. Font, however, dismissed it as "fables." (This from a man whose predecessors in the region quested for cities of gold and believed California was an island ruled by women.) A subsequent editor of his diary labeled the narrative "dreary rubbish" and did not bother translating it. Font himself laughed at his informant's "little yarn." The man declined to tell him any more of it.[21]

The man's story and Font's snickering capture the collisions of himdags that began to remake the landscape of A'al Vaipia and its surroundings in the eighteenth century. The priests, soldiers, settlers, ranchers, miners, and governors who came to the Papaguería all believed that civilized people stayed put. They aimed to do so in the Sonoran Desert and use the region as a stepping-stone to places beyond. As Spaniards tried to live out their vision amid the thornscrub of the Sonoran Desert, they built landscapes—literally raising rafters—to suit their purposes. Their incursion was yet another source of impermanence in the O'odham world and could not but influence the sons and daughters of I'itoi. They incorporated some of the change, while retaining the capacity to reject the impositions of the Spanish himdag, even sometimes violently, as Font would see at the end of his journey.

Although it is possible that the ill-starred companions of Álvar Núñez Cabeza de Vaca stumbled into or near the region in the 1530s, the first well-documented Spaniards in the Papaguería were a detachment from Francisco Vázquez de Coronado's expedition under the command of Melchior Díaz. On January 18, 1541, possibly within a dozen miles or so of A'al Vaipia, Díaz died of a wound resulting from an accident with his lance. Subsequent Spanish explorers found the area more promising, even essential to their aims. Colonial interest in the area quickened when the Jesuit priest Father Eusebio Kino came to northern Sonora in 1687 and founded Misión de Nuestra Señora de los Dolores on the Río Dolores, which would serve as his headquarters. Kino came to the northern Mexican frontier to evangelize Indians to Spanish ways of worshipping and living and to explore the land to facilitate further efforts at conversion. He built churches, established livestock, planted and irrigated crops, baptized, married, and buried.

Constantly on the go between the many settlements he founded and the lands he had not yet seen, he covered thousands of miles and encountered thousands of people. During the 1690s, Kino established numerous missions in the Altar, Magdalena, and Santa Cruz river valleys.

Between 1693 and 1706 he sought to prove that California was a peninsula, not an island, and to discover a land route by which Sonoran settlements could provision a mission system in California. On October 7, 1698, he and a party large enough to require some eighty pack animals hauled westward through a pass in the Ajo Mountains into what is today Organ Pipe Cactus National Monument. They continued south, across the modern international border to an O'odham village on the banks of the Sonoyta River that Kino called San Marcelo de Sonoídag. He and his companions camped there, a little east of the future town of Sonoyta, about thirteen miles east of A'al Vaipia. Kino praised the settlement's "abundant pasturage and water," irrigation canals, and fields of squash. His military escort Captain Juan Mateo Manje estimated that approximately eighty villagers lived there, twenty-four of whom Kino baptized that afternoon. He called it "a post very suitable for a great settlement."[22]

Indeed, Father Kino returned there twice annually during most of the next several years and worked hard to build it up. In 1699, he introduced thirty-six head of cattle and some horses with which, as Manje said, "to start a settlement." For Spaniards, the preexisting village of Sonoídag did not truly constitute a settlement until livestock grazed its pastures. Whenever Kino came by, the villagers streamed out along the road to greet him miles before he reached the village. They prepared a house for Kino and served him meat, wheat, maize, beans, and calabashes. There were a thousand souls in the vicinity, and even more farther away. Many of them gathered, undoubtedly including some from A'al Vaipia, to meet Kino on his visits. In 1701, Kino decided to haul his own kind of rafters. He ordered twelve small beams cut, likely from willows along the Río Sonoyta, and erected a church, which he named Nuestra Señora de Loreto, having just carried an icon of her for months across the Papaguería. By the following fall, he found it "roofed and well whitewashed" by the villagers. Kino next directed them to construct corrals and a new ditch for irrigating the ever-expanding fields and conveying water to the houses.[23]

The landscape Kino constructed at San Marcelo facilitated practice of the Spanish himdag. Spaniards liked to stay put. They drew boundaries around pieces of land and established exclusive access to resources within. The crown claimed sovereignty over vast swaths of continents, including the right to tax, regulate trade, command labor, employ violence, and exclude other peoples. It also granted parcels to missions, explorers, settlers, miners, and the military as well as to communities. Instead of surviving in the desert by spreading risk through mobility, tapping a wide variety of resources, and extracting the minimum needed to get by, Spaniards sought to establish ownership over fixed places and extract a surplus that could be exchanged with other peoples who extracted different resources from other fixed places. Sometimes ownership rights to land went to individuals or households. In many cases, however, the rights were communal. Persons or families could claim usufruct rights to lands held in common for grazing, hunting, timber, and other uses. In all of these cases, the Spanish himdag implied staying put within defined boundaries and then forming connections to other places.

San Marcelo de Sonoídag became a base camp to which Kino and his companions returned semiannually to rest and reprovision, slaughter some livestock for meat to consume on their journey, and then continue their exploration to support, as Manje put it, the "discovery of lands and tribes to the north, and also for the support of the fathers of California." Corrals, domestic animals, and the whitewashed walls and rafters of the church made the place familiar and comfortable for them. As Kino wrote in 1701, "It was a great relief to all and a great comfort . . . that in a country so far inland we should find this refreshment." In 1702, Kino boasted to his superior that the areas he had explored now contained five priests, five missions, 3,500 head of cattle, acres of wheat, maize, and beans, and as many varieties of "vegetables, garden products, and fruit trees as in Europe." There were vineyards, pack trains, oxen, level roads, abundant pastures, timber, and minerals. From this landscape, he observed, "it will be possible to trade by sea and land with other near-by and remote provinces," including New Mexico, New Spain, and New France, and from there to reach Europe, Japan, and China.[24] A few miles from A'al Vaipia, San Marcelo de Sonoídag anchored the global Spanish empire in a remote locale.

Staying put sparked conflict, however. Although the date is not known, Apaches had migrated to the eastern rim of the Papaguería, probably sometime between when I'itoi led the O'odham against the sivanyi and when the Spaniards arrived. Although some Ndee, as they called themselves, farmed during the summers in the mountains, they generally relied on hunting and gathering. In fact, one of the O'odham names of the nomadic Hia C'ed O'odham was *S-o:bmakam*, Apache-like people. Although the label has had derogatory connotations, some Hia C'ed O'odham today reinterpret it proudly, emphasizing the common historical mobility of the two groups. Construed this way, linguist Ofelia Zepeda acknowledged, it is a very apt description of the two groups' ecological strategies. By the late eighteenth century, the Apaches had acquired horses, and the Spanish and One-Villager settlements provided a strong attractant. Raiding sedentary agricultural communities became a calculated ecological strategy to extend the Apache resource base. Raiders targeted livestock, produce, tools, and other items useful for thriving in the Sonoran Desert. The first documented military confrontation between O'odham and Apaches occurred in 1694. Thereafter, O'odham and Spaniards often allied against their common enemy, resulting in retaliations and counterretaliations that escalated into episodic warfare over much of the eighteenth century.[25]

The scant detail of Spanish journals makes it difficult to know precisely what effect all this had on Quitobaquito. At the time, A'al Vaipia was one of several wet spots along the Río Sonoyta. Although farms today suck the river nearly dry by pumping groundwater, Kino and other explorers of his era indicated that it flowed aboveground most or all of the way to the sea. On his first visit to the river, he remarked on its many *carrizales* (fields of reeds) and *tulares* (fields of bulrushes), both indicating well-watered places. Ducks and birds alighted in the marshes, and there was "excellent pasturage for the cattle." Kino first came to A'al Vaipia on the afternoon of October 7, 1698, and named it San Serguio, honoring the saint whose feast day it was, and referred to is as "the good place." To lighten his load the next morning, Kino left some baggage and mules in the care of the San Serguio denizens and continued along the Sonoyta River to the sea. Upon returning two days later, he was pleased to see that the "loyal natives had taken care of everything very well." Although he passed by it repeatedly over the next several years, Kino made only one additional reference to it. In October 1700, he mentioned receiving "good refreshments" from the people of an unnamed village west of San Marcelo, probably A'al Vaipia. He "spoke the word of God" and baptized three adults, whom he christened Ygnacio, Francisco Xavier, and Francisco de Borja. Two leaders from the village accompanied him to Nuestra Señora de los Dolores.[26]

Spanish explorers rarely returned to this "good place," with its marsh, ducks, good pasturage, and trustworthy locals. Perhaps, because there were other watering places along the south-bank trail they usually followed, they declined crossing the arroyo to the north side. A'al Vaipia was only a half-day's journey from San Marcelo, an inconvenient overnight camp for sojourners eager to make tracks. Or was it, as some scholars have surmised, because Native guides conducted them away from the populated village? A third, intriguing possibility is that A'al Vaipia lay in an ecological and cultural borderland that Kino and his compatriots did not quite know how to use. Kino found Sonoídag, with its greenery, fruitful fields, irrigation works, fat cattle, whitewashed church walls, and friendly, industrious Natives, a comfortable place. Because the village was larger than Hia C'ed O'odham settlements, but scores of miles from the usual haunts of the Akimel O'odham, it seems likely that these people were Tohono O'odham who stayed put more than usual because of the river. Villages to the west, however, even well-watered ones like A'al Vaipia, received less favorable ratings. Manje repeatedly described inhabitants west of San Marcelo derisively with phrases such as "naked Indians, very poor, who sustained themselves with roots, locusts and wild fruits." He did not identify what they called themselves or give their place a saint's name. Kino often failed to mention the people at all. These Natives, whom the Spaniards so easily dismissed, were probably the No-Villagers, the Hia C'ed O'odham. At the time, the always blurry boundary between semisedentary and fully nomadic peoples of the Papaguería may have fallen somewhere in the thirteen miles between San Marcelo and A'al Vaipia. The oasis and lands west were not culturally or ecologically conducive to building landscapes suitable to staying put. The Hia C'ed O'odham accepted this, so they rejected Manje's 1694 suggestion that they resettle "on some river with more fertile lands . . . , where it would be possible to send them a priest."[27] So did the Jesuits, who never founded a fixed settlement in the vast Papaguería north and west of San Marcelo.

Spanish failure to settle beyond the vicinity of A'al Vaipia indicated that, at the end of the eighteenth century, naked people still called most of the shots in the Papaguería. For several decades after Kino died in 1711, Jesuit priests superintended San Marcelo. In the long run, however, the Spaniards' himdag was not well suited to the Sonoran Desert. Missionaries had to build churches from adobe instead of stone, which European parishes favored, and the structures' roofs were flat instead of arched. Iffy experiments with growing Old World wheat often gave way to fields of New World corn, which was better adapted to the locale ecologically. Sometimes hunger drove the colonizers to hunt feral cattle, as the Apaches and O'odham did, or to gather useful wild plants. Such "hybrid spaces," as historian Samuel Truett has called them, revealed the degree to which the environment demanded concessions of the Spaniards even as they modified landscapes with the hope of re-creating European comforts.[28]

Indigenous peoples, too, thwarted Spanish aspirations. Apache raiding drove settlers to abandon the countryside for the safety of presidios at Tubac and Tucson. Other times the would-be colonizers simply retreated south, abandoning all they had invested in remaking the landscape. Even the O'odham, whom Kino described as so kindly, fiercely resisted Spanish evangelizing as early as 1695. Frustrated by rigid mission life, military abuse, and other transgressions, they attacked missions and other settlements across the Papaguería in November 1751. Although the Spaniards regained control by March 1752, more than a hundred of them fled south to Mexico, while a hundred more, including many priests, were killed.[29] Among the dead was Father Henry Ruen, rector at San Marcelo.

Missionary efforts in the Papaguería never quite regained their footing in the aftermath. Political rivalries in Europe led the crown to expel the Jesuits from the Americas in 1767, and the Franciscans, who replaced them, concentrated their evangelizing energies instead along the California coast. The ongoing search for a route to California brought Father Font and the Anza party past Casa Grande in 1775. On their return from the coast, they stopped at Sonoídag, where they found the ruins of Kino's Loreto church, burned in 1751, and a white cross at the foot of a saguaro cactus marking the grave of Ruen. The party paused briefly to pan for gold, but finding none and seeing only twenty O'odham, the party hurried on to a better campsite. San Marcelo de Sonoídag was no longer a place where Spaniards wanted to stay put. Nor was it a stepping-stone to empire. Passing that day by a site that was likely A'al Vaipia, Font described it merely as "some deserted little huts."[30]

Actually, it was probably not deserted. To the Spaniards, who invested heavily in staying put with ditches, corrals, and whitewashed churches, unoccupied was the same as abandoned. To the O'odham, however, empty did not necessarily

María "Chona" Encarnación, ca. 1930s. Photo by Ruth M. Underhill. Courtesy of Denver Museum of Nature and Science, Underhill Collection.

mean deserted. To a person who has many villages, the fact that they are in one does not imply they have abandoned the others. Instead, their absence when Font passed by more likely reflected a landscape that the People had designed to permit moving about. By attempting to build a landscape in which to stay put, the Spaniards changed some things for the O'odham. Much else, however, persisted, including the Natives' movement through a landscape they had built to accommodate impermanence.

Through a Native Lens

Font's travel accounts are the last written records of Quitobaquito prior to the 1850s. There are, however, descriptions of places like it. In 1933, a ninety-year-old Tohono O'odham woman named Chona gave an oral history to the anthropologist Ruth Murray Underhill. Chona's own memory stretched back to the 1840s, and she also knew stories from her parents and grandparents. Like many O'odham memoirs, her narrative shows great concern for the ways of distant ancestors.[31] Her account describes traditions that she perceived to be quite ancient and thus can take us back generations and provide hazy glimpses of a time before Font passed by the deserted huts near Quitobaquito and even before Kino stopped at the good place. Chona grew up in the village of Mesquite Root, at the base of the Quijotoa Mountains, roughly sixty miles northeast of A'al Vaipia, and inside the present boundaries of today's Tohono O'odham Nation. Although she never visited the oasis, she knew places like it, and her travels ranged widely across the Papaguería. Her observations can help us conjecture about the landscape at A'al Vaipia between Font's passing by and the end of Spanish rule in North America in 1821. The Spaniards had thought of the Papaguería as mostly empty, worthless space dotted with discrete, fixed places at which to farm, mine, ranch, or baptize. Chona, in contrast, conceived of her world as a ring of concentric circles radiating outward—her house, her village, her people's homeland, and beyond. A'al Vaipia was surely embedded in such a world. This O'odham organization of space and movement through it persisted during the century and a half of Spanish colonization and enabled the People to absorb their encounter with the Spaniards while remaining separate, independent, and always in the process of becoming.

In the long sweep of O'odham history, the Spanish incursion was yet another case of impermanence. Like the periods of drought, flood, frost, or heat, or like the epic battle against the sivanyi, it was another turn of dynamic history to which the People responded. Chona's life marked the legacy of Spanish colonization's influence on O'odham life. Her community kept livestock, for example. They also ate wheat, an Old World crop, and traded for cloth from Mexico. Her full Spanish name, María Encarnación, indicates cultural and probably genetic interchange among her people and Spaniards and Mexicans. When her first child was born, she went to the medicine man to be ritually cleansed, but she and her husband also took the infant to a priest to be baptized. They did this, she recalled, because "we were modern." And when her father, José María, died, the burial combined O'odham and Roman Catholic rituals. "We did not bury him in a cave . . . as our people used to," she told Underhill. Instead, they dug a grave, as they had learned from Mexican priests. Into it they placed his "blanket and pillow" instead of his mat, "because we did not sleep on mats any more." Given the common Spanish and O'odham military alliances, perhaps the most Hispanicized thing about her was the fear of Apaches that pervaded her life. She described her community's numerous conflicts with their mounted rivals, including a harrowing story in which three Apaches chased Chona and her husband after the couple had journeyed alone to pick figs in Mexico.[32] The bulk of her narrative, however, emphasized Native cultural traits that persisted.

Chona began her interview by talking about her childhood house. She and her family lived in a round grass hut, not unlike ones in historical photographs of Quitobaquito. In the mornings, when the light hairs of I'itoi were just visible on the eastern horizon, she awoke to her father's commands to his children. Boys, go out and run so you will be swift in war. Girls, get up and grind corn to feed men who fight the enemy. The house ensured safety from the highly charged world outside. Once, when her father returned from a raid on the Apaches, in which he had killed a man, he was full of power, too powerful to see his children. It might have made them sick. They stayed inside the house with their grandmother while their parents each went to separate huts until he was purified. Later, he took a doll made of an Apache's hair and ceremonially adopted it as his child and invited it into the house. He passed it around to his wife and children, each of whom did the same. It lived in their hut thereafter, and it was a helper to the family.[33] The family's grass hut was impermanent, an appropriately low investment of labor in a place that might or might not harbor people for very long. For a child who recalled morning rituals, her father's advice, and the safety of remaining with her grandmother, and who learned that even the boundary between O'odham and Apache could be permeable, Chona's house of grass and branches was a place that enabled reproduction of culture across generations.

Many huts together made up the village. Chona called Mesquite Root "a good place," the same phrase that Father Kino had applied to A'al Vaipia. To both of them, the term connoted a location near things they valued. Mesquite Root was near a seasonal wash flanked by fields, the kind of setting that Corn had recommended to the People long before. As they had for generations prior to the Spanish arrival, her people sang to make the crops grow. In addition, prickly pears, a staple of the O'odham diet, grew thick nearby, never more than four steps apart. There were birds and rabbits, cholla nuts, ironwood and mes-quite trees, and a pond.[34]

Besides access to material abundance, the village landscape perpetuated social relations. Considered "dangerous" and capable of sapping the strength of men around them, menstruating women retreated to a small grass hut that Chona called "the Little House." When she was an adult, her hut lay across a gully that ran behind her house. Some spots in the village were reserved for men to gamble, smoke, discuss how to ready boys and girls for war, and make col-lective decisions—there being no higher political authority in the decentralized O'odham world than the village. Other spaces were women's domain. Under ramadas, not unlike the ones at A'al Vaipia, women told stories while they wove baskets or ground corn or cholla seeds into flour. The stories were didactic and enforced cultural norms. According to one, a woman who started menstruat-ing but did not tell anyone or go to her Little House was struck by lightning. Others warned that girls who thought too much about boys risked having a snake come and make love to them. Both sets of spaces maintained gender traditions. Still other spots were ambiguously gendered. One of Chona's first husband's siblings, Shining Evening, possessed a feminine spirit inside a man's body. Chona used both male and female pronouns to refer to them and called them a "man-woman." Shining Evening lived in their own hut and typically joined the women in work, but Chona appreciated the physical strength that Shining Evening brought to the more demanding female tasks such as hauling full baskets or grinding corn at the metate.[35]

The villagers cleared still other places for a racetrack. Racing was a popular sport, and both men and women participated enthusiastically. Chona loved to race and once won a girdle, a red dress, and a Mexican scarf from a competitor less swift afoot. The racetrack also served as a gendered training site in the essential skill of running. Chona recalled her father encouraging children to practice running, boys to "be swift in the time of war" and girls to flee "when the enemy shall come."[36] Like the village as a whole, the racetrack physically manifested on the landscape the O'odham strategies for survival in the desert. Both reflected the practical activities needed for persistence and also expressed the social norms that held the community together culturally and enabled the himdag to endure over generations, even in the face of Christian baptism, disease, and mine labor.

Beyond the village lay a cornucopia, an expansive homeland filled with resources to support a flourishing culture. Because no single place offered everything, however, tapping the cornucopia required movement. Men went out hunting and raiding. Women foraged for seeds, cactus fruit, and other plants. Young girls carried water. In the month of Pleasant Cold, Chona remembered, after the rains had ceased and the pond at Mesquite Root had dried up, she and the other village girls would "run for water far, far up in the hills and across the flat land" to fill their families' jugs. "But," Chona recalled, "we did not stay at Mesquite Root all the time." Sometimes the villagers followed the men into the mountains to hunt deer. At other times, they traveled over the Mexican border to pick the century plant. On other occasions, they went up into the hills and crafted makeshift greasewood shelters and stayed many days picking green chollas. Chona also remembered frequent visits to the "River People," the Akimel O'odham. These visits were equal parts ceremonial, social, and economic. Rituals of song and dance followed footraces, and the Tohono O'odham came home with horses and other gifts from their One-Villager cousins. Another example of movement was the Salt Pilgrimages men made to the Gulf of California. In addition to returning with salt for use and trade, Chona's first husband received a vision. On the shores of the Sea of Cortez, he met Coyote, who conferred curing powers on him. Thereafter, the new medicine man traveled and healed throughout the homeland. The payments from patients made him rich. Chona felt his sojourns also expanded her freedom. The village boundaries, ill defined as they were, circumscribed women's movement. "I could not go out alone on the desert as [my brothers] did," Chona told Underhill. "That is man's work." She later counted herself fortunate that both her first and second husbands took her on their travels. "I never had to stay home."[37]

Together, Chona's memoir, Spaniards' diaries, O'odham stories, and the environment itself sketch a portrait of what A'al Vaipia might have been like at the end of the Spanish period. Since no diarists mention a dam or a pond, it seems unlikely that there was one. *Carrizos, tules,* and ducks did indicate that A'al Vaipia was wet, though, and water all but guaranteed settlement of some sort, at least some of the time. The village probably consisted of a cluster of grass houses, one to a family. Unmarried adult children built their own huts, as Shining Evening did, and daughters who married went to live in their husbands' villages, as Chona did, perhaps at Sonoídag or even farther afield. Little Houses, secluded from the other structures, probably ringed the cluster, physically marking gender difference. Also signaling gendered behavior were the ramadas, where multiple generations of women worked and chitchatted, thankful for the shade and company. Maybe there was a racecourse. There were fields nearby, certainly growing corn, but also perhaps beans, squash, melons, and maybe even Spanish wheat. Wheat and corn meant there would be metates, such as the one with which I'itoi ground his grain at Baboquivari Peak. The people sang to make the corn grow, and they may have irrigated the crops too. Young girls could have carried the water from the springs or the Sonoyta River, or perhaps the villagers dug ditches. They might have tended a few livestock on the outskirts of the cluster of huts and penned them up in corrals. If they did, they probably did not invest much labor in infrastructure because it was not a place for alighting permanently.

Periodically, the villagers would have left in groups or sometimes all together. Perhaps some went to Dolores and learned about baptisms and burials from priests there. For certain they traveled to the sea, returning materially and spiritually richer, with fish, shells, and salt in their baskets and stories of Coyote on their lips. They probably journeyed to Mexico to glean fields or pick figs and to the Santa Cruz and Gila Rivers to race and to harvest the One-Villagers' yield. The No-Villagers went to the Colorado River to exchange news with the Quechans and journeyed to the north and east to take vengeance on the Apaches. A'al Vaipia was a place that could adapt well to a shortage of monsoon rains or an abundance of pitahaya blooms in another district, a place that could incorporate the benefits of domesticated animals and see wisdom in other people's religious ways. They could abide light-skinned strangers on their southern and eastern margins and even take advantage of a bolt of cloth or a pair of trousers without altering their own culture much. A'al Vaipia's villagers did not submit to the sedentary River People, the mobile Apaches, or the missionaries. When the Spaniards tried to confine them to particular spaces or habits that did not suit them, they pushed back, just as their origin stories indicated they had against the sivanyi. In sum, A'al Vaipia was a landscape designed to promote a livelihood, a himdag, that could accommodate impermanence and permeable borders while persisting in recognizable form over the long run. It lasted well into the nineteenth century.

Coyote's Laugh

When Font heard his guide's "little yarns" about the building of Casa Grande, he snickered, and, like Coyote's, his laugh was transformational.[38] It signaled the arrival of a new European worldview, one that was oblivious to much of the O'odham himdag and often dismissive of what it did understand. The O'odham tolerated the impermanence of their shaking world and adapted. The Spaniards sought to extend their control over their world and over other peoples' too. Even in only partially succeeding in the Sonoran Desert, the Spaniards exposed the O'odham to a big world that included a universal religion, global commercial networks, long-distance imperial control, hierarchical power held tightly at the center, and transformative institutions such as landownership and domestication of animals. For the moment, the O'odham himdag and landscapes, designed to accommodate impermanence, could adapt to the slow pace and modest scale of change. Gendered spaces, decentralized political authority, and movement across permeable social and physical borders did not yet give evidence of dramatic change. The Spanish empire fell to Mexican independence between 1810 and 1821, and on the horizon loomed two nation-states in North America, each committed to boundary making and industrial capitalism, which together would speed up and intensify the pressures on the landscape. Soon, A'al Vaipia would become ensnared in power structures of the big world, forcing the O'odham to raise new rafters.

| # "And They Had Water"

Multiethnic Settlement at Quitobaquito, 1821–1916

ONE DAY, SOMETIME in the second decade of the twentieth century, a little girl peered into the shop at Quitobaquito. Her wide eyes beheld rows of cans whose colorful labels brightened the store's shelves. Beatrice Melvin was delighted that day. Usually, her parents left her at home with her grandmother at Bates Well when they traveled to Quitobaquito to shop or work the plot of land they had there. But this time, they had let her tag along as their wagon rattled south- ward down almost the same path that Hohokam traders had followed with salt and shells hundreds of years before. The settlement around the springs was an exciting place for a seven- or eight-year-old girl. While her parents tended to their affairs, she could watch the donkeys pull the arrastras "around and around" to grind the wheat. She also loved to munch the fruits—pomegranates, figs, watermelons, and cantaloupes. "And they had water," she later recalled. "It was just coming the water out and it's coming big. We went up there and we drank and drank. . . . Oh, it was good."[1]

After the oral traditions that illuminate A'al Vaipia in the precontact and colonial periods, Beatrice's memory, related in a 1983 interview, provides a sec- ond snapshot of the oasis prior to the arrival of the National Park Service. Her memory captures what Quitobaquito became by the early twentieth century: a multiethnic settlement of farming families who engaged in commercial trade and enjoyed the ample fresh water. Although few indigenous sources survive, other records, primarily from white settlers and travelers, allow us to fill out Beatrice's perspective. Her father, Tom Childs, for example, born in 1870, married an O'odham woman, Martha García. He learned the tribe's language and culture and lived among them for many years. He knew many people who had been in the region in the 1840s, including tribal elders and his own father, also named Tom Childs. Alberto Celaya, a Mexican born in the 1880s, also knew American, Mexican, and indigenous old-timers. He grew up among Hia C'ed O'odham thirty miles south at another oasis, Quitovac, Sonora, learned to speak O'odham, and moved to Sonoyta as an adult. His grandfather had lived at Quitobaquito. Other information comes from the Norwegian ethnographer Carl Lumholtz, who traveled the region in 1909 and 1910. He observed the land and people, including Hia C'ed O'odham elders, whose presence at A'al Vaipia stretched back at least to the 1860s, likely earlier. Besides Lumholtz, railroad and border surveyors and other scientific expeditions visited the Papaguería and recorded their findings. The memories of all these people and those they knew stretched back to midcentury and earlier, telling the story of men and women who came to Quitobaquito and inscribed their aspirations onto the landscape until tin cans from eastern factories found their way to an oasis in the Sonoran Desert.

The mixed-race child in a store gazing up at shelves of merchandise from all over the continent highlights the changes that had transformed the land and people of Quitobaquito and throughout the Papaguería over the previous century. For twelve thousand years, the region's peoples had accommodated impermanence and built that tolerance into the landscape through seasonal movement and reliance on a diverse resource base. Then in the nineteenth century, ethnically varied newcomers tried to impose permanence. Equating civilization with sedentarism, they preferred to stay put and engage in the movement of goods instead. They exchanged what they extracted from the land locally for the contents of brightly colored cans and other items manufactured or processed in far-off ecosystems. And they remade Quitobaquito's landscape to accommodate this himdag. They developed property lines, roads, stores, fences, corrals, arrastras, and irrigation ditches. They introduced new species and chased native ones away. They destroyed some habitats and created others. Broadly, they transfigured the landscape at Quitobaquito in three main ways. They laid borders, improved infrastructure, and connected the oasis to other places. All of this had a dramatic impact on the O'odham, especially the No-Villagers. Fences, new interlopers occupying resource-rich places, private property, Indian reservations, and imposition of the international boundary constrained the old O'odham ways that had relied on mobility across extensive spaces. As they increasingly intermarried with other ethnic groups and scattered in pursuit of wage labor, they became nearly invisible to the newcomers. By the time Beatrice was a teenager, A'al Vaipia's O'odham families had dispersed to Dome, Chico Suni, and Ajo. Almost no one lived at Quitobaquito anymore. This diaspora laid the groundwork for twentieth-century occupants to remake Quitobaquito to give the illusion that no one had ever lived there at all.

Boundaries

Newcomers from the United States and Mexico, who began coming to the Papaguería in the 1840s, held widely different views of space and borders than the Native locals did. As the linguist Ofelia Zepeda, herself a Tohono O'odham, observed, her people "often do not rely on maps to help them distinguish what is their territory. Most people know their territory by travel from point to point." In a 2022 interview, one Hia C'ed O'odham elder described a place's location as "two washes away" from another. At places like A'al Vaipia, Tohono O'odham and Hia C'ed O'odham overlapped, interacted, and intermarried, blurring the physical and cultural boundaries between the groups.[2] To Spaniards, Mexicans, and Americans, however, maps were everything. With colors and sharp lines, maps precisely demarcated spaces, indicating where one people's territory stopped and another's started, where one individual's property ended and another's began. They believed that control over such spaces, whether national or individual, was inviolate, an inalienable right. The intersecting territories, shared sovereignty, and usufruct access to resources that characterized O'odham understanding of land use had little place in—indeed was inimical to—the boundary marking by newcomers. In fact, because the Papaguería, with its absence of fences, permanent structures, and other improvements, did not fit their imagination of bordered, uniquely claimed spaces, it looked empty and unused to colonizing Euro-Americans of the early nineteenth century—there for the taking. They imagined the western third of the continent as a blank spot on the map, waiting, as divinely ordained, for them to come and draw the boundaries on maps and inscribe them on the land. The sequence of Spanish, Mexican, and finally American incursions into the Papaguería between the late eighteenth and mid-nineteenth centuries was partly a story of the gradual and steady, though ultimately incomplete, replacement of indigenous borders with Euro-American ones.

The rise of a treacherous travel route, the Camino del Diablo, exemplifies the beginning of this transition. Native guides had led Kino and his companions over routes humans had traversed for thousands of years. English, Russian, and eventually American competition for Spanish holdings in western North America renewed Spain's interest in these trails in the 1760s. In addition, a series of discoveries of gold in northwestern Sonora and southern Arizona starting in November 1770 at Cieneguilla, south of Altar, and continuing into the late nineteenth century, lured thousands of Spanish, Mexican, indigenous, and mixed-race prospectors and their suppliers to the region. In 1750, Jesuit priest Jacobo Sedelmayr journeyed from Sonoyta to the Colorado River. In the 1770s, Juan Bautista de Anza led a pair of military expeditions over a similar route in hopes of scouting a connection between Sonora and California settlements. Another party, under Pedro Fages, trekked the route to punish Quechan Indians who had resisted Spanish domination in 1781. Following in the steps of Kino and generations of Indians, late eighteenth-century Spaniards' expeditions established a difficult but viable route that hopped from watering place to watering place, connecting Sonoyta with the Colorado River, roughly following the modern Arizona-Sonora border and passing right by Quitobaquito, which, circa 1830, the American immigrant Tom Childs Jr. noted hosted a small Hia C'ed O'odham settlement. An extension reached down to mines in Quitovac,

Caborca, Cieneguilla, and Altar. This network of routes came to be called the Camino del Diablo, or Devil's Road. Because in guiding Europeans Native guides often steered clear of territories held by their rivals in favor of areas occupied by allied groups, the Camino itself blended geographies of water and indigenous political rivalries.[3]

The influx of people who traveled the Camino during the Mexican period between 1821 and 1854 tested whether European and O'odham understandings of borders could coexist. One oral tradition held that when a village of people left one place, they always left someone there to signal their intent to return. Camino travelers, however, did not recognize this as a claim to space. The colonizers, seeing no boundaries or permanent structures, imagined they were crossing borderless, unused, unclaimed space. And yet in the parched environment of the Papaguería, everyone eventually had to converge at the handful of lush spots, and when they did, these two ways of marking off the land clashed. Bandits drove horses stolen in California along the route and sold them in Sonora. Mules, gold, and other commodities also traveled the route. At first, indigenous miners, including the O'odham, and Mexicans worked the strikes together, but the newcomers increasingly pushed them away from the best deposits and water sources. In 1838, Altar official Santiago Redondo wrote of the "discontent" he had witnessed among the O'odham at Quitovac, Sonoyta, and elsewhere. They seethed, he said, at the "insults and even extortions they have suffered at the hands of unscrupulous Mexican miners, and also . . . the enormous amount of water taken from them." Redondo understood that this was partly a disagreement about how to define borders. The Mexican interlopers perceived the land as unused, but "the Papagos consider [it] as theirs by right of residence there from time immemorial." As Redondo feared, Mexicans and the O'odham went to war over these disputes over access to space in the early 1840s.[4]

Traffic further picked up along the Camino in the 1840s, as did conflict. Prior to the California gold rush of 1849, a handful of American adventurers crossed the route, though most non-Native sojourners were Sonorans and other Mexicans. As late as the 1840s, the O'odham still moved about heedless of Euro-American borders. As they had for generations, they fished in the Sea of Cortez and moved seasonally to gather roots, berries, cholla buds, and pitahaya fruit. They hunted antelope, mountain sheep, and other game and traded at Mexican and later American settlements. But movement was getting harder. In the aftermath of Mexican independence in 1821, miners, ranchers, and others streamed into O'odham homelands in northern Sonora, occupying the places with the best grass and the most water. Crowded out and unable to pursue their mobile himdag among so many Mexicans trying to stay put, the O'odham gradually moved northward, eventually into what is now southwestern Arizona.[5]

The Sonoran miner and merchant Francisco Salazar traveled the Camino del Diablo in 1850. "Los Americanos," he said, preferred to travel in the cooler winter months, but he made his journey in the spring and summer to avoid attacks by Apaches, who generally kept to the north in Arizona's highlands during the hotter months. Again, the geography of the Camino blended Native and Euro-American concerns. In planning a route, wayfarers had to consider trade-offs among water availability, temperature, and the location of the Apaches. Salazar may have miscalculated with his summer safety theory, however. Probably not all attacks were the work of Apaches. Deprived of some of the most valuable places on their seasonal rounds, the Hia C'ed O'odham increasingly supplemented their meager subsistence by plundering the supplies of travelers on the Camino del Diablo. They were a threat in any season. A pair of Hia C'ed O'odham men who later lived at Quitobaquito confessed to Childs that they had murdered a Mexican family traveling along the trail, a story that Childs's wife confirmed. After attacks like these, the Hia C'ed O'odham assailants quickly melted into the crusty terrain of the Pinacate region, where authorities could not find them. Travelers also abused the Hia C'ed O'odham, however. As Childs would later note, "in the early days," the Areneños "had a pretty rough time with some of the early prospectors and hard characters who traveled through their country." Whether the assailants were Apache, O'odham, Mexican, or American, the time and route of travel on the Camino del Diablo depended as much on the desire to avoid violence from other groups as it did on the need for water and mild weather. Sonorans pushed the O'odham north to the Camino, and the O'odham promptly preyed on Sonoran travelers, who in turn modified their travel plans to avoid attack. Quitobaquito sat in these borderlands, where no single conception of boundaries yet prevailed.[6]

As assaults on travelers continued, a Mexican posse kidnapped about a hundred Hia C'ed O'odham sometime in the late 1840s or early 1850s and took them to Caborca. Other Sand People fled to American territory at Yuma and Gila City, but a dispute with locals chased them to Quitobaquito, then still in Mexico. Around 1851, an unidentified disease, possibly yellow fever, wiped out much of the Hia C'ed O'odham population, reducing them to perhaps only a few families. The Norwegian ethnographer Carl Lumholtz learned this from the elderly Quitobaquito medicine man Wialos Velasco. Like the Sonorans before them, American colonizers took the best lands, including at Quitobaquito and Ajo. Waves of colonization, armed conflict, and disease launched a diaspora of Hia C'ed O'odham that scattered them from their longtime haunts in the Pinacate to Dome (near Yuma), Sonoyta, Caborca, Ajo, and elsewhere. Among the new people moving to Quitobaquito were the family of Beatrice's indigenous great-grandfather, Juan José García, as well as Luis Orozco, whose descendants would live at the oasis even after the national monument was established.[7]

In some ways, the first Americans to come to southern Arizona were no less mobile than the O'odham. Among the earliest was Tom Childs Sr., Beatrice's white grandfather. He came from Mississippi, by way of California, in 1847 at the age of fifteen and built himself a cabin on the north bank of the Gila River, which then marked the border between the United States and Mexico.

Pinacate, 2015. The austere Pinacate region of northwestern Sonora is the traditional heart of the Hia C'ed O'odham homelands. Today its geologic and cultural features are preserved in a UNESCO biosphere reserve, El Pinacate y Gran Desierto de Altar, in northern Sonora. Photo by Comisión Mexicana de Filmaciones. Courtesy of Wikimedia Commons.

Living alone, he farmed a little, hunted, fished, prospected, and rounded up stray cattle left behind by travelers en route to the California goldfields. He traded with O'odham, Quechans, and Maricopas and moved around to acquire other resources he needed and to duck conflicts among rival tribes, with whom he wished to maintain good relations. For a while, he operated a sawmill south of Tucson and prospected for silver in Sonora. On one occasion, some O'odham showed him the copper deposits at Ajo. After serving in the Confederate Army during the Civil War, he returned to southern Arizona and operated a stagecoach company, caught on as a wagon master for Charles T. Hayden, father of future US senator Carl Hayden, and then bought a ranch in the 1860s. In trying to make a living for himself, he had ranged from Yuma to Nogales, nearly three hundred miles apart, and none of his enterprises landed him anything resembling permanence. Apache raids, dishonest associates, floods, distance from reliable markets, and plain hard luck kept him on the move and always a step behind the prosperity he longed for. In 1875, he and his wife, Mary, and their five-year-old son, Tom Childs Jr., moved to the young town of Phoenix in search of the stability the era prescribed for American family life.[8]

A. B. Gray, however, envisioned a world in which fellow southerner Childs and other white immigrants might prosper. A Virginian by birth, Gray served as a commissioner on the team that surveyed the international boundary after the United States seized much of Mexico's northern lands during the Mexican-American War. In 1854, while surveying a route from Texas to California for a possible southern transcontinental railroad, he wrote what is likely the first English reference to the Hia C'ed O'odham, describing them with the usual tropes of nakedness and their primitive, unpalatable diet.[9] In the land itself, though, he saw great promise. The Papaguería's copper deposits, he said, would become "unquestionably of great value," especially for "being situated in the neighborhood of the contemplated railway." Of the soil, he wrote, "I have no doubt the finest cotton will soon be extensively raised and brought to its highest state of perfection by proper cultivation." Between the Santa Cruz and Colorado Rivers, he found "no heavy grades or difficult excavation . . . and no short curves." A railroad, he had argued in a previous document, would encourage settlement of people eager to develop private property—to mine ore and cultivate crops. Moreover, he promised, a railroad "would be a surer protection than a Chinese wall, and the settlements which would spring up along it, and the rapid communication it could furnish, would cause the Indians . . . to abandon their predatory habits." The straight lines of railroads and well-bordered cotton fields would bring order to the abundant but uncultivated Papaguería and allow proper, civilized people to stay put. "What is now a waste in the hands of the savages might become a thriving country."[10]

Just prior to Gray's 1854 survey and partly because of his advocacy of a southern railway route across the Papaguería during his work on the 1849 border survey, the United States acquired more territory from Mexico. Known as the Gadsden Purchase, the arrangement moved the international boundary south to its present location and brought Ajo, Tucson, and the Gila River into US territory, while leaving Sonoyta and the Pinacate in Mexico. Quitobaquito now sat north of the border, but only by a few hundred feet. Major William Emory headed the American half of a binational commission charged with surveying and marking the new border. Working under him, Lieutenant W. M. Michler directed the team that charted southern Arizona in 1855. After arriving by sea and ascending the Colorado, he and his men surveyed the area around Fort Yuma. From there, they attempted to work their way east across the Sonoran Desert but were halted by shortages of water and supplies. Michler then took the alternate tack of ascending the Gila River and then the Santa Cruz to Tucson and working his way west from there with an elaborate supply chain. The hardships continued, however. At one point, the party had to transport its gear by hand three miles up a rocky hill that the mules and wagons could not traverse. Over a three-day span, they made only seventeen miles as they battled the "impassable mountains; massive rocks and steep precipices." The trail grew somewhat easier after that ordeal, but "the animals had become so injured and lame by the sharp angular rocks that they had to be taken away to be reshod, and many of them to be replaced." The men toiled in heat that sometimes exceeded 110° Fahrenheit and put up with snakes and other "strange bedfellows" that crawled into their blankets at night. They finished in August, working by firelight at night, as the temperatures made daytime labor impossible.[11] All this just to mark an imaginary line in remote country. The O'odham must have thought they were crazy.

The white boundary makers, however, did not always look favorably on the locals, either. Michler did speak well, if briefly, of Quitobaquito, which he called "an Indian village" with "fine springs." His geologist Arthur Schott observed that the Natives were "favored with spring water flowing out in abundance," and that they raised cattle. The reports disparaged the rest of the country, however. "The soil is sandy," Emory stated, and "bare of vegetation," "a hopeless desert." But, like Gray, he imagined that railroads, wells, and irrigation works might tap "immense" and "immeasurable" capacity for producing crops and raising stock.[12] In short, the Papaguería was not yet a good place for people to stay put. But with the proper improvements that would enable enterprising people to import supplies, extract the resources, and transport them out, it might become so.

The Boundary Commission's observations about indigenous peoples also indicate American zeal for drawing borders. The Pimas, the descendants of the One-Villagers, whose sedentary farming most resembled the American visions for settled agriculture of small holders on private property, received high praise from the commissioners, who found the Pima lands "fenced in, and irrigated by many miles of acequias." Emory called them "semi-civilized," and their villages "the most considerable and interesting settlement in the new territory." He admired their "proficiency" in farming, warfare, and morality. Michler called them "good husbandmen and farmers" and "a wealthy class of Indians." His "eyes were gladdened with the sight of rich fields of wheat ripening for the harvest," and he appreciated that the Pimas and other sedentary Indians had "learned the value of American coin, and [that] you can use it in the purchase of anything." They also understood property and "were anxious to know if their rights and titles to lands would be respected by our government." Emory believed "they have undoubtedly a just claim to their lands," and he did everything in his power "to silence their apprehensions," informing them that "by the terms of the treaty, all the rights that they possessed under Mexico are guarantied to them by the United States; a title to lands that was good under the Mexican government is good under the United States."[13]

References to the Apaches, however, who did not abide by the boundaries of private property and international agreements, were usually preceded with adjectives like "wild" and "marauding." Meanwhile, the Hia C'ed O'odham were barely taken notice of at all, being named but once in a several-hundred-page report. Emory urged Congress to pass legislation to secure the sedentary peoples their rights, but the Hia C'ed O'odham, who moved across borders and did not use fences or coin, remained largely invisible.[14]

Thus, the boundary surveyors' writings revealed the American vision for separating land use among distinct users and separating their plots, to which they had exclusive title. So too did Congress's 1863 designation of Arizona as a territory—another well-defined, colored spot on the map—as did the numerous mining claims and land patents filed in southern Arizona over the next few decades, all with clearly delineated borders visible on the land, or at least on papers in file drawers in Washington, DC.

Michler's surveyors placed markers VII and VIII in the vicinity of Quitobaquito, but both would soon disappear, along with many others the team had laboriously positioned.[15] Emory had predicted that Native Americans might move or destroy them, but other people tampered as well. Mexican and American settlers disassembled the monuments and used them for building materials. Others moved them to extend their property a bit here or there. Some vandalized them in protest. Although early boundary-drawing efforts yielded mixed results, Americans in the Papaguería would keep trying. A well-bordered landscape, where national sovereignty was clear and property rights secure, was essential before farmers, miners, ranchers, and railroad companies would invest in the improvements necessary for staying put.

A Dam

A man named Dorsey made the improvements that enabled folks to stay put at Quitobaquito. The tall Georgia frontiersman, who appears in documents variously as Andrew, Adolph, Andres, Arnold, or simply "A.," came to Quitobaquito in the 1860s and built or moved into an adobe house. He opened a store, grew pomegranates and figs, prospected, and erected a mill. He named the settlement Fremont. Local lore credits him with making the most dramatic change to the oasis: he built a dam. Michler had identified the springs and a village but did not mention any hydraulic infrastructure. Schott called it a "ciénaga," Spanish for swamp or bog. Spaniards frequently gave that name to wet spots that lacked flowing water, but they did not usually apply it to clearly improved places. That and the fact that Schott noted even modest improvements elsewhere (such as the "miserable huts" and irrigation of a "small patch" at Sonoyta) make it unlikely that he and Michler had found anything as substantial as a dam and failed to mention it.[16] So Dorsey must indeed have been the first. His earthen barrier backed up the waters running from the hillside and created a small pond a little less than an acre in size, making it, until the era of big reservoirs, one of the largest bodies of perennial surface water in the Sonoran Desert. Below the dam, he dug irrigation ditches to carry water from the reservoir to his fruit trees and other crops. Over the next few decades, O'odham, Mexicans, Americans, and others flocked to Fremont. By attracting new labor and enlarging the scale of irrigation, the dam expanded the available resource base and launched the chain of improvements at Quitobaquito that Beatrice Melvin would behold manifested in the tin can labels.

Other newcomers added to Dorsey's improvements. Two other Americans, Albert Steinfeld and J. C. Waterman, came in the 1870s and opened a mill. They also operated a store, either competing with Dorsey's or, more likely, given the small size of the settlement, taking it over. Mexicans, too, settled at the pond and built adobe houses. A family named Lopez herded goats. Meanwhile the vicinity filled with Mexican and American farmers, merchants, ranchers, and prospectors. Although Sonoyta declined during this period, a few miles west toward Quitobaquito, Mexican entrepreneur Cipriano Ortega built the hacienda Santo Domingo, around which coalesced a thriving community on the banks of the Sonoyta River, complete with a motorized mill by the 1880s or 1890s. Ortega visited Quitobaquito often, established a mill there as well, and generally tried to keep the community under his thumb.[17]

Transportation infrastructure ranked among the most consequential improvements. By the late nineteenth century, a new thoroughfare, Pozo Nuevo Road, closely followed one branch of the old salt trails in use since ancient days. It ran from the settlement at Bates Well, where Beatrice lived, south to Quitobaquito and the east-to-west-running Camino del Diablo. Instead of couriers with shells or macaw feathers, however, wagons filled with produce, ore, ranching implements, and manufactured merchandise now rattled over the desert. Hand-dug wells, cowboy line camps, and other nodes of activity dotted the sides of the road, and as always, Quitobaquito was in the thick of things. Miners from the Ajo copper deposits and the Growler Mountains, which span the northern boundary of the modern Organ Pipe Cactus National Monument, hauled ore down Pozo Nuevo Road, turned west at Quitobaquito—perhaps watering their stock at the pond, picking up a few supplies, or exchanging news at Dorsey's store—and continued to the Colorado River, where they loaded their treasure aboard ships bound for faraway markets. Even more importantly, in 1881 the Southern Pacific Railroad Company completed the first southern transcontinental railway across southern Arizona, fulfilling A. B. Gray's old dream and providing employment for many in the area. Later in the 1880s, another railroad branched across the border into Sonora. With an increasing number of permanent buildings, infrastructure features, and a growing population, Quitobaquito and its surroundings began to embody the American and Mexican desire to establish economic enterprises that allowed them to stay put.

Long ago, I'itoi had turned into a spider and stilled the earth with his web, but with all these changes, the Hia C'ed O'odham world was once again unsteady. The diaspora that had begun in the 1840s and 1850s continued and intensified for the rest of the century until almost no one remained living in the Pinacate. Tom Childs later reported that some had gone to work in the placer mines near Yuma and then labored for the railroads. Perhaps drawn by the agricultural possibilities created by the dam, many drifted to Quitobaquito. In 1863, the Indian agent Charles D. Poston estimated that that 250 O'odham lived there. Although surely an overstatement, it nevertheless indicates considerable population growth. The earliest historically identifiable O'odham individual was Juan

José García.[18] As a teenager in the 1880s, Childs used to visit Quitobaquito, becoming friendly with two of García's sons, José Agustín and Tomás, the latter of whom would become Childs's father-in-law. Childs traveled throughout the Pinacate with José Agustín, including one sojourn on which they encountered a Hia C'ed O'odham man named Juan Caravajales. Childs called Caravajales the Hermit of the Tinajas de los Papagos (the Hermit of Papago Tanks) because he and his wife were allegedly the last Hia C'ed O'odham still living in the Pinacate. For decades, Caravajales guided Childs on trips over the sand and badlands of the Areneños' deserted Pinacate heartland. The two climbed mountains and traversed lava flows. Caravajales pointed out empty huts, overgrown croplands, abandoned watering holes, and shell workshops, from which ancient peoples had carved ornaments that they traded as far as the Navajo villages in the Four Corners area. One trip brought the two men to a cave wherein the Hia C'ed O'odham believed I'itoi dwelled. An unscrupulous white explorer would later idly divulge the cavern's contents, but Childs maintained silence for the next sixty years. "What we found in the sacred cave of the Papago," he said, "I cannot tell." Whatever remained in Elder Brother's hideaway, the Hia C'ed O'odham had left the Pinacate by the 1880s. Caravajales pointed and said "huhuku o'otam," which means "all gone people."[19]

At their new hearth at Quitobaquito, in the second half of the nineteenth century, they mixed traditional ways with new ones. They still gathered and ate cactus fruits but also sold them at market. They used mills to grind Old World wheat but still did so using donkey power (in contrast to the mechanical engine that powered Ortega's mill at Santo Domingo). At Quitobaquito, there were several stone mound shrines to I'itoi, atop which O'odham passersby since prehistoric times had traditionally placed small green branches and other gifts. With the coming of whites to the region, the O'odham acquired cigarettes, which they added to their offerings. When those began to be stolen, however, the O'odham reverted to twigs and stones. The village consisted of many traditional grass huts and a few adobe houses, built, according to Mexican old-timer Alberto Celaya, by Mexicans. In burial practices, as in other aspects of their changing himdag, they incorporated elements of Mexican, American, Roman Catholic, and traditional customs. Quitobaquito's blend of traditional ways and "the white man's . . . habits," as Childs put it, showed the growing but not yet complete influence of American patterns of staying put.[20]

The O'odham who lived at the improved Quitobaquito were more sedentary than they had been, but they did not quite stay put, exactly. Hia C'ed O'odham elder Marlene Vazquez, recalling stories from her grandmother, said her people moved regularly between Dome (near Yuma), Pinacate, and Quitobaquito. Runners and traders crossed the border back and forth freely to work or trade or gather salt. Expertly, they navigated the rough, desiccated terrain, choosing their route to pass by tinajas, the rock ponds that captured water and had long enabled travel in the region. Their journeys, however, were hardly nomadic. They left family members at the village, to which they returned again and again. "When they [American and Mexican governments] started putting [international] boundaries in," Vazquez said, "my ancestors were still . . . going back and forth to go home and back to A'al Vaipia." Mobility sparked sporadic conflict with Mexicans into the 1880s. On occasion, O'odham crossed the border near Quitobaquito to rob travelers, steal cattle, and commit other crimes. Then they returned north to the United States to escape punishment. Meanwhile, the hacendado Cipriano Ortega and other Mexicans routinely crossed the border to terrorize the O'odham on the US side. Local legend held that the Natives knew the location of a silver strike, possibly belonging to José Agustín García. Coveting these riches, Cipriano Ortega harassed and threatened the locals, trying to wangle from them the treasure's whereabouts and causing them to flee Quitobaquito periodically, only to return months or years later. In the 1880s, many fled to live near Ajo but returned to the oasis before the decade was out.[21]

Around this time, Luis Ortega, no relation to Cipriano, moved to the oasis with his family and stayed almost to the turn of the century before moving to Darby Well, south of Ajo. Speakers of the Hu:hu'ula dialect, the Ortegas were likely Two-Villagers, Tohono O'odham. Luis's sister Rita met and married the Hia C'ed O'odham Tomás García in Gila Bend in the 1870s. Tomás had lived at Quitobaquito but left to work for the Southern Pacific. Rita and Tomás married and were back at the oasis by the 1880s.[22] Their daughter Martha was Beatrice's mother and Tom Childs's wife. The association of the Childs, García, and Ortega families was but one of many interethnic unions among Hia C'ed O'odham, Tohono O'odham, American, and Mexican families at and near Quitobaquito during this period of human movement and shifting borders. The Hia C'ed O'odham still moved about, only instead of migrating seasonally to pick cactus fruit, gather salt and shellfish, or celebrate feasts, it was now pocketbooks, mine whistles, and schedules of wagon and rail deliveries that set them on the move. And for most, Quitobaquito, with its springs, ditches, dikes, orchards, pond, and wagon roads, had replaced the Pinacate caves and shell manufactories as the hearth to which they periodically returned.

One of the refugees from Cipriano Ortega's harassment was Luis Orozco. In 1887, he moved to Quitobaquito and began to farm. His son, José Juan Orozco, was born there around 1890, and José Juan's son Jim is said to have been born about 1905. Like Dorsey, whose time at the oasis they overlapped, the Orozcos cultivated fruit trees and other crops with irrigation water from the pond. The family did not own the land, and they paid no attention to the international border, working both sides of it. After Dorsey left, they maintained the waterworks. With brief exceptions, José Juan lived the rest of his life at Quitobaquito.[23] His son Jim would be the last proprietor there.

All the improvements and the coming and going amounted to a small settlement at Quitobaquito circa the 1910s. The water engineer Herbert V. Clotts,

Pit house. House made of saguaro ribs and mud occupied by Jim Orozco. Courtesy of Western Archeological and Conservation Center, National Park Service, Organ Pipe Cactus National Monument, Catalog 15919.

who visited the oasis, noted four houses, twenty-five people, three wells, eight acres under cultivation, fifty cattle, and eight horses. When Lumholtz toured southern Arizona and Sonora in 1909 and 1910, he acknowledged that most of the region was "suitable only for cattle and horse raising," but, he added, "more of it than people realize can be brought under cultivation." He had no doubt "that through human agency, large parts of it will some day delight the eye with waving fields of grain and orchards of fruit."[24] The wells, roads, ditches, dams, and stores that people built at Quitobaquito and nearby in the second half of the nineteenth century enabled him to see the promise of the country. Improvements, however, mattered little on their own. Even if you spent all your time growing figs and wheat and developed sophisticated mechanisms for watering them, you could not survive at Quitobaquito without links to people who wanted to buy the fruits of your labor. Improvement was only as good as the density of a locale's connections to other places.

Connections

In the summer of 1854, the prospectors of the Arizona Mining and Trading Company equipped themselves in southern California. Mexican-American War officer Peter R. Brady led them, and they counted A. B. Gray among their financial backers. Gathering horses, supplies, and wagons, they headed east to Fort Yuma, where they joined Brady's old friend Tom Childs Sr. From there, the party barreled up the Gila River and then hacked its way through desert thornscrub to abandoned mines at Ajo, where Spaniards, O'odham, and Mexicans had intermittently worked surface deposits of copper for at least a century. For two years the men and the O'odham workers they hired drilled holes, filled them with black blasting powder, and blew up hillsides. They lugged water by wagon from the Gila some forty miles way. Supplies came at intervals of weeks or months, probably hauled from the nearest settlements at Tucson, Sonoyta, or Caborca. They ate rancid food, slept in shacks, and endured illness and injury without a doctor. Finally, they had enough ore to sell. Dorsey, who had not yet built his dam at Quitobaquito, handled the freight. One day in 1856, teams of horses, mules, and oxen pulled sturdy wagons filled with ore, with water barrels hanging off both sides, away from Ajo and down the Gila to Fort Yuma. There the treasure was packed onto boats, floated down to the mouth of the Colorado River, and reloaded onto seaworthy vessels bound for Swansea, Wales, via San Francisco and the tip of South America. Swansea refiners smelted the copper, and months later, somehow, a $5,000 payment made its way back to Ajo. On the second foray of this elaborate journey, however, the ship sank near Patagonia, sending years of hard work to the bottom of the Atlantic. The company, Arizona's first incorporated mining firm, folded in 1859. Although resolute in the face of hard work and poor living conditions, the miners could not overcome the distance and danger separating them from supplies, markets, and capital. Later, the elder Childs and his son Tom tried working Ajo again in 1887. By this time, the advent of telephones and electricity had sparked global demand for copper, and the Southern Pacific Railroad connected Ajo not only to new smelters in Arizona, but to the world. In 1912, the Childses sold their claims for $90,000. When Americans tried to stay put in the Papaguería, a fine line divided bankruptcy from fortune, and which side of the line they landed on had a lot to do with connections.[25]

Another example is the International Boundary Commission's border resurvey. When it took to the field on February 2, 1892, the outfit sported three commissioners, sixty civilians, and a fifty-soldier military escort (which later grew to as many as eighty-eight). It had seven four-mule baggage wagons, three six-mule water-tank wagons, three two-mule light spring wagons, one two-mule buckboard, one four-mule ambulance, twenty-five mules for packing (eighty-three mules in all), and fourteen saddle ponies. It carried five officers' wall tents, twelve conical wall tents, and twenty small wall tents. In May, another wagon was added. The outfit had mail service, a hospital, surveyors, draftsmen, cartographers, a blacksmith, a wheelwright, masons, carpenters, photographers, naturalists, an astronomical team, and tools for all of them.[26] When the weather turned cold in the mountains of New Mexico in late fall 1893, the commission packed everything up, hauled it over to Yuma, and started working back toward the east at lower, warmer elevations. The railroad brought them water, which they hauled in wagons from the line to the work sites.

When the entourage came to Quitobaquito in 1894, it likely outnumbered the village in both animals and people and probably surpassed it in supplies as well. The party's naturalist Major Edgar Allen Mearns described Quitobaquito as "a small garden" irrigated from springs that flowed into "a shallow, artificial lake." The village had "three adobe dwellings, a warehouse, and a corral . . . and a small house at the garden." The commission's official report indicated that two Mexican families dwelt there, with unnumbered Native Americans in the vicinity. The irrigated fields, it said, lay on the Mexican side. In 1900, when the geologist and ethnologist W. J. McGee traveled along the border, he reported that the Boundary Survey's wagon and mule tracks were still visible on the land, as were tent pegs, ash heaps, rusted cans, and empty pickle bottles.[27] This ability to tap human labor, horsepower, dollars, equipment, water, and even pickles in other places and move them efficiently into and across the Sonoran Desert freed the surveyors from the seasons and provided food, hydration, and security. Essentially, it eliminated most of the physical challenges that had historically constrained the actions of all who had migrated through or settled in the Papaguería before. Because they could stay connected to other places while in the desert, they managed to mark a line much more accurately than previous surveyors had and achieved more widespread agreement on both sides that the boundary was legitimate.

Now that the United States had a line, however, it needed a good line rider to enforce it. Almost inevitably, the imposition of a border invited someone to seek advantage by connecting the two sides. Although immigration from Mexico was freely allowed, illegal smuggling of guns, liquor, and fugitives plagued the border. As the United States opened checkpoints where it could inspect and tax people and goods that entered, livestock drovers and others with something to sell in the north started crossing in remote areas to avoid the duties. Most alarmingly, southern Arizona had also become an entrepôt for Chinese immigrants, who evaded the 1882 Chinese Exclusion Act by immigrating to Mexico and crossing the desert into the United States. In 1904, the US Customs Service hired lawman Jeff Milton to travel the countryside and thwart illegal entries. New York Zoological Society director William T. Hornaday, who met Milton in 1907, described him as a big man of "good humor" and "restless energy." Although Milton was officially stationed at Sonoyta, the bulk of the unauthorized traffic lay to the west, so shortly after his appointment, he relocated to Quitobaquito semipermanently. From there, he chased down hundreds of migrants and also found that saving the lives of the endangered desert wayfarers was as much a part of his job as apprehending them.[28] The Chinese he did not catch went to work for railroads, mines, and other employers in Arizona and throughout the West. They also worked in service industries, especially restaurants and laundries, and as domestic laborers. Even as American sensibilities held that civilized peoples established boundaries, the enterprises they undertook behind the border required connections to laborers from beyond it.

Staying put also required moving things about. That meant either going to get them, the way the Hia C'ed O'odham had for centuries, or bringing them to Quitobaquito. No man profited more from the expanding connections than Mikul García "M.G." Levy. Levy was born in Texas in 1859 to parents of Spanish extraction, including a Jewish father. Although Judaism usually passes through the maternal line, Levy was later remembered as a Jew by Childs and Celaya, so it seems likely that he identified that way. He was a man of medium size, who walked with a limp from an injury he sustained in his younger days.[29] University educated in Germany, he was remembered for his intelligence, good manners, and enterprise.[30] Levy was the one who brought the tin can labels to Quitobaquito.

Kirk Bryan, a geologist who toured the Papaguería in 1917, indicated that Levy opened a shop at Quitobaquito in 1888. Childs agreed with that date, though the 1970s park historian Wilton Hoy thought that estimate possibly too early. Over the next several decades, Levy owned stores and mines on both sides of the border, including his most lucrative venture, the Victoria Mine, which he purchased from Cipriano Ortega. Fourteen miles east of Quitobaquito, the Victoria mine yielded $40,000 of silver during the time Levy owned it. His most romantic escapade, however, was the permit he received to prospect among the rubble of the old Spanish mission of San Marcelo, where, according to legend, the fathers had buried golden treasure. He found nothing, of course. Both Celaya and McGee placed Levy at Quitobaquito in 1900. McGee visited him while traveling with a pack train from Sonoyta carrying casks and kegs, hay, and grain to the west. Perhaps the driver dropped off or picked up supplies from Levy along the way. Most of the shopkeeper's merchandise, however, came by mule train from a supplier in Caborca, Sonora. His business was a sizable operation according to old-timer Robert Binion, who recalled that Levy had "quite a store," doing more than $10,000 in business annually. One of Levy's shopkeepers was José Lorenzo Sestier, a French immigrant, whose tombstone still overlooks the lagoon at Quitobaquito a few hundred yards to the north-west.[31] Another shopkeeper was José León, half Mexican and half O'odham and the husband of Victoria León, for whom Levy named his prized mine.

Levy's business, like that of Dorsey and all the other merchants at Quitob-aquito over the years, was predicated on the movement of goods, not people, and he made a small fortune in the desert this way. After digging ore out of the ground, shipping it off, and importing new manufactured goods with the proceeds, selling them, and then investing the profit in mines for nearly two decades, Levy seems to have left Quitobaquito sometime in the middle of the first decade of the twentieth century, heading for Ajo and continued financial success. But the phenomenon of Quitobaquito attracting goods from outside while shipping off the food and minerals extracted in the vicinity did not leave with him.

Tom Childs also moved things in and out of the region to enable himself and his neighbors to stay put. Childs frequented Quitobaquito from the 1880s to 1910s and resided there for a few years in the early twentieth century. Sometime between 1903 and 1905, he rebuilt the now-departed Dorsey's dam and irrigation ditches, which had washed out, and he began raising crops. To feed his Hia C'ed O'odham relatives and neighbors at Ajo, Childs once drove his six-mule wagon to Phoenix and returned with a cartload of food and other necessaries. On another occasion, Childs and his prospecting partner, Quitobaquito resident Rube Daniels, pulled their wagon up to the store in Gila Bend. They filled it with beans, flour, canned milk, assorted canned goods, salt pork, sugar, coffee, and mining gear. Sometime later they rolled back into town, the earlier rations used up and the wagon reloaded with ore ready to be sent to El Paso for smelting.[32]

Although he moved about quite a bit throughout his life, the plan of his Hot Shot Ranch south of Ajo and roughly forty miles north of Quitobaquito shows a substantial place of permanence. Stepping outside for his morning rounds, Childs could have faced the sun rising over the mountains, a water tank and windmill immediately in front of him. Walking past the schoolhouse on his property and bending north around the woodshed would have taken him past a reservoir and fenced corrals to check on the hogs. Beyond the pen, he would have been able to see his cultivated fields, and behind him lay a slaughterhouse and facility for processing hides. When he turned back west, the soap factory and chicken coop sat on his right, the machine shop straight ahead, and a Hia C'ed O'odham village full of friends and relatives behind those buildings. Winding his way south around the barn, he could have finished his stroll by passing under a pair of trees, likely cottonwoods, and let himself into the ranch house yard through the gate, where he could have washed up before turning left into the dining room. The well-bounded space represented American mastery of landscape that enabled staying put in southern Arizona.[33]

In addition to extending Quitobaquito's connections geographically, Childs stretched them across social borders as well. Childs's dinner table at the Hot Shot Ranch reputedly could seat seventy-five guests, hosting O'odham, Americans, and Mexicans, often at the same time. Earlier, when Childs had lived at Quitobaquito, he, Daniels, and at least one other American, John Merrill, had all married Hia C'ed O'odham women. Arizona's miscegenation laws, however, blocked Childs's interracial marriage to Martha García, so the couple crossed the border and wed in Sonoyta.[34] Ironically, the border the nation erected to separate itself from Mexico also provided cover for Americans to circumvent the social boundaries that separated them from Native Americans.

By the turn of the century, then, Quitobaquito was a surprisingly diverse place. The community's inhabitants included Tohono O'odham, Hia C'ed O'odham, Mexicans, Americans, Frenchmen, Italians, a Jew, and at least one Black man. Intermarriage yielded offspring of many combinations of these. The village also attracted Asian migrants. One quintet of Japanese travelers passed through Quitobaquito on foot from the south in 1907. They were "tired, hungry, [and] heated," according to Hornaday, who was visiting at the time, and they "knew nothing of the next water." They had only two canteens between them and were headed across the desert without a guide. Tom Childs and Rube Daniels gave them food and tobacco and a place to rest, and the wayfarers purchased some flour and bacon. Hornaday, who, appallingly, had once caged an African man for display in the New York Zoo's ape exhibit, grumbled that the "little hamlet is hybrid."[35] The world was pouring into this remote oasis, reflecting the ability of industry to project power to faraway places, tap their resources, and spur people to respond with migration, resettlement, and new forms of production and social relationships.

The effects of connections to the wider world did not pass over Quitobaquito's Native American inhabitants. Thirty Hia C'ed O'odham, including José Juan Orozco, are buried in a cemetery not far from the pond. Around the graves, archaeologists have identified offerings that were left, most from the period between 1890 and 1930. They include metal implements, metal and glass containers, corsets, shoes, and grommets. There are jackknives, hammers, tobacco tins, spice cans, wire cables, doorknob shanks, casters, and more—all manufactured in some faraway place with resources from other ecosystems and shipped into southern Arizona and paid for with the profits from bringing the fruits of mining, farming, and stock raising to market. The names on the cans testify to early industrial America's burgeoning manufacturers: Armour Packing, Schilling's Best Coffee, Calumet Baking Powder. There are tin cans with crimped and soldered seams, machine-made implements, and milled lumber. This remote patch of desert was once connected to the factories of industrializing America, and even Native Americans were using the resulting products in their daily lives. As Celaya observed, the O'odham ate new foods more and gathered old ones less. The men wore pants and shirts. They stopped placing twigs and stones on the shrines. "They are more civilized," he said.[36]

Along with cultural transformation came dependence. All those monuments the Boundary Commission laid along an imaginary line and all the fencing around property like the Hot Shot Ranch constrained where indigenous peoples could go—where they could farm, pick cactus fruit, dig roots, draw water, or let their cattle roam. The seasonal mobility and diversified resource base that had historically enabled them to cope with the difficult Sonoran Desert environment were incompatible with the activities of neighbors who marked off land, fenced it, claimed exclusive use within the boundaries, and occupied it permanently until they sold it to the next owner. To get by in this increasingly bordered landscape, the O'odham of Quitobaquito and elsewhere began migrating to work for mines, ranches, and railroads, enterprises that in turn relied on bordering the land. Thus, their new movements tragically contributed to the very processes that forced them to abandon their old mobile himdag. As white newcomers refashioned the landscape with roads and railroads, stores and fences, windmills, wells, and irrigation works, staying put became more and more viable, and moving about less so.

Increasingly, the O'odham relied on this network of things moving about. As Celaya recalled, the O'odham who worked at Quitovac, Sonora, labored at a placer mine and purchased their food and clothing from Caborca suppliers. North of the border, Chona continued her seasonal movements but for very different reasons than she previously had. "In the winter, when the horse pond dried up," she recalled, "we did not go to [work for O'odham in] Mexico." Instead "we went to Tucson and worked for white people." With her wages, she bought processed foods, silk shawls, shoes, calico cloth, and canvas bags. Although she declined her husband's urging to purchase a sewing machine, mass-produced goods of the American industrial revolution circulated in a national marketplace and made their way as far as the Papaguería. By the second decade of the twentieth century, most Hia C'ed O'odham had abandoned Quitobaquito to look for work in Ajo, Gila Bend, and elsewhere. Only José Juan Orozco and his family remained. But an international boundary ran through his homestead, with the lagoon and most buildings on the north, fields on the south, and irrigation ditches crisscrossing the invisible line. He could not prove title to the land he worked to support his family. He could not even prove his citizenship, whether he belonged north or south of the line.[37] Soon other boundaries would further hem him in.

In 1916, the United States even fenced the O'odham. The Bureau of Indian Affairs established the Papago Indian Reservation, today called the Tohono O'odham Reservation, on a swath of land spanning a hundred miles east to west between Tucson and Ajo and a hundred miles north from the Mexican border. Effectively, the federal government drew lines on maps dictating that the Tohono O'odham belonged inside but not out. Although not moved into the reservation, the Hia C'ed O'odham too found it especially problematic. The government did not recognize them as a distinct people. The remoteness of their territory, their historical mobility, the continued residence of part of their population in Mexico, their dwindling numbers, their intermarriage with other ethnic groups, and their dispersed wage labor conspired to make them invisible. The boundary-loving people in power in the United States liked to separate things—nations, residences, hog pens, and ethnic groups—into distinct spaces. Peoples whose lives crossed social and physical boundaries were not supposed to exist. Just because the government could not see them, however, did not mean that they disappeared. José Juan Orozco, Martha García Childs, and others persisted. Their descendants would continue the struggle against invisibility and the boundaries that made them so.

New Visions

In 1900, W. J. McGee traveled the Camino del Diablo with a stop at Quitobaquito. In his account of the expedition published in *National Geographic* in 1901, he extolled the people he called the "Papago" (he did not distinguish between Tohono and Hia C'ed O'odham either). They descended, he said, from "peaceful and pastoral . . . desert irrigators" and "wandered afar in search of water, [and] located fields and villages even by the temporary wettings of chance storms." The environment was difficult, but rich, and "into this complex mechanism, the prehistoric forbears of the Papago insinuated themselves so gently as scarcely to disturb the relations of parts; into the same mechanism the Papago themselves pushed their way harmlessly." With the "violent entry of the Anglo-Saxon," however, "the weaker organisms withered before him." Perhaps this was inevitable, McGee and many others of his day lamented. After all, "it is the way of the western world to grow in population and wealth, to increase in industrial and intellectual tension." Still, he acknowledged, something was lost in the process. "Resources began to suffer; the forage grew scant . . . cacti withdrew . . . big game became wary and betook to other ranges. . . . With the decimation of plants and the trampling of stock the soil grew less retentive of the scant moisture . . . so that meager ground-water disappeared [and] . . . the smaller springs went dry." With this "degradation, the Papago tribesmen withdrew." McGee counted them, too, among the "weaker organisms" that gave way when the "Anglo-Saxon came with that intense energy which balks at no obstacle, brooks no delay."[38]

"The dark lines of the picture," McGee offered, however, "carry a brighter complement: Science." He urged Americans to learn the "wisdom . . . the imperative necessity" of using resources "by patient adjustment of industries to natural conditions." To McGee, conservation was salvation. By careful, rational management of land according to scientific principles, resources might be stewarded, and the devastation of the past avoided and perhaps even remedied in the future. This kind of thinking swept the American scientific and political elite in the last decade of the nineteenth century and the first decade of the twentieth and became the template for resource management down to the present.[39]

One version of it held that some lands—those of particular scenic, scientific, and historical significance—should be reserved and their resources not developed at all, at least not for extractive purposes. People should pass through these lands only as visitors, never as permanent residents. An early expression of this vision came with the 1906 Antiquities Act, which allowed presidents to designate by executive order national monuments to protect "objects of historical or scientific interest." Another expression was the 1916 Organic Act, which created the National Park Service. The act directed the agency to manage some of these reserved lands as parks, with twin objectives: "to conserve the scenery and the natural and historic objects and the wild life therein and to provide for the enjoyment of the same in such manner and by such means as will leave them unimpaired for the enjoyment of future generations."[40] Over the next century, these goals would apply to more than four hundred national park units, to which millions of tourists flocked every year.

Although intended as a way to live more gently on the land than had the prospectors at Ajo and other Americans of the industrial era, parks were also yet another way of drawing boundaries, claiming sovereignty within, and regulating who could use the land inside and what they could do with it. This, along with the NPS's mandate to preserve in perpetuity, meant that parks were intended to stay put and thus derived from many of the same values that brought borders, improvements, and connections to Quitobaquito in the second half of the nineteenth century. In the decades after the 1916 establishment of both the National Park Service and the Papago Reservation, many who thought like McGee began suggesting reserving a bordered piece of the Sonoran Desert, including Quitobaquito, to save it from the ravages of human beings. This thinking anticipated the subsequent logic underlying the North Puerto Blanco Drive wilderness sign's portrait of Organ Pipe's past as untraveled, uncultivated, and devoid of human activity. At the time McGee wrote his lamentation, however, José Juan Orozco was trying to stay put at the oasis, finally consummating Kino's two-hundred-year-old hope for the O'odham. He had not, as McGee had said of the Papagos, "withered away" along with "weaker organisms" in the face of the Anglo-Saxons' "intense energy." He had not "insinuated" himself into the land "so gently as scarcely to disturb" it. Even as McGee was heralding this narrative, José Juan Orozco was giving the lie to it.

| Science, Conservation, and NPS
Placemaking at Quitobaquito, 1900–1962

IN 1903, DANIEL T. MACDOUGAL, assistant director of the New York Botanical Garden, traveled to Arizona. He came as the representative of the Carnegie Institution, founded the year before with the enthusiastic support of President Theodore Roosevelt and the deep pockets of steel titan Andrew Carnegie. It was already one of the nation's premier scientific organizations. After scouring the Southwest and northern Mexico for a suitable site, MacDougal selected a hill on the outskirts of Tucson for the world's first laboratory devoted to desert study. Opening that October, the Carnegie Institution's Desert Botanical Laboratory sported an ingenious ventilation system that kept its researchers cool indoors even when the outside temperature reached 120°F. From this agreeable setting, scientists investigated the mysteries of life in extreme arid environments. They studied botany, biology, meteorology, geology, geography, hydrology, and more, a range of interests unlike anything anyone had ever pursued in the Sonoran Desert. To be sure, early Spanish explorers and the US boundary surveyors had done a little science, and of course indigenous peoples had developed keen understandings of their environment, but the region had seen nothing on the scale of the Carnegie Institution's well-funded efforts to systematically count, measure, collect, name, and classify the entirety of the region's living things and to understand them in relation to one another and their physical surroundings. In November 1907, MacDougal, now the lab's director, and several colleagues including the flamboyant head of the New York Zoological Society, William T. Hornaday, brought their scientific curiosity and appetite for adventure to Quitobaquito.

For hundreds of generations, peoples at Quitobaquito had imprinted their aspirations onto the land, constructing landscapes conducive to pursuing their own constellation of objectives and calculated to respond to the desert's potential uncertainties. The scientists from the Desert Botanical Laboratory brought yet another vision to the oasis. In contrast to everyone who had come to Quitobaquito before, they were a materially comfortable people. They were the beneficiaries of the improvements of industrialization that were enabling Americans to perceive the environment not only as an obstacle to be overcome or a collection of resources to be extracted, but also as something of scientific, aesthetic, recreational, and spiritual value. In his account of the expedition, *Camp-Fires on Desert and Lava*, Hornaday wrote that he had long "been keenly desirous" of discovering the geographic point at which bighorn sheep could no longer tolerate the environment's "fierce heat, and scanty food and water" and thus reached the southernmost extension of their range. He expected to pinpoint this locale in the Sonoran Desert. He also said that "with the three jolly good fellows whose company I shared, I could enjoy exploring any country this side of the Styx. Indeed, I would take my chances with them beyond it."[1] Thus they went into the desert partly for study and partly for fun.

These intentions contrasted with those of previous desert dwellers who sought from the landscape long-term livelihood and community. Ironically enough, another distinction between scientists and their predecessors is that the scientists imagined no people in the desert. Hornaday opened his book by proclaiming the trip an "exploration of a genuine terra incognita." On maps, their ultimate destination, the Sierra Pinacate, was "blank," and "not a soul . . . knew" even about its "lava." He dismissed the knowledge of the area's "few Papago Indians and perhaps half a dozen Mexicans," explicitly placing them apart from the "thinking world," to whom the area was "totally unknown." He reveled in southern Arizona's "boundless" spaces, "the cleanness of the face of Nature," and the "absence of . . . dirty humanity."[2] In sum, MacDougal, Hornaday, and their companions hoped to discover not an impermanent place where people had long lived, adapted, and made landscapes, but a timeless quarter that human beings had not disturbed.

The only problem was that such an undisturbed quarter had never existed at Quitobaquito, at least not for twelve thousand years. It would have to be created. To bring about such a place, people and the imprint they had left on the landscape would have to be actively removed and replaced with a new landscape deliberately constructed to appear timeless and empty of people. Hornaday and other white visitors had accomplished this rhetorically. With the support of the Desert Botanical Laboratory and others, Organ Pipe Cactus National Monument would be founded in 1937 and charged with carrying it out physically. The Park Service would remove the Orozcos and their improvements in an attempt to remake Quitobaquito into a bordered, peopleless pleasure ground where visitors could study and enjoy land fixed in time and preserved unchanging. Thus, the new park was to be a maker of landscapes, not just a container for them. By attempting to preserve an inherently dynamic landscape in a fixed state, however, park officials ended up transforming it. Historian Laura Alice Watt called this phenomenon the "paradox of preservation."[3] Bordering and freezing—constraining a landscape in space and time—guided the Park Service's remaking of Quitobaquito between 1937 and 1962. It converted a landscape where people had lived and worked into one where they visited and played. The paradoxical consequences of that transformation turned Quitobaquito into a landscape of exclusion.

A Comfortable People Come to the Desert

By the early twentieth century, industrialization was making people in southern Arizona and across the nation more comfortable. The profits of mass production and mass distribution found their way into the pockets of men like Carnegie and their lawyers, accountants, and middle managers, creating a class of Americans freed on a scale not seen before in human history from having to produce daily to meet their basic needs. They labored for wages and bought what they needed. Increasingly, many of them had a little left over for spending, which enabled them to travel and recreate. Often, their play mimicked the physical labor they no longer had to do to sustain themselves, and Americans hankered for outdoor recreation opportunities. Only a people who no longer had to chase food, sleep outside, struggle across difficult landscapes, and protect themselves from the elements would want to hunt, camp, or hike for leisure. Only those with reliable streams of sustenance would go into the wilds for the sole purpose of observing and recording what was there. As the very industrialization that made them wealthy and comfortable also simultaneously worked over the California redwoods, Rocky Mountain heights, and southwestern deserts, the industrial class sought to preserve a few places for outdoor play and study. A measure of this transformation and a harbinger of the support for desert preservation that would soon result in the establishment of Organ Pipe Cactus National Monument was the popularity of John C. Van Dyke's 1901 *The Desert.* The Rutgers art professor sojourned in the California, Arizona, and Mexico deserts and then wrote the lyrical but scientifically sound volume, which changed the way Americans thought about deserts.[4] By the 1930s, some of these well-fed, well-clothed, well-hydrated folks, including the scientists working comfortably in the Desert Botanical Laboratory, would inscribe their comfortable himdag on a piece of the Papaguería by establishing a national monument on the US side of the border.

They hoped to make it a landscape of leisure. Although important to human well-being, the ends they pursued were not generally directly essential to human sustenance. Among them were science, education, outdoor recreation, travel, physical vigor, aesthetics, and natural and historic preservation. Enjoyment, of course, was not new to the desert. As Chona's memoir testified abundantly, the O'odham danced, sang, drank, gambled, raced, and feasted with a vengeance.[5] They also, however, hunted, hauled water, bore children, ground cholla buds, harvested the One-Villagers' fields, and extracted Ajo copper for Tom Childs Sr. and his Arizona Mining and Trading Company. They filled most of their time with the hard work necessary just to make their landscape habitable. What distinguished the landscape that twentieth-century newcomers built was that so much of it was designed to promote leisure and to obscure labor. To be sure, plenty of people worked in this landscape. Scientists researched. Park staff managed and interpreted resources. Employees served throngs of tourists at restaurants, gas stations, grocery stores, shops, and motels. Construction workers laid asphalt, installed visitor center plumbing, and raised border fences. Most of this labor, however, took place to enable someone else's leisure. Labor and leisure coexisted in the O'odham landscape and in the scientists', but in the first two-thirds of the twentieth century, the balance between them flipped.

Scientists led the way toward this metamorphosis. Over the next several decades after its founding, the laboratory's staff and many other researchers went out into the desert frequently. They checked rain gauges, collected specimens, and examined rocks. In addition to the 1907 MacDougal-Hornaday expedition, Carl Lumholtz conducted an anthropological expedition in 1909 and 1910, and the irrigation engineer Herbert Clotts explored the Papaguería in 1914 and 1915, reporting on both indigenous peoples there and their natural world. In 1916, Congress authorized a survey of watering places and roads in the Southwest, including southern Arizona. The goal was "a systematic program for making the desert safe and accessible." To carry this out, the Harvard geologist Kirk Bryan drove all over southern Arizona in 1917, using his speedometer to assess distances. He set out markers and recorded conditions on roads so obscure that they were sometimes barely passable. As a result of his travels, he authored a pair of publications in 1922 and 1925, which for the first time charted the roads and water sources in the Papaguería and provided more "comprehensive and accurate descriptions of its geography, geology, and hydrology than have hitherto been published."[6] Bryan's expedition and others like it were a first step in creating a new way of staying put—that is, enabling sedentarism by making the desert widely known and therefore accessible.

The Desert Botanical Laboratory's Godfrey Sykes, who had traveled with MacDougal and Hornaday on their Sonoran Desert junket, embodied the scientists' zeal for knowing the desert. In July 1925, Sykes traveled the Camino del Diablo not for gold or salt or macaw feathers but out of curiosity. Hardly a drop of rain had fallen the previous winter, and he wanted to see how desert life was faring. Following some of Bryan's routes, he traveled alone in a "heavy touring car." The rise of auto travel had by this time made the desert less dangerous and more accessible than ever, but he nevertheless ran into trouble. Windblown sand obscured the road and drifted deep enough to mire his vehicle. For four midday hours, he shoveled his way out, cutting branches and laying them beneath the wheels to increase traction, and deflating and repumping the tires. Meanwhile, the mercury in his thermometer climbed to 115°. Knowing he carried plenty of food and water, the ever-curious man of science seized the opportunity to test how a human body performed under extreme circumstances, regularly measuring his pulse as he labored and wishing he had the means of taking his temperature as well. He later boasted that he had twice "approach[ed] the danger point . . . the sudden checking of perspiration," but he avoided collapse by lying for a few minutes in the shade of his car. The physical toll of his afternoon's toil cost him fourteen pounds and "some slight digestive trouble," not enough to dissuade him from repeating the journey later in the summer.[7]

For early Spanish explorers, California-bound argonauts, and even the desperate Japanese border crossers that the MacDougal-Hornaday expedition encountered, the Sonoran Desert could be a place of suffering, and not infrequently death. Sykes's desert was a place of scientific inquiry and testing of masculine vigor for people who lived in material comfort and therefore did not have to exert themselves every day just to live. He and others of his era traversed the desert as leisured people, not to work to modify it for human convenience or to extract something marketable, but rather to appreciate its beauties and unlock its mysteries. In 1934, Desert Botanical Laboratory director Forrest Shreve summed up the distinctiveness of this new view. "The man of practical affairs," he wrote for *Scientific Monthly*, "looks ruefully at the desert as a great waste. . . . His conception of utility is the prevailing one, which concerns only the physical welfare of man." But a scientific man "can see in the desert many uses of a wholly different type—humanistic, intellectual and esthetic. He can see the desirability of having a little-coveted region in which it is possible for people to dwell simply and cheaply, with the opportunity to wander, to think, to paint, to study." The desert's value for "inspiration [and] scientific work, is worth many times its marginal value in the world of commodities."[8]

As had long been the case in the Papaguería, however, this new vision clashed with old ones. Even as scientists cataloged plant species and marveled at the desert's beauties, other people continued to exert energy to rearrange the landscape to make it more suitable for humans. That is, they worked. In 1911, John Greenway acquired and began expanding the New Cornelia Mine in Ajo and made it one of the state's earliest large-scale copper extraction operations. As the New Cornelia grew, mine workers came to stay in Ajo, and so did shopkeepers, schoolteachers, machinists, and others who served the miners. Hoping to match the New Cornelia's success, smaller-scale prospectors scoured the surrounding mountains, including the Quitobaquito Hills, looking for valuable minerals. In 1917, Robert Louis Gray Sr. began running cattle in the Ajo Mountains, along the international border, and near Quitobaquito.[9] His efforts blossomed into a local family cattle enterprise that endured into the 1970s.

As it had for centuries, the oasis attracted plenty of human activity, as desert dwellers and visitors of diverse origins and ambitions used the oasis to sustain themselves. Meanwhile, homesteads sprang up near Quitobaquito. Newcomers by the names of Johnson, Oldham, Jenkins, Montgomery, and others squatted on surrounding lands to try to make a living, and Greenway contemplated extending his railway to Quitobaquito and into Mexico. José Juan Orozco, who applied for American citizenship in 1924, continued to ranch a bit, farm a bit, and maintain the irrigation canals supplied by the pond, family operations that had been going on since the 1880s. He even dug a new well a few miles to the north on Pozo Nuevo Road. It came to be called José Juan's Well and Pozo Nuevo (Spanish for "New Well"). A small mining district of more than thirty claims mushroomed in the hills above the springs. In 1917, a handful of US infantry also camped briefly at the pond while trying to secure the border from followers of the Mexican revolutionary Pancho Villa. Operating from Quitobaquito and surrounding water sources, American bandits rustled cattle from Sonoran herders and drove the animals north across the border, beyond the jurisdiction of Mexican authorities. Mexican thieves did the same in the opposite direction. During Prohibition between 1920 and 1933, smugglers ran whiskey over the border near Quitobaquito and other places.[10] Smugglers, rustlers, Asian crossers and their pursuers, revolutionaries, and soldiers moved about, while farmers, miners, merchants, and ranchers tried to stay put. Quitobaquito did not make any of them rich, but it was a good place where they could get by in a difficult environment.

Although the O'odham people's moving and staying adaptations had long shared the desert, American labor and science did not easily coexist. Whether sedentary or mobile, labor left its imprint on the fragile desert environment, which alarmed those who wanted to preserve it. Cattle overgrazed the grasses, fouled water sources, eroded hillsides, and ate cactus. Miners dragged heavy equipment across the land and carved tracks that tore up vegetation and accelerated erosion. As one observer said of the desert's slowness to erase any disturbance: drive twice in the same spot, and you have a road. Wildlife shied away from human activities. At Quitobaquito, for example, bighorn sheep had been hunted and scared off, even though as late as the 1890s, they were reported to be abundant in the hills near the springs.[11] Scientists like Shreve and others who valued the desert for its intellectual and cultural benefits rather than material production worried that the sheep and pristine expanses of cactus could not survive the labors of the extractors. Scientists, too, wanted to stay put, but they wanted to do so more gently. They sought to prevent the desert landscape from disappearing under the pressure of grazing, mining, homesteading, and other staying-put activities. At the most basic level, labor sought to modify the desert, while science preferred to keep it as it was.

For most of American history, labor had the legal upper hand, but by the 1920s, there was a limited but growing precedent for preservation of Sonoran Desert lands for public benefit. Withdrawal of lands from private exploitation began in 1907, when President Theodore Roosevelt set aside a sixty-foot strip, the so-called Roosevelt Reservation, paralleling and adjacent to the border for activities related to securing the international boundary. In 1923, President Calvin Coolidge designated the quarter-mile radius around Quitobaquito Springs, within which the Orozcos still lived, as a federal water reserve. The Orozcos retained the right to use the water, though they did not own the land. The state of Arizona in 1929 passed a Save the Cactus law forbidding unauthorized collection of cacti. In 1930, President Herbert Hoover reserved some land on the US side of the border north of Sonoyta for a customs station.[12]

In the early 1930s, a few people began to envision a much larger federal reserve to protect hundreds of square miles. The NPS was looking to systematize its plans for expanding to new kinds of parks, including ones in the southwestern desert, to protect exemplary species. In 1931, Edwin McKee, a naturalist at Grand Canyon National Park, began discussing with the Desert Botanical Laboratory's Shreve the possibility of establishing a national monument "featuring desert vegetation." Intrigued, the Grand Canyon superintendent wrote to the National Park Service director, who sent Yellowstone superintendent Roger Toll to tour southern Arizona and southern California by auto in early 1932 to look for suitable locations. Toll recommended three sites for desert parks, including territory west of the Ajo Mountains between Ajo and Sonoyta. There was "no better Organ pipe [cactus] area," he reported, and the expanse boasted "a liberal growth of sahuaro" too. Anticipating future land-use controversies, he urged that the proposal for the reserve should come from Arizonans, not the Park Service. Accordingly, later that fall, Shreve and a team of scientists from the University of Arizona and the Desert Botanical Laboratory visited the area and endorsed the idea. Arizona congresswoman Isabella Greenway—the widow of the New Cornelia Mine and railroad entrepreneur John Greenway—also favored a park, saying in a 1934 letter to National Park Service director Arno B. Cammerer that she was "intensely interested in preserving this unusual grove of cacti and ha[d] felt for years that a National Monument should be established." The Tucson Natural History Society and the Pima County Board of Supervisors both passed resolutions in favor of a monument in early 1934. The Ajo Chamber of Commerce also endorsed it. Support came as well from the Papago Reservation via Office of Indian Affairs head John Collier—with the request that the Tohono O'odham be allowed to continue their historical use of the park. There is no record of what the O'odham thought of all this; likely they were not consulted. In 1935, the NPS directed its southwestern monuments chief, Frank "Boss" Pinkley, to conduct a survey to draw the exact boundaries. As Cammerer wrote to Representative Greenway at the end of 1935, the Park Service believed that "national monument status would be the best form of land use for these areas."[13]

As advocates worked out the justification that they hoped would win the presidential approval required for a monument to be designated, they articulated a new strategy for flourishing in the desert, a version of staying put, but doing so gently. Above all, this variant involved drawing boundaries around lands for natural preservation, particularly for scientific purposes. The Park Service had charged Toll with finding places to protect stands of cacti. In his report, Toll identified three great species of the southwestern flora—the saguaro, the Joshua tree, and the organ pipe cactus—and recommended a preserve for each, one in California, one on the outskirts of Tucson, and another in the heart of the Papaguería. The Papaguería monument, Toll and others pointed out, would protect most of the

Organ pipe cactus near Quitobaquito Pond, 2019. *Stenocereus thurberi* thrives in the monument, one of the only places in the United States where it grows. Photo by Jared Orsi.

sizable stands of organ pipe cactus, *Lemaireocereus thurberi* (now *Stenocereus thurberi*), north of the border. So important was this species to their vision that they named the proposed park Organ Pipe Cactus National Monument.

Even at the time, however, the organ pipe cactus was never the sole purpose of the reserve. In his report, Toll also extolled the saguaros, chollas, and other plants, as well as the area's birds, bighorn sheep, javelinas, Gila monsters, rattlesnakes, and more. The "scenery," he averred, "is equal to any." Geologist E. R. Pohl wrote in August 1936 that the area "represents a paradise of investigation to the petrographer and petrologist." He also gloried in the "great expanse" of desert valleys and quoted a previous scientist who had labeled it a "strange wonderland, isolated and different from the rest of the country." University of Arizona biologist Walter P. Taylor added that most of the nation's reserves were at high elevations. America needed to preserve some scientifically valuable lowland places. The 1906 Antiquities Act had stipulated that national monuments had to be of historical or scientific value. Clearly, the area north of the border and west of the Ajo Mountains qualified.[14]

Indeed, the advocates sought to protect not just one species or even a list of them. Rather they sought to preserve intact an entire ecological community. "The interrelations between the life and the environment," Shreve wrote, "are intimate and intricate. Every aspect of the desert is closely tied to every other aspect of it." And to study such relationships, he wrote in 1936, science cannot confine itself to the lab but rather must include "widely extended observation in the field." As wildlife biologist W. B. McDougall would later remark, "This is primarily a biological monument." He believed it would never be "very popular with the majority of tourists." Nevertheless, it had "very great scientific and educational value as a sanctuary for the Organ Pipe Cacti and the Gaillard Big Horns, together with the other plants and animals which help to make up a unique ecological community." To men like Toll, Shreve, and W. B. McDougall, the conclusion was inescapable. To preserve species and to understand them and their ecological relationships, it was necessary to mark off permanent space—a lot of it—for a preserve, where it would be possible, as Shreve put it, "to see the whole pattern and design of desert life."[15]

Preservation, then, would enable the desert ecological community to stay put. Scientists and other park advocates aimed to fix the species and their relationships to each other and to the land in both time and space—to prevent the desert ecosystem from ever changing within the park borders and to prevent outside things from entering and defiling it. Identifying, marking, and even fencing the boundaries—to keep out poachers, livestock, and anything else that would move across the park's borders—preoccupied park advocates and early staff from the beginning. The list of mobile things the reserve would need to keep out was long: poachers, cactus collectors, private cattle, Native Americans' sheep and goats, vehicles, homesteaders, and prospectors, for starters.[16] Like miners staking out claims or ranchers fencing range, the NPS aimed to claim a piece of property and stay put.

To staying put in space, the NPS also added freezing time. Most advocates agreed with the geologist Pohl, who appreciated that this piece of the Sonoran Desert represented "what is probably the most ancient and most continuous desert in the world, conditions such as are found there today having apparently continued with but few interruptions since pre-Cambrian times, more than 500 million years ago." He was wrong—the Sonoran Desert has a rich history of transformation over time—but it *appeared* to them unchanged, and advocates wanted to keep it that way. For example, W. B. McDougall advised in 1937 that "any change in the environment, such as the introduction of domestic animals would result disastrously to these plants. It is of national importance that the environment be maintained in its present condition. . . . The environment of this unique plant life [should] be studiously protected and kept unmodified."[17] The "present condition," of course, included livestock, but that was beside the point for a people pursuing permanence.

Amid this zeal to preserve time and space, even the historically mobile O'odham peoples had to ask permission to use the reserve. Their representatives in Washington haggled with the NPS to adjust the monument boundaries to accommodate Native American grazing and water sources. And on June 2, 1936, Office of Indian Affairs commissioner John Collier wrote to the director of the National Park Service endorsing the proposed monument, noting that a "definite statement should be made in the proclamation . . . that the right of picking the cactus fruit within the area will be reserved to the Indians." It was granted—apparently on the grounds that the O'odham's pitahaya harvests were part of the unchanging past the Park Service sought to preserve.[18] Even so, the fact that the O'odham now had to request permission to enter lands that they had historically moved freely across indicated the degree to which staying put had trumped moving about in southern Arizona.

While the NPS was imagining converting part of the Papaguería to a monument for nature preservation, another Department of the Interior agency, the Office of Indian Affairs, was removing and transforming the region's longtime inhabitants. Manuela Carmello, who descended from A'al Vaipia residents, and her husband, Alfonso, by the 1920s lived at a Hia C'ed O'odham village called Darby Well just south of Ajo and forty miles north of the oasis. In the 1920s and 1930s, the Office of Indian Affairs paid Alfonso and Manuela five dollars apiece for their three girls and sent them to an Indian boarding school at Fort Yuma. Boarding schools such as the one at Fort Yuma forbade the use of Native languages and replaced traditional dress with uniforms. Office of Indian Affairs staff believed removal of children would civilize them. It was, commissioner of Indian Affairs John Collier said, an "upbuilding task." Believing that Native adults were poor parents, the upbuilders sought to cultivate in the children "reason," "loyalty," "service," "health," and "efficiency," on behalf of "country, community, and home."[19] To accomplish this, whipping, although technically forbidden, was common and widely seen as a necessary tool. So was manual labor, and the students were often put to work in fields or farmed out to local landowners to pick cotton and melons. On occasion, Alfonso and Manuela traveled some 150 miles to see their daughters but were turned away after a brief visit, the school staff probably wanting to minimize contact between the students and any potential traditional influence of families. Sending children away to such a place must have been a heart-wrenching decision. Some families hid their children. Others refused to participate in tribal censuses, fearing that the enumerations were a way for the government to find students for the schools. But times were hard in the Papaguería, and there was a severe shortage of local schools and a surfeit of children. Alfonso Carmello weighed his options and decided to get his kids an education.[20]

Desert conservation and Native upbuilding, divesting both land and people of their indigenous heritage, were two heads of the same colonial coin. Nowhere in southern Arizona could this be seen more clearly than at Baboquivari, the mountain where I'itoi lived. Located on the Papago Reservation, the 7,730-foot pink granite peak was the most sacred of places to the Tohono O'odham. Foresters, however, had long dreamed of building a fire lookout station there. Rumor held that from the top you could see all the way to the Sea of Cortez nearly two hundred miles away. Although for a long time the mountain's steep slopes held them at bay, they appear to have given no thought to the spiritual desecration a station would inflict on the home of the O'odham Creator. Finally, in 1933, the Papago Reservation superintendent and forester launched the assault. Indian crews under white supervision hammered and dynamited their way upward.

They sliced a series of landings into the sheer granite face of the monolith and bridged them with redwood staircases. By December, they clambered onto the summit and established the fire lookout. "Baboquivari is taken," an article trumpeted. "Baboquivari has at last been conquered and put into service which will save many dollars. . . . This is conservation at its peak."[21] In the imaginations of conservationists, both land and people in the Papaguería needed to be a little less Indian. Boarding schools, fire lookouts, and a new national monument would be among the institutional tools for accomplishing that.

On April 13, 1937, when President Franklin Roosevelt signed Executive Order 2232, creating Organ Pipe Cactus National Monument under the Antiquities Act, the US government added a piece of the Papaguería to the national land grid that parceled territory by ownership within straight lines. The proclamation ensured that from the Papago Reservation's western boundary to the third meridional section line through townships 17, 16, 15, and 14 south, range 8 west, and from the international boundary north to the third latitudinal section line through township 14 south, ranges 8, 7, 6, and 5 west, the National Park Service would try staying put gently. When the ink dried on Roosevelt's signature, Quitobaquito lay inside those straight-edged borders. In the summer of 1939, wildlife technician Andrew Nichol conducted one of the first NPS surveys of forage and water conditions on the monument lands. Although he lamented that human activity had driven all mammals from Quitobaquito, he also predicted that "when poaching is finally stopped here, these springs will be the most important wildlife center on the Monument."[22] One problem, though, was that José Juan Orozco was still trying to stay put there as well, and what the park called poaching, he thought of as subsistence.

Erasing Himdags: *Park Management of Quitobaquito, 1937–1962*

In 1937, NPS staff began converting Organ Pipe Cactus National Monument from an executive order into a park. The materials prepared for the first master plan identified the main subjects for visitor interpretation as biology, geology, Papago ethnology and history, and archaeology. Quitobaquito would have been an excellent place—perhaps the best in the park—to interpret all these topics. The materials, however, barely mentioned the oasis at all. Quitobaquito, long a place of human presence and even in the 1930s a site of grazing and homesteading, did not match the early park leadership's conception of what a nature preserve should be. Moreover, it was inaccessible. A trip to Quitobaquito, one park document observed, would appeal only to "the more hardy breed of tourists," who did not mind "getting stuck in the sand" or "dragging bumpers on steep ditches." Instead, the master plan materials called for confining monument visitation to an area adjacent to a highway to be built between Ajo and Sonoyta. Monument headquarters, with a parking lot, nature trail, and interpretive area, would abut the thoroughfare, and a four-mile side road into Alamo Canyon would take visitors to a picnic area east of the highway and through a sample of the desert's wonders. The "greater portion of the monument," the report said, "is to be kept in its primitive condition" and open only to people interested in "serious study." "No interpretational devices are planned . . . for these portions of the monument."[23] Staying put gently, then, meant protecting the land in a state similar to an imagined distant past that had few or no people in it. This vision, of course, brought the park immediately into conflict with the people who occupied it in the present and made environmental preservation into an act of landscape creation.

Within months of the monument's establishment, Robert Gray, whose family had ranched the preserve's lands since 1919, filed a request to continue running cattle there. A year later, the park granted him the first of many grazing permits that would allow the family's stock to munch native grasses into the 1970s. In 1938, Albert Long, president of the Arizona Small Miners' Association, complained to Arizona senator Carl Hayden that prospecting was being excluded from the monument. Under pressure from Hayden and over vehement protests by scientists and conservationists, Congress passed legislation in 1941 to permit mining in the park as a wartime measure. In May 1939, the commissioner of Indian affairs asked permission for the Tohono O'odham to graze stock in the southeastern portion of the preserve, which abutted the Papago Reservation. The monument leaders acquiesced, provided that it was only cattle and not sheep or goats. An official agreement to this effect was signed in 1940. The preoccupation of monument management for the first three decades was to manage the park in a way that would minimize these conflicts, giving in enough to prevent them from becoming public relations disasters that would undermine the entire concept of national monuments, but not enough to allow local extractive uses to destroy this remnant of pristine Sonoran Desert. Against this backdrop, on July 28, 1938, the Office of Indian Affairs filed a request on behalf of José Juan Orozco to graze a hundred head of cattle near Quitobaquito. When the acting director of the National Park Service acceded to this petition on August 26, it launched a nearly twenty-year struggle between the Orozcos and the Park Service for control over Quitobaquito and what should move and what should stay put there.[24]

Contrary to the monument's preservationist aspirations, the Orozco homestead was not pristine wilderness. Dorsey had moved some 350 cubic yards of earth to construct the dam, and the family and others maintained it for seven decades. After the dispersal of the pond's O'odham community in the 1910s, the Orozcos stayed on; José Juan's son Jim grew up there and continued in residence as an adult with his wife, Mary Antonia. José Juan's brother and sister-in-law lived there briefly in the 1920s. Thereafter, until the 1940s, no one but Orozcos lived there, though many O'odham visited, and some continued to regard it as tribal land, in the tradition of common ownership they had practiced for centuries. They continued to visit A'al Vaipia as late as the late 1950s. Hia C'ed

Orozco homestead, 1939. Park Service and other federal officials met here frequently with the Orozcos between 1937 and 1957 to negotiate the family's presence in the park. Photo by Natt Dodge. Courtesy of Western Archeological and Conservation Center, National Park Service, Organ Pipe Cactus National Monument, Catalog 15919.

O'odham elder Marlene Vazquez recalled as a child her grandmother piling the family into an old Plymouth and hauling them down to the cemetery near the pond to "keep tradition" and pay respects to deceased family members. When Park Service personnel inspected the dam in December 1950, it impounded about 2.4 acre-feet of the springs' flow. Nearby, the Orozcos had constructed a one-room adobe house, a two-room adobe house, a saguaro rib house, and another adobe house on the Mexican side of the border. They had also built a corral. Twelve hundred feet of ditch—ten inches wide and six deep—carried water from the springs to the pond and the Orozco compound. Another two thousand feet brought water from the pond to fields on both sides of the border. Cottonwoods and other shade trees had been planted, and the residents had cut wood for fuel and construction. The family cultivated fifteen acres at the time, but that figure had been as high as eighty, according to a 1912 War Department map. In the fields grew eight fig trees, about thirty pomegranates, some corn, and some melons, none of them native to the Sonoran Desert.

The fields spanned the border, crossing the sixty-foot Roosevelt Reservation and a parallel reserve the Mexican government had designated on its side. Orozco cattle grazed in a five-to-six-mile radius around the pond. He cleansed them in a dipping vat. He also owned a grinding mill. To stay on the right side of the animal spirits, he cremated the bones of the game he shot. To the Orozcos' consternation—although they held no legal title, they considered the land theirs—a camp of the US Border Patrol joined them at Quitobaquito in the mid-1940s to monitor the problem of Mexican cattle carrying hoof-and-mouth disease into the United States. The federal agents made themselves comfortable by erecting tent-frame structures, driving their automobiles into the site, and piping some of the springs' flow to their camp.[25] Thus, well into the twentieth century, Hia C'ed O'odham at Quitobaquito lived an adapted version of their people's traditional ways. The Orozcos took advantage of modern opportunities of staying put, but they still ignored the border, hunted game, and moved about when they wanted to, and they built a landscape to accommodate this. They stayed put more than their ancestors had, but this modified himdag nevertheless proved anathema to the Park Service's conservation values.

The Orozco compound at Quitobaquito showed that, contrary to NPS visions for preserving a peopleless, pristine desert, indigenous peoples did not inhabit the Sonoran Desert only in the past. Their presence in the here and now constituted an administrative challenge for park managers. On August 1, 1941, the monument's first custodian, William Supernaugh, along with three white officials from the Papago Reservation and another man, paid a visit to José Juan Orozco to put a stop to his alleged violations of park policies. Orozco, Supernaugh complained, was shooting deer. He had even been caught the previous August jerking venison at his homestead. Orozco countered that he had killed the animals on the Mexican side of the border. But that was not all. The custodian charged that Orozco had torn down a previous settler's cabin and erected a new one of his own on the spot. When monument officials ordered him to tear down or move the new structure, he delayed, then later rebuilt it. He cut wood and brush for his corral. He also allegedly harbored smugglers and other illegal border crossers.[26]

The purported transgressions did not just violate monument regulations but also challenged the officials' core vision of the park as a place for staying put in time and space. As park and Office of Indian Affairs staff explained in a separate visit to José Juan Orozco, they objected to his hunting "because the Park Service wants to keep the wildlife in a natural state."[27] To impose its vision of preservation, the staff needed things inside the park to stay inside and things outside to stay outside. But smugglers and hunters who crossed boundaries moved in and out of the monument's jurisdiction, thus evading the control park managers wished to exercise. Moreover, in hunting, cutting wood, and erecting, dismantling, and moving structures near Quitobaquito, the Orozcos were merely continuing to do what human beings in the area had done for millennia. Up to 1937, none of these had been a crime, but the monument changing the rules to preserve an imagined pristine past that had no people in it made their actions illegal. What the Park Service viewed as deterioration of nature's past, the Orozcos experienced as cultural continuity.

The first direct conflict between the Orozcos and the Park Service involved a fence. From the beginning, officials deemed fencing to be among the most important steps to establish the monument. Among their other concerns, the staff worried that without barriers, livestock from the Papago Reservation would stray through the passes in the Ajo Mountains and onto monument lands. World

War II put the brakes on all construction projects at Organ Pipe and across the entire Park Service, so little was accomplished in the way of fencing at first. But the end of the war and an outbreak of hoof-and-mouth disease among Mexican livestock in the mid-1940s renewed officials' interest in fencing at Quitobaquito and all along the international boundary. Monument officials' desire to keep the in, in and the out, out clashed with the O'odham habit of movement. The fence would bisect the Orozcos' homestead. Ditches from the pond ran right across the international boundary. The Orozcos moved animals, machinery, and tools across the border to work their fields, which also straddled the line. A fence to exclude diseased Mexican cattle would make this daily movement, on which the family's subsistence depended, impossible. NPS acting regional director John M. Davis worried that "we could be justifiably criticized if we should arbitrarily divide Jim Orozco's farm by a fence."[28]

So officials made another trip out to the Orozco compound. Participants' recollections of this meeting differed widely. The Park Service claimed to have offered to build Orozco a gate through which he and his stock and materials could pass. Officials asked that he keep the gate closed, to prevent diseased animals from entering the monument. Jim Orozco, in contrast, told Tom Childs that the government was prohibiting his water use and had ordered him to leave Quitobaquito. He asked Childs to help him keep his ranch. Childs wrote to longtime family friend Senator Carl Hayden, addressing him as "Dear Carl" and saying that as long as he could remember, and long before that, the Sand Papagos had used the land and water at Quitobaquito. If the senator would do anything to help the Orozcos remain at Quitobaquito, "you will have done a nobel deede for the one who rightly owns [it]." Hayden, who had previously intervened in Organ Pipe management on behalf of the Grays and Albert Long, asked NPS director Newton Drury to explain.[29]

Drury's carefully worded two-page response explained that the Orozcos did not have title to the land, that the Park Service did not object to their water use, and that the monument officials had offered to build a gate. He opened and closed the letter by assuring Hayden that there must have been some miscommunication "due to linguistic difficulties." The family spoke "very little English." Much as Orozco had used the international boundary to avoid culpability for hunting violations, NPS officials now hid behind alleged language barriers to refute Hayden's implication that they had handled Orozco roughly. The linguistic miscommunication may or may not have been an accurate assessment on Drury's part. Although some government documents echo Drury's claim of Orozco's limited English, other evidence attests that Jim Orozco spoke English, Spanish, and Piman, and that he had friends among people of all three cultures. The meeting at Quitobaquito may have been more amicable than it was rendered in the circuitous Orozco-Childs-Hayden retelling, but it is also not hard to imagine that the often-brusque Supernaugh had issued veiled or direct threats to intimidate

Orozco. Certainly, he was hoping by this time to move the family from park lands eventually. The International Boundary and Water Commission had already advised the regional NPS officials that it was "possible for the National Park Service to cause the removal of Mr. Orozco's buildings from the National Monument." And, as Drury put it more politely to Hayden, the Park Service was hoping to acquire the family's water rights, or at least "all rights appurtenant to land use and development," and to get "Orosco to move his buildings to the land he occupies in Mexico." Although the fence—with gate—was completed in 1948, acquiring the Orozco interests would be a larger task.[30]

José Juan Orozco died in his one-room adobe house at Quitobaquito in April 1946. His son Jim and Jim's family continued to live there, but the patriarch's death opened the way for the Park Service to eliminate the family's interests from the monument. First, it declined to renew the grazing permit, which had expired with José Juan's passing. Next, NPS officials moved to acquire the remaining Orozco holdings. Supernaugh visited the oasis in December 1950, along with NPS water resource specialist A. van V. Dunn and the agency's land attorney Merritt Barton to begin assessing the claims the family might hold. Days later, the assistant regional director for the NPS Southwest Region, P. P. Patraw, suggested that the Orozcos held no title to land but that their water rights and an easement along the ditches might be purchased by the government. This, he said, would work best via a condemnation suit, which would allow the courts to establish the contents and value of the Orozco interests.[31]

Even though Jim Orozco consented to the condemnation, the process moved slowly. At one level, the transaction was simple. The federal government was going to pay Orozco to take his cattle and belongings and move his family away from Quitobaquito. Initially, Orozco assented to this arrangement, though he would later change his mind. In the American property law system, designed for the management of individual people staying put in precisely defined places, however, the transaction involved much more. The value, location, and contents of Orozco's interest had to be precisely defined. Did he own any land or water rights? If so, how much, and did his ownership derive from occupation and use of the site and its resources or was it by inheritance from José Juan? If the latter, had the estate ever been probated, and if so, was it by the state of Arizona or the Papago agency? Were there any other heirs who could claim a share? Who owned the rights to the well Orozco had previously transferred to the Grays without proving that he even owned them himself? His water use had to be measured. The land had to be surveyed and the boundaries determined. All this—and more—generated thousands of pages of paperwork. Not until October 1957 did the grinding federal bureaucracy and the state court system clear the way for $13,000 cash to change hands and the Orozcos to move from Quitobaquito, leaving behind their buildings, ditches, figs, and pomegranates, along with a host of new management questions for the park.[32]

Razing Arizona

Now that it had control of Quitobaquito (the Border Patrol had moved out in 1952, with the declining threat of hoof-and-mouth disease), the park had to figure out what to do with this site that it had initially considered marginal to the monument's mission. In late October, a frustrated superintendent James Eden wrote to NPS regional director Hugh Miller that Orozco still had not left his compound. Although the O'odham man had received payment and promised to move, "in true Indian fashion," Eden wrote, Orozco had not yet vacated the homestead. Eden was anxious "to start cleaning up around the springs and pond and tearing down everything in sight." As Eden later wrote, he believed that the "only objects of historic value" in the park were "archeological artifacts." There were "no important historic structures." Accordingly, in 1959, the park's long-range development plan allocated $4,000 for removing buildings and erasing evidence of human presence, ranking the erasure as a top-priority project.[33] They were going to construct a new landscape at Quitobaquito without people, something that had not existed since I'itoi had rewarded his followers with land.

Adobe ruins. Collapsing buildings of the Orozco homestead, 1954, three years before the National Park Service acquired the site. A Park Service document said of this scene, "Now the adobe buildings are fast falling to ruins and returning to the earth from which they came." Like generations of Americans before them, Park Service officials alleged that the absence of improvements to the landscape justified the taking of indigenous lands. Photo by Moulton Smith. Courtesy of Western Archeological and Conservation Center, National Park Service, Organ Pipe Cactus National Monument, Catalog 15919.

Razing Quitobaquito. In 1962, the national monument dredged the pond at
Quitobaquito and razed the historical structures belonging to the departed Orozco
family and others who had lived there. Courtesy of Western Archeological and
Conservation Center, National Park Service, Organ Pipe Cactus National Monument,
Catalog 15919.

Without consulting any O'odham people, historians, or archaeologists and
operating out of the staying-put-gently preservationist paradigm that had long
guided management of Organ Pipe, the Park Service obliterated the family's
seventy-year residence at Quitobaquito. Beginning on January 8, 1962, workers
hired by the Park Service did away with the fields and razed the remaining buildings. They hauled away old tin cans and other debris and pulled up fences. In
concession to the fact that full erasure of human presence would have required
destroying the scenic pond and arboreal surroundings, the workers left the dam,
remnants of the orchard, and some of the ditches. By March 1962, when NPS
regional naturalist Natt Dodge visited the site, the metamorphosis was nearly
complete. The fields and buildings were gone. The lagoon had been fenced to
keep cattle out, and the Park Service had "cleaned up all unsightly debris left
there by the family of Indians." All this, Dodge marveled, "has been carried out
with a minimum of damage to the natural features of the site." The "natural
conditions," he predicted, "will restore themselves in a reasonably short time."
But, as Hia C'ed O'odham elder Marlene Vazquez later remembered it, "They
wiped out everything, making it look like nobody had ever lived there."[34]

Few people lamented the demise of the ramshackle homestead. Scottsdale, Arizona, resident E. Donald Kaye, however, felt differently. After reading about the destruction in the *Arizona Republic*, Kaye wrote to the secretary of the interior, Stewart Udall: "I like the old adobes and I think they should be preserved particularly when there is known history connected with them." He asked the secretary to "do something about some of your 'mad housekeepers' in the Park Department." The Park Service's response was that Orozco's structures dated to the twentieth century and were "of no known historical significance."[35]

The monument's stance in this regard was very much in keeping with environmentalist passions of the day. The threatened damming of Echo Park in Dinosaur National Monument sparked a wilderness movement in the 1950s that found its way into mainstream American politics and culminated in the passage of the Wilderness Act of 1964. The Wilderness Act allowed Congress to designate lands to be preserved in a pristine state, untainted by human influence, something that Quitobaquito clearly was not. The law defined wilderness as a place "untrammeled by man, where man himself is a visitor who does not remain . . . an area of undeveloped Federal land retaining its primeval character and influence, without permanent improvements of human habitation, [and] which is protected and managed so as to preserve its natural conditions." This was exactly the opposite of why the O'odham valued the oasis. As longtime Tohono O'odham Nation official Verlon Jose would later put it, his people held A'al Vaipia sacred precisely "because people lived there." It was "age-old ancestral ground."[36] Against such a backdrop, bulldozing buildings and erasing evidence of cultivation made sense to the Park Service's mostly white custodians, but to the O'odham it was desecration.

Kaye, however, proved to be prophetic. Organ Pipe's early commitment to preserving a pristine, unpeopled park by minimizing roads and interpretation and simply letting nature take its course did not square with the NPS's midcentury Mission 66 program, which aimed to invigorate visitor services at national parks across the nation. In addition, the rise of an ambitious ecology movement led to a growing sense that parks should actively manage nature, not just keep hands off. The idea of staying put gently was taking on new meanings, and management of Organ Pipe Cactus National Monument, especially Quitobaquito, would have to change accordingly. One day, the "old adobes" and "unsightly debris" would be missed.

| # The Folly of Freezing Time
Impermanence at Quitobaquito, 1962–1994

FOR A CENTURY AND A HALF, across the globe, conservationists have driven indigenous peoples off their lands. Having accomplished this at Quitobaquito, Organ Pipe Cactus National Monument set about building a new landscape there, continuing a twelve-thousand-year-old tradition of shaping the environment to serve cultural aspirations. In addition to erasing the physical presence of the Orozcos, park staff sought to reestablish pristine conditions, as if the oasis had never been touched by humanity. Believing the oasis to be poor habitat for its desert pupfish inhabitants, the park reinforced the dike and realigned and cleaned out the channels. It dredged 4,164 cubic yards of earth from the pond, "restoring it," in the words of the official completion report, "to what is believed to be its original size."[1] This was a curious statement. Even though park staff did not know what the oasis's pristine condition before human modification looked like or when that might have existed, achieving that mythological state was vitally important in the staff's eyes, even if it involved some guesswork—and heavy machinery.

Nobody who participated in erasing the Orozcos' past and deepening the pond, however, would have anticipated what happened at Quitobaquito next. In 1994, the park reversed itself and nominated the oasis to the National Register of Historic Places, essentially proposing to preserve the human history it had obliterated thirty years before. Larry Van Horn, the author of the nomination, averred that memory of Quitobaquito's human past should be preserved because it "shows the march or movement of history from Paleo-Indian to Anglo times." The nomination also cast Quitobaquito as a place to and from which people had historically come and gone, and he maintained that this movement itself should be preserved.[2] The nomination celebrated both change over time and movement in space, and it integrated cultural preservation with natural, a double departure from the earlier attempts to freeze time at the moment of the pond's "original," unpeopled state.

Bookended by the erasure of the Orozco homestead and the National Register nomination, this chapter traverses the environmental and cultural changes between the 1960s and 1990s that prevented park staff from establishing an unchanging pristine natural landscape at Quitobaquito. No sooner had the park restored the pond than the earth around Quitobaquito began, as it had in the very beginning, to shake. The reconstituted pond turned out to be neither original nor better for wildlife. In addition, the aspirations with which Americans built landscapes changed dramatically as well. New laws called for environmental protection and also demanded cultural resource preservation and visitor services. In the 1960s, then, both ecology and culture proved to be unstable, complicating the intention to reestablish an original natural landscape and maintain it permanently. As a result, in the 1970s and 1980s, the monument floundered toward preserving its history and archaeology, a shift that even extended to the first tentative collaborations with the living sons and daughters of I'itoi. By the 1990s, the monument began haltingly to integrate natural and cultural resource management and to tolerate, even value, change in both. But unlike I'itoi, an early maker of landscape at Quitobaquito, the Park Service never managed to spin a web that prevented continued change. Instead, the tumult of the 1960s to 1990s continued to alter the conditions under which the park operated, thwarting efforts to freeze time at Quitobaquito. In this context, preserving what it had once expelled made perfect sense.

Bumbling, Fumbling, and Tinkering

Up to this point, the Park Service had predicated most of its management of Quitobaquito on freezing time. Monument staff relegated human beings to a distant past in which they were few, primitive, and exerted little or no impact on the environment. That is, they did not make landscapes, at least not ones that lasted or that mattered. In this world, nature remained in balance, undisturbed by the activities of people. Officials took it as their mission to re-create this imagined historical moment in time and keep the oasis from changing. Freezing time, however, was difficult to achieve in practice. Not only did history and nature both prove maddeningly dynamic, but so did present culture. New environmental and racial values began to take root in mainstream American politics after World War II, as Organ Pipe was being formed, and flowered in the 1960s and 1970s. As they did, they produced a new legal and cultural environment. The Wilderness Act (1964), the National Historic Preservation Act (1966), the National Environmental Policy Act (1969), and the Endangered Species Act (1973) placed new and sometimes conflicting requirements on national park resource managers. Cultural shifts, such as the continued expansion in vacationing and the era's social liberation movements, especially the American Indian Movement, also changed the country's priorities for what national parks should be and do. In the 1960s and 1970s, Organ Pipe resource managers struggled to glue Quitobaquito to a historical moment that may or may not have ever existed, even as the world moved under their own feet. The unfortunate results of this fraught enterprise led University of Arizona environmental scientist Peter Bennett in 1981 to bemoan the "bumbling, fumbling and tinkering that has been Quitobaquito's fate since the National Park Service undertook its stewardship."[3]

Even as the bulldozers wiped away the last traces of the Orozcos, postwar affluent society made Americans into a nation of vacationers. This revolutionized park policy at the national level and introduced to the oasis a new type of people, visitors. These human beings held aspirations distinct from those of most who had come to Quitobaquito before. They liked to hike, picnic, watch birds, and feel as if they were away from their busy homes. They also needed to park their cars, dispose of their trash, and empty their bladders. And they expected to do all this in relative comfort, even in the desert. Catering to them shaped the landscapes the park made and challenged its attempts to preserve a pristine environment. This expansion of travel resembled the one that industrialization had produced at the end of the nineteenth century, but this time on an even larger scale. Rising wages, paid time off, and earlier retirement gave even working-class Americans larger amounts of disposable income and time to spend on leisure. Thirty cents a gallon at the pump did not hurt, either. Celebrating the national parks as preserves of the nation's most spectacular scenery, democratically open to all, writer Wallace Stegner dubbed them America's "best idea." As vacationers took to the roads to see the nation's public lands, the Park Service in 1956 launched Mission 66, a ten-year development program that aimed by 1966 to construct adequate facilities for the eighty million visitors expected to enjoy national parks by the year of the NPS's fiftieth anniversary.[4]

Like other parks, Organ Pipe kicked off its efforts by preparing a prospectus. Touting the monument's "American Heritage," the document advocated for preserving the Sonoran Desert "unimpaired for the enjoyment and inspiration of the American people." Accomplishing this called for a $3 million makeover including roads, trails, campgrounds that could accommodate big RVs, interpretive exhibits, campfire talks and other public programming, motels, stores, cafeterias, and a visitor center. Meeting the needs of the estimated eight hundred thousand annual visitors (ninety thousand of whom would likely want to camp) expected by 1966 also required enlarging the staff and constructing the attendant residential and administrative facilities and utilities. Quitobaquito, a potential visitor magnet in park personnel's eyes by this time, was the only site specifically named in the prospectus. It noted that a visitor who hiked at the oasis would be "treading in the footsteps of early pioneers of our history." To facilitate this stepping back into history, the park's 1956 Mission 66 plans called for a campground at Quitobaquito as well as a two-way road to get there. Neither of these materialized, but when the Orozco homestead clearing got underway several years later, it included much to attract visitors. While removing the evidence of past peoples, the Park Service built a landscape welcoming to present ones. Work crews installed interpretive signs to explain avian and aquatic life at the pond. They also built a nature trail around the lagoon, a parking lot at the pond's edge, and a fence to keep cattle out of the area.[5] This was a very different vision from the early park managers' plans to keep visitors away from Quitobaquito and other places in the backcountry unless they had the hardiness and scientific interest to encounter it in its raw state.

Not only was American vacation culture driving landscape change at the oasis, so was the local environment itself, especially something very small. *Cyprinodon macularius*, the desert pupfish species that lived in the Sonoyta River drainage basin, was collected by the United States and Mexican Boundary Survey and identified in 1853 by Spencer F. Baird and Charles Girard. "Body elliptically elongated, an inch and six-eighths long," they wrote in a journal article, "above reddish brown, yellowish beneath." It was an unassuming description for a creature that, more than any other, would shape Quitobaquito management for half a century after the elimination of the Orozco homestead. Although the Quitobaquito variety would later be identified as a separate species, ichthyologist Robert R. Miller investigated the oasis in 1953 and pronounced it a fine habitat for what was then still believed to be *C. macularius*. But as late as the mid-1960s, little was known about the pupfish except that they were rapidly disappearing. Alkali bulrushes and other plants that had once been kept at bay by cattle grazing and trampling began to invade the pond and ditches after the Orozcos' stock had departed. The encroaching vegetation choked the lagoon and prevented water from getting from the spring, through the ditches, to the pond. This, and the sediment that had washed into the pool over the years, was the reason for the dredging of the pond in 1962. Work crews captured the pupfish and moved them to a temporary location while the scouring took place. After the dredging and dam work, they restocked the fish. The 1962 completion report indicated that the pupfish were recovering nicely.[6]

That assessment, however, was a miscalculation built on the Park Service's fetish for pristine conditions. In restoring the pond to what they believed were the original depth and size of Dorsey's pool, park managers actually created a body of water that was colder and deeper than was optimal for pupfish. So the monument next constructed a shelf along one part of the pond, to create a warm, shallow breeding ground. As the vegetation problem persisted over the next few years, the Park Service, working with the Arizona-Sonora Desert Museum, also installed concrete ditches and underground piping to convey water from the springs to the pond and maintain constant water levels.[7] Before the park's devotion to what it believed were original natural conditions, human alterations of damming and grazing had enabled pupfish to flourish for at least a century. Once homesteading ended, it became necessary to engineer a new environment to mimic the benefits of the built landscape that the park had destroyed in its pursuit of a peopleless primeval environment.

Picnic tables, 1973. The Park Service installed a picnic area, nature trail, interpretive signs, restroom, parking lot, and other amenities to accommodate visitors during and immediately after the Mission 66 era. Courtesy of Western Archeological and Conservation Center, National Park Service, Organ Pipe Cactus National Monument, Catalog 15919.

Post-Orozco Quitobaquito did, however, turn out to be good for current people. As expected, they flocked to the oasis, provoking yet more new ecological changes and management challenges in the process. The proximity of the parking lot to the shore encouraged members of the exasperating human species to release pet fish, ducks, and turtles into the pond, and on occasion to plant palm trees. The most threatening exotic was the golden shiner, a common bait fish, which was probably introduced by well-meaning anglers. By the time it was discovered in the pond in 1969, it was thriving in the deep, cool waters the dredging had created, outcompeting the beleaguered native species. A scientist at the University of Arizona's Cooperative Fisheries Unit predicted that the golden shiners would eventually drive the pond's pupfish to extinction. So the Park Service removed the pupfish again, poisoned the pond, drained it, refilled it, and replaced the pupfish.[8]

Other management changes were afoot as well. That summer, partly in response to the exotics concern and partly in response to rising visitation numbers, the monument relocated the parking lot a few hundred feet to the east, farther from the shore. It also installed pit toilets, benches, picnic tables, garbage cans, and additional interpretive exhibits. Simultaneously, the park started monitoring flow from Quitobaquito Springs on a monthly basis, an operation that would be upgraded to continuous measurement in 1981 in response to fears that groundwater pumping for agriculture on the Mexican side of the border might be lowering the water table that fed the springs. In 1975, the park launched a program to evaluate the pupfish population annually. In 1976, the monument earned designation as a UNESCO Biosphere Reserve, and in 1978, Congress compounded the contradictions of the oasis when it declared approximately 97 percent of Organ Pipe, including Quitobaquito, as wilderness under a sweeping bill that expanded trails, park boundaries, and wilderness acreage nationwide.[9]

By the end of the 1970s, after all the modifications, Quitobaquito was a place of paradoxes. Historical remains of past people had been eliminated in the name of restoring original ecological conditions, and they had been replaced with an improved road, a parking lot, pit toilets, and a picnic area so that present people could enjoy the pristine nature. And that pristine nature consisted of a pond impounded by a dam and ditches built in the 1860s and continually maintained and upgraded since then—often by purportedly ecologically minded Indians—until it became prime habitat for a fish species that required draining, dredging, building shallow breeding grounds, poisoning, channel modification, exotic species extirpation, parking lot relocation, palm tree removal, water monitoring, and other life support to ensure its survival. Visitors enjoyed all this while strolling in the shade of cottonwoods and other trees planted by previous residents. Confounded, Peter Bennett wrote in 1981 that because of these human modifications, "the area cannot be strictly managed as a natural area. Since the historical structures have been removed, it cannot be managed as a historical site." Quitobaquito was a human-made natural resource. The Park Service had few guides for managing such a thing. Clearly, though, with annual visitation to the oasis numbering in the thousands and the pupfish census numbers diving from 7,295 in 1975 to 1,800 in 1981, erasing historical human presence and letting nature take its course could not preserve the oasis.[10] It needed a new approach.

In 1979, the park began to tackle these paradoxes in its "Interim Management Plan for Quitobaquito Oasis." Sometimes called the Cunningham Plan, the document explicitly acknowledged Quitobaquito's multifaceted significance—ecological, historical, and recreational—and recognized that the oasis required active management to perpetuate its value in all three areas. The Park Service, the report indicated, should "manage Quitobaquito as a prehistoric and historic site," "maintain the existing ecosystem" through limited "manipulative changes," and "provide for public access and enjoyment." Along with a host of interpretive and visitor access measures, it recommended revegetation with native species, restoration of the pond inlet for flood-control purposes, and ongoing maintenance of water flow, ditches, and springs.[11] In sum, it suggested ways to manage Quitobaquito as a multifaceted, dynamic place that was neither purely natural nor fully artificial. This was a far cry from bulldozing buildings, fencing a remnant of pristine desert, keeping cattle and people away, and letting nature take its course.

Short and conceptual rather than detailed and practical, the report elicited criticism from various environmental scientists, notably Peter Bennett. He objected that the purpose section did not adequately spell out the goals and reasons for ecological maintenance and visitor access and that the report assumed many environmental facts without providing evidence. Moreover, he said, its recommendations were insufficient to achieve even the vaguely stated goals of the purpose section. In short, he opined, "it would be an inadequate guide for the resource manager." Perhaps for these reasons, the plan was never implemented, and in 1981, Bennett would observe that "a comprehensive coherent resource management plan for Quitobaquito based on multidisciplinary input" was still "urgently needed."[12]

Even so, by 1979, park staff thought about Quitobaquito quite differently than they had when bulldozers and backhoes had cleared the Orozco homestead and scoured the bottom of Quitobaquito's pond. The dynamic interaction of people and nature that had characterized Quitobaquito's deep history and continued to manifest even after the park's establishment had forced monument personnel to reckon with an ecosystem that, as it had in the time before I'itoi, was still shaking. Faintly, they could imagine building a landscape that was good for nature, history, and visitors, but they lacked the clarity of purpose to implement it. Instead, a series of fruitful ad hoc efforts from the late 1970s to the 1990s continued creeping toward an approach that integrated past and present, nature and culture, and tolerated impermanence.[13]

The "Last" Sand Papago and the Discovery of History

On January 19, 1977, the *Arizona Republic* announced the death of Jim Orozco, an "aged Indian" and the "last known full-blooded Sand Papago." Freezing time had long relied not only on the physical removal of people from landscapes but also on their conceptual removal from the present as well. In numerous statements like the Orozco obituary, scholars, park officials, and others—even some O'odham—declared that the Hia C'ed O'odham had vanished. Such pronouncements consigned them to a past for which the park bore little responsibility. But of course they had not vanished. In fact, Orozco's sale of Quitobaquito angered some of his people who were still alive and holding strong attachments to their homeland. They considered the oasis a communal place, not subject to sale by an individual or a family. As tribal elder Marlene Vazquez later put it, although the Hia C'ed O'odham moved about considerably, "they always went back home to A'al Vaipia because that was their home." Indians who stepped out of the past to express opinions about non-Natives' remaking of the landscape in the present were inconvenient for the park. Staffers preferred the ancient and now silent makers of potsherds, stone tools, and broken shells, ancients who had no voice to object when non-Native scientists imagined past landscapes without people. The 1979 interim management plan, however, indicated that the importance of culture and history were rising in park managers' estimation. For example, the plan listed prehistoric and historic preservation among its management objectives for the oasis. It also noted the site's "importance also to Sand Papagos living today."[14] Few Organ Pipe documents up to this point had ever acknowledged that contemporary Native Americans had any claim on park sites. Small as it was, this simple statement departed from the park's previous archaeological studies, which had generally cast the O'odham as residents of a bygone past who had left bits of evidence of their exotic, unchanging existence. Legal and political changes of the 1960s, including the National Historic Preservation Act (NHPA) of 1966 and the social liberation movements for Native Americans and other peoples of color, brought O'odham peoples out of the frozen past and into the evolving present, where they could influence management decisions at Quitobaquito. This discovery of history implied that the landscape had historically undergone change and likely would in the future and nudged the park toward integrating its management of nature and culture.

The monument's interest in history goes back to its founding. The first line of Franklin Roosevelt's executive order stated that the reason for establishing the monument was that the lands contained "historic landmarks" and "various objects of historic and scientific interest." Despite this rich history, however, the park initially gave scant attention to this founding mandate. But the legal and cultural flux of the 1960s and 1970s began to change this. The NHPA established the National Register of Historic Places and provided additional protections for sites listed on it. It also established and helped fund and review state and tribal historic preservation programs. Finally, its section 106 required that all activities on federal property, conducted with federal permits, or receiving federal funding include an assessment of the potential impact to historic resources.[15] The legislation led Organ Pipe Cactus National Monument and other parks to pay attention to historic landscapes such as Quitobaquito. Subsequent archaeology in the park would move beyond merely documenting exotic bygone pasts and instead would shape landscape building at the oasis in the present.

In 1967, historian Richard Brown and seasonal ranger Wilton Hoy produced a study, "Historic Sites and Structures Inventory for Organ Pipe Cactus National Monument," which acknowledged the park's legal obligation "to treat [historic] sites and structures with care to preserve their environmental and architectural integrity." Accordingly, the authors identified eighteen sites of historical significance in the monument and recommended focusing attention and resources on preserving these effectively, especially the three primary ones, rather than spreading resources thin by trying to preserve every potential site. Quitobaquito, the authors averred, was "the most important historic site in Organ Pipe" because of its "comprehensiveness of association." Surface water had long attracted people, and thus all of the region's main historical themes, including Native American use, Spanish exploration and missionization, travel along the Camino del Diablo, American pioneering, transportation and communication, and the international boundary survey, "converged" there. Without the benefit of subsequent archaeological studies that definitively established material evidence of the network of trails near Quitobaquito, Brown and Hoy lamented that so few physical remains were left and that the park interpreted history there only as a "sideline" to natural history. The authors nevertheless contended that the remaining resources—the spring, ditches, pond, dams, faint traces of the Orozco homestead, and the oasis's status as one of Kino's stops and its proximity to the Camino del Diablo—justified expanding historical interpretation. Historic and environmental preservation, Brown and Hoy insisted, were compatible. After all, people and animals had come to Quitobaquito "for the same reason: water." Acknowledging the necessity of ongoing environmental management, they advised that it be conducted with greater sensitivity to historic preservation.[16]

The Park Service immediately began practicing, in token fashion at least, what Brown and Hoy had preached. Under the requirements of the National Historic Preservation Act, the park undertook assessments to determine the potential cultural resource impact of its various rehabilitation projects at Quitobaquito. In preparation for the relocation of the parking lot in 1974, for example, NPS archaeologist Sam Henderson visited the site to collect any significant artifacts. Expecting to find only a "small amount of material," he set up no grid, and his "actual collecting consisted of gathering any material that I thought significant to the history or archeology of the location. Whenever in doubt, objects were accepted without ponder." He sent them to the Arizona Archeological Center for further study. "This measure of mitigation," he concluded, "should allow archeological clearance to be granted," which it was. Despite the survey's efforts, the parking lot construction unwittingly plowed up and destroyed the remains of a Native American campsite, possibly of ancient origin.[17]

A more rigorous study was done in 1976 in connection with a proposed realignment of the nature trail at Quitobaquito. This time, the project did not move forward, and it was because of the results of an archaeological survey. Nancy Curriden, the archaeologist in charge, surveyed the surface of the area proposed for construction but emphasized that such a procedure could not determine whether any subsurface resources were present. She noted the extensive damage already done to the area, including by the 1974 parking lot construction, and she contended that Henderson's collection of artifacts without provenance made it even more important to preserve other potential undisturbed sites at Quitobaquito. On these grounds she recommended against trail realignment and instead urged the undertaking of a more systematic survey. The subsequent survey named materials from the historic period, including "thick green bottle glass, which probably dates prior to the 1920s and square handmade iron nails," among the valuable objects in need of preservation at the site. It takes only a little imagination to picture such items being purchased off the shelves of Levy's store by people such as Beatrice Melvin's family, who were still living at the time the survey was done. In contrast to Superintendent Eden's 1962 lack of interest in the Orozco homestead, the NPS now considered twentieth-century historic artifacts worth preserving, once they met the National Historic Preservation Act's test of being at least fifty years old. This second survey confirmed Curriden's initial assessment.[18] For perhaps the first time since the founding of the park, human history received consideration on par with natural history in a management decision at Organ Pipe.

The first systematic archaeological survey of the Quitobaquito area finally came in 1977. It was led by Arizona State Museum head of cultural resource management Lynn S. Teague. The goal was to locate and map all prehistoric and historic sites at Quitobaquito. Over the course of five days of surface investigation, Teague's team identified and precisely located and documented the provenance of objects from nine different clusters of material that irrefutably showed continuous human presence at Quitobaquito from as early as roughly 8000 BCE. The findings provided "time depth" to human use of the area, Teague reported, and would allow for interpretation of changing human subsistence habits over a long period. Although acknowledging that the exact significance was difficult to assess because of the considerable disturbance to the area, Teague noted that Quitobaquito represented the northernmost extension of Sand Papago materials, which made it the only such resource in the United States. She also observed that because a few former inhabitants of the village were still alive, the site provided an opportunity for ethnoarchaeological research. It also showed the integration of the Hia C'ed O'odham into commercial society, a story that could and should, Teague thought, be told through interpretive exhibits to give visitors a fuller understanding of the area's history. She recommended further study and excavation.[19] Teague's report departed from previous park thinking: indigenous peoples changed over time, the historic period was worth preserving, and contemporary O'odham peoples might have something to contribute to understanding and managing the park. It would be a long time before such approaches would entrench themselves deeply in staff's minds, but this was a start.

Meanwhile, O'odham politics and identity evolved, as did the place of Native peoples in American society generally. At first, few Hia C'ed O'odham visited Quitobaquito after the Orozcos left in 1957. Later, some of them told linguist Ofelia Zepeda that "there was no reason for [us] to go back." Apparently, releasing pet turtles, picnicking, bird-watching, and imagining no one had ever been there before did not much interest them, and unlike many of the nation's non-Native vacationers, they had not experienced the national parks as America's best idea. In the 1970s, the Red Power movement pressed for sovereignty through both the construction of intertribalism based on shared indigenous experiences and the rejuvenation of individual tribal identities. Heightened identification with indigenous heritage trickled down from national politics to individual identity. For example, Lorraine Marquez Eiler, a great-granddaughter of the García family who had lived at Quitobaquito in the nineteenth century, recalled hearing elders talk about being Hia C'ed O'odham as she was growing up at Darby Well, but she did not understand much about tribes or reservations or federal recognition. As a high schooler, she moved to Ajo and began to inform herself more. She realized she was Native, even though as a Hia C'ed O'odham she had no official membership in a recognized tribe. As an adult in the 1970s, however, she began investigating why this was. She sought membership in the Tohono O'odham Nation and encouraged others to do so as well, eventually getting elected to the tribe's legislative council. In this context of Native political empowerment and heightened interest in connecting with their heritage, both the O'odham and the national monument began to look at Quitobaquito history anew. As Hia C'ed O'odham elder Miguel Velasco put it at a 1983 meeting with younger Natives, the old people "are all gone. . . . All that is left are you people. . . . Now [you] want to know of them."[20]

One of the nine cultural loci that Teague and her colleagues surveyed at Quitobaquito was the Hia C'ed O'odham cemetery of thirty-four graves, which dated to the decades around the turn of the twentieth century. José Juan Orozco was the last to be buried there, in 1945. Vandalism and natural deterioration had left the graveyard in a dilapidated condition. Descendants felt that the state of the graves dishonored their ancestors, and Park Service officials pragmatically worried about the public health impact. Surviving documents are not clear about who initiated the idea, but on August 15, 1977, monument superintendent Ray Martinez and Fillman Childs Bell, daughter of Martha García and Tom Childs and sister to Beatrice Melvin, convened a meeting at monument headquarters with thirty-five descendants of ancestors buried at the cemetery. The attendees explored several options and agreed on a plan for rehabilitating the graves. Accomplishing this spawned an unprecedented partnership between the O'odham and Organ Pipe Cactus National Monument. First, they collaborated to conduct extensive oral histories and ethnographic research to inform the park about the names and genealogies of those buried there, about Hia C'ed O'odham burial customs and lifeways, and about Quitobaquito history. Throughout, Bell played a key role as both informant and liaison between the Park Service and Hia C'ed O'odham. She coauthored both the Park Service's ethnographic report and a journal article about the project in *Kiva*. Together, they made the story of the Hia C'ed O'odham, past and present, known on a wider scale than ever before. "This report is primarily for the descendants of the Sand Papagos," the final document began. In October 1980, after continued consultation with descendants and after preparing an impact assessment and obtaining clearance from the Arizona State Historic Preservation Office in compliance with NHPA section 106, the Park Service modified the cemetery landscape to match its new sensibilities, covering the graves with steel mesh and stones to prevent future vandalism and deterioration.[21]

Inspired by how much the interviewees had to say beyond the simple question of who was buried in the cemetery, the Park Service commissioned a more extensive oral history project. This one was led by Ofelia Zepeda, a Tohono O'odham poet and University of Arizona linguist. She finished it in 1984. Most previous ethnographic studies of the O'odham peoples had focused on the Tohono O'odham and Akimel O'odham. These studies relegated the Hia C'ed O'odham to the mysterious status of a people largely thought to have melted into Sonoran and Arizona society in the late nineteenth century and disappeared. As late as the 1970s, they were a people dimly understood by outsiders. The pair of Park Service ethnographic studies, however, established for the first time a compendium of information about the Hia C'ed O'odham and their transformation in the twentieth century and enabled them to tell that story. Most importantly, the interviews challenged the misapprehension that they had disappeared and showed that they were a living people, whose history was still unfolding and who should be, along with the many indigenous peoples who had inhabited and visited the area over thousands of years, a centerpiece of park management and interpretation at Quitobaquito.[22]

By the mid-1980s, virtually every historical, ethnographic, or archaeological study of Organ Pipe Cactus National Monument had ended by recommending further investigation. In 1989, funding finally became available for a large-scale systematic archaeological study of the park. Between 1989 and 1991, the NPS's Western Archeological and Conservation Center in Tucson conducted inventory surveys across the monument. The project covered 7,675 acres and 188 loci at 178 sites. Under the direction of archaeologist Adrianne Rankin, the crew logged 752 person-days between June 13, 1989, and May 2, 1991. The result was an 853-page report that identified, dated, and cataloged artifacts, described site locations and historical contexts, and evaluated conditions, research potential, and National Register eligibility for each site. Quitobaquito and its vicinity contained nine sites, all of which Rankin found to be eligible for the National Register, thus requiring section 106 compliance prior to future landscape modifications. In her report, Rankin proposed twenty-one new projects, including mapping, historical research, test excavations, submission of National Register nominations, and an archaeological job-training program for Native Americans. In 1993, Rankin proposed a survey specifically for Quitobaquito. It would encompass 250 acres around the pond and spring, and its goal was to "locate and identify all archeological resources, both prehistoric and historic, that are associated with use of the springs and pond in the Quitobaquito Basin." The proposal promised to assess the site's integrity, threats, and scientific potential and to make management recommendations. She carried out the survey between May and July 1993.[23]

Rankin's survey capped a two-decade period during which the park began to embrace its human past and lived up to the instructions in its founding executive order to preserve objects of historical interest. During this period, the monument moved from disregarding human history entirely to performing required cursory, haphazard archaeological studies, and then finally to comprehensive research. Along the way, the park collaborated with newly interested and assertive O'odham to document their past. Not only did the goal of historic resource management shift from erasing to preserving, but the decision-making process transformed as well. In 1962, the superintendent had decided to bulldoze the Orozco homestead on his own, perhaps in consultation with a few staff members. The decision to restore grave sites, in contrast, involved meeting with Hia C'ed O'odham individuals, accepting their input, empowering one of them to play a central leadership role, writing an impact assessment, and ensuring compliance with section 106 requirements. In addition, women figured prominently throughout the process. Park Service documents from the Orozco removal barely acknowledged the existence of Jim Orozco's wife, Mary Antonia, and almost all NPS staff named in the records were men. In contrast, Fillman Bell, Dorothy Hall from the State Historic Preservation Office, archaeologists Nancy Curriden, Lynn Teague, Adrianne Rankin, and Yvonne Stewart, linguist Ofelia Zepeda, and a host of female O'odham informants were essential to the archaeological and ethnographic undertakings of the 1970s and 1980s. Thanks to a suite of new laws and new players at the table, the park was slowly taking account of its history.

"Natural Landscapes Can Be Cultural Landscapes": Integrating the Management of Environment, Culture, and History

Now that the park had discovered history, it needed to figure out how to manage the oasis with this new awareness. Two NPS documents from the 1990s illustrated the park's incomplete progress along that path. In 1994, the NPS Western Regional Office submitted a National Register nomination for Quitobaquito that cast the site as significant for representing both people and the environment, with both changing over time and changing each other along the way. While the preparation of the nomination was underway, park personnel were also hard at work on a new general management plan. Published in 1997, it featured Quitobaquito prominently, and it too emphasized the integration of natural and cultural resource management. By the end of the century, in the words of Rankin, the Park Service understood that "natural landscapes can be cultural landscapes" and vice versa.[24] Managing Quitobaquito with that insight was quite another thing altogether.

In the early 1970s, the National Park Service directed that historic structures should not be destroyed or modified without permission from the Washington office. Organ Pipe superintendent Edward C. Rodriguez approvingly noted that this measure "should eliminate the danger of loosing structures as occurred at historical Quitobaquito," and he listed the oasis among the monument's sites suitable for nomination to the National Register. In 1977, NPS historian Jerome Greene drafted nominations for several places in the park, Quitobaquito among them.

Claiming significance for all chronological periods, including prehistory, Greene's nomination emphasized that Quitobaquito represented archaeology, agriculture, conservation, exploration, settlement, and transportation. In 1978, the keeper of the National Register approved four sites, but not Quitobaquito. There is no record of the reasoning, but the nomination fit poorly with the era's prevailing historic preservation thinking, which favored the protection of great buildings associated with famous people, events, or places. In its impulse to capture a structure at a dramatic moment in history and to preserve it in that state in perpetuity, this approach was not unlike the environmental preservation in the early years of Organ Pipe Cactus National Monument.[25] In its broad sweep of time, emphasis on historical change, and proposal to designate the site of a nonextant ramshackle homestead of a little-known Native American family in remote Arizona, the nomination was a long shot to impress National Register reviewers.

The national preservation movement, however, was maturing beyond its great-buildings approach. In the 1970s and 1980s many preservationists embraced the idea of cultural landscapes, which increased attention to vernacular architecture. Increasingly, preservationists aimed to save places that, according to architecture scholar Dolores Hayden, combined "natural landforms and buildings that define a particular place or region." Perhaps because the Park Service acquired so many places like Quitobaquito that defied categorization as either human or environmental, the NPS provided much of the intellectual and practical impetus behind the cultural landscape preservation movement, officially recognizing such places as a distinctive landscape type. It described one type of cultural landscape, a historic vernacular landscape, as one that "evolved through use by the people whose activities or occupancy shaped that landscape." Meanwhile, an ethnographic landscape contained "natural and cultural resources that associated people define as heritage resources."[26] Quitobaquito may have flunked the great-old-buildings test that the superintendent applied in 1962, but it seemed to fit nicely as a cultural landscape.

In 1994, now with deeper archaeological knowledge as a result of Adrianne Rankin's surveys, the park once again nominated Quitobaquito, this time as a cultural landscape. This nomination was also rejected, possibly on the grounds that bulldozing and other NPS activity had damaged the site's historical integrity. Although again there is no record of the rationale for the rejection, the nomination's conceptualization is instructive. Adopting a cultural landscape approach, the author of the nomination, Larry Van Horn, a cultural anthropologist with the NPS's Denver Service Center, emphasized the way that Quitobaquito portrayed human interactions with the natural environment, especially their change over time. He nominated Quitobaquito as a historic district, rather than as a historic site, meaning that it was a collection of twenty related sites, including archaeological deposits, prehistoric and historic trails, Sestier's grave, the locations of Levy's store and the Orozcos' buildings, and the dam, ditches, and pond. The period of significance spanned from 9000 BCE to 1944 CE. The Hia

C'ed O'odham cemetery was not included. The oasis was significant, Van Horn argued, as "a cultural landscape that reflects the occupation and interaction of several different ethnic groups with the springs, basin, flats, and hills . . . from prehistoric times to the present period." He maintained that "the idea of a cultural landscape, may be useful to appreciate the overall historical narrative of . . . peoples or cultural groups over time adapting to and utilizing this permanent water source." He also added, "The march of prehistory and history . . . is what Quitobaquito is all about."[27] The Park Service had once tried to freeze time at the oasis. Now it was attempting to preserve the phenomenon of change itself.

History that moved and marched and in which nature and culture intertwined in a way worthy of preservation required a tolerance for impermanence and implied new management strategies. The park staff began work on a new general management plan in 1987. The monument's last master plan had been completed in 1964, a product of the Mission 66 era. Park staff in the 1980s deemed it "outdated" and, with considerable understatement, noted that "several significant changes have occurred since then." For example, the Park Service had to comply with a long list of regulations dealing with pollution, clean air, floodplain management, endangered species, wilderness, archaeological resources, historic structures, environmental justice, illegal border crossers, and Native American graves, human remains, sacred objects, and artifacts of cultural patrimony. Planning in the 1990s, therefore, was a different sort of process from the top-down command-and-control procedures with which the Park Service had erased the Orozcos' homestead. Drafts of planning documents were now to be reviewed by other agencies, and hundreds of pages of public comment were compiled. Park staff met with environmentalists, neighboring communities, other government agencies, O'odham, and others and tried to incorporate their input. Stakeholders, the new general management plan stated, cared "strongly" and "deeply" about pupfish, archaeological remains, visitor access, and more, and sometimes their objectives were "mutually exclusive." Consequently, during the planning process "tempers" sometimes ran "high."[28]

The environment was no less unruly. As pupfish numbers continued to fall, the US Fish and Wildlife Service listed the species as endangered in 1986. Then, in 1987, studies revealed that it was actually a different species, *Cyprinodon eremus*, endemic to Quitobaquito and a few other smaller springs and wells nearby. Several thousand years ago, regional geologic uplift had severed surface water connections between Quitobaquito and the Sonoyta River, and during the resulting isolation, *C. eremus* had evolved into a species distinct from the better-known *C. macularius*, which swam in the Sonoyta River. The well-being of *C. eremus*, however, came partly at the expense of another rare species, *Kinosternon sonoriense*, the Sonoran Desert mud turtle. Like human structures and virtually everything else other than pupfish, the turtles had been removed or destroyed during the pond drainings that the park undertook to save *C. eremus* in the 1960s and 1970s. By the late 1980s, the pond's turtle populations had dropped from a few hundred in the 1950s to between fifty and one hundred. As park staff mitigated the decline, however, they encountered a complex ecology. The omnivorous *K. sonoriense* eats vegetation, fish (which it is not very adept at catching), and aquatic invertebrates, the latter of which it competes for with pupfish. Increasing pupfish numbers meant less nutritious diets for turtles, which compensated by eating more plants. A 1996 study revealed the pond's *K. sonoriense* population to be underweight and undernourished.[29] In this context of uncertain politics and ecology, the park undertook its new master plan.

Funding shortages and the messy democratic tangle of legal compliance and public input periodically delayed the process, but by the mid-1990s, staff had produced several key planning documents. Collectively, they revealed the ways in which park managers responded to both the ecological changes at Quitobaquito and the cultural changes in America between the 1960s and 1990s. Notably, the plan aimed to "establish a mutually agreeable relationship with the Tohono O'odham" and to "preserve and continue their important relationship with this ecosystem." Later it stated that "natural" and "cultural resources" were "inextricably linked." The plan's statement of the park's "significance" listed both natural and cultural features, calling it a "globally significant ecosystem," "the most biologically diverse protected area in the Sonoran Desert," "a site of cultural resources," and a site of "intersection of three cultures . . . that is significant archeologically, geographically, and internationally." Biodiversity, globalization, and multiculturalism reflected late twentieth-century sensibilities that the world was dynamic and changing fast and that places, people, and concepts once thought of as separate suddenly seemed intricately connected. The plan also indicated that the UNESCO biosphere designation, because it sought to preserve remnant ecosystems while also better understanding human interaction with the environment, "underscores the importance of preserving the rich history of the Tohono O'odham and Hia C'ed O'odham." The materials also suggested upgrading the monument to Sonoran Desert National Park to better reflect Organ Pipe's diverse features and to protect it from being closed because of dwindling budgets.[30] In sum, the planning effort reflected the post-1960s rising respect for indigenous cultures, the integration of people and environments, and tolerance of impermanence.

The plans for Quitobaquito captured all this in microcosm. It was, the report said, "an area which holds many precious resources, natural, cultural, and ethnographic." The plans called for making the area around the lagoon a wilderness subzone. The parking lot would be moved again, about half a mile from the pond to an already disturbed site. An orientation sign and interpretive information would greet visitors as they exited their vehicles, and a vault toilet and shaded picnic tables would be handy nearby. Those who wanted a stroll could approach the oasis via a handicapped-accessible trail that would lead to scenic views and good birding at the pond's edge. A few of the social trails that crisscrossed the habitat around the pond would be formalized. Most would be eliminated. The main trail would then loop around, avoiding sensitive archaeological and ecological sites, and return hikers to their cars. The specifics of the design and construction would be guided by a multiagency task force to include members of the Tohono O'odham Nation, the Fish and Wildlife Service, the Arizona State Historic Preservation Office, and the National Park Service. It would draw on expertise in archaeology, anthropology, landscape architecture, and wildlife biology. The park aimed to build a landscape at Quitobaquito in which visitors would enjoy a better experience, while pupfish, turtles, and ancient remains would be disturbed less.[31]

Today, more than a decade past the 1997 general management plan's intended ten-to-fifteen-year time horizon, little of it has been implemented. There is no Sonoran Desert National Park, nor has one seriously been considered. Pupfish and turtles still struggle at Quitobaquito, and the oasis has not yet become the cornerstone of balancing nature, culture, and visitor management that the plan suggested it could be. In this regard, the plan resembles the intriguing but dead-end 1994 National Register nomination. Nevertheless, the two documents, with their tolerance for impermanence, recognition of connections between nature and culture, and valuing of indigenous peoples as both worthy of historical interpretation and contemporary partnership, illustrated how far the park had come since it ran off the Orozcos and attempted to establish imagined pristine conditions and prevent them from changing. How this new thinking could be practiced at Quitobaquito, however, remained elusive. By the end of the century, the park imagined the oasis quite differently and held new aspirations for the kind of landscape it wanted to build there. These ideas found expression in the pages of National Register nominations and ambitious planning documents but proved difficult to implement on the ground. Limitations on funding and reluctance to jettison old imagination held action on these new ideas in check, and despite four decades of archaeological studies, pond draining, and parking lot moving, the monument had so far accomplished little in the way of building the new landscape it envisioned. As monument staff groped toward practical implementation of their aspirations, the oasis came under pressure from an old problem that manifested with intensified urgency. The world at Quitobaquito was still shaking.

| "America's Most Dangerous Park"
Bordering Space at Quitobaquito, 1937–2013

THE PARK COULD NOT FREEZE TIME at Quitobaquito, and nor, it found, could it border space. This chapter is about the consequences of trying. In his 1991 novel, *Language in the Blood*, Kent Nelson described Quitobaquito as remote, sensual, and dangerous, a place where few went, but where those who did might discover what they were made of and what their limits were. His protagonists operated an illegal humanitarian smuggling ring that passed near the oasis en route from the Gulf of California to the north, like travelers for thousands of years before them. Only instead of carrying salt and shells, these adventurers guided refugees of Central American Cold War violence to the United States. It worked—except for the rattlesnake bites—because Quitobaquito was isolated. No one supposed people could be smuggled through such a difficult and out-of-the-way place. Tijuana, Juárez, Nogales, and other urban centers attracted the bulk of the transborder traffic. Consequently, for most of the book, the smugglers managed to sneak people over the border to Quitobaquito and out of the park under the noses of unsuspecting monument officials and the Border Patrol.[1]

Within a decade, fiction became prophesy. On any given night for much of the first decade of the twenty-first century, it was not uncommon for more illegal border crossers to be sleeping in the park than recreational campers.[2] This was alarming. Freezing time has always presupposed controlling space. The park used physical and metaphorical boundaries to ward off anything that might disrupt pristine conditions. Now, border crossers incised new trails through the fragile desert ecosystem, trampled plants, scattered trash, and even occasionally started grass fires. Federal responses proved equally deleterious. Fences, roads, patrols, surveillance systems, and escorted visitation gave the wilderness a militarized atmosphere. Physically, the measures damaged the environment and impeded age-old patterns of human movement. Symbolically, they expressed a national preoccupation with keeping the oasis—indeed the entire park, state, and country—free from intrusion. In the 1990s and early 2000s, border-making came to define Quitobaquito, and as it did, it reinforced the site's recent tendencies toward exclusion, undermining some of the very values the monument was established to protect.

The Long History of Borders and Border Crossing

Border violations in the Southwest long predate the twenty-first century. In 1960, the park maintained essentially no law enforcement presence. In the 1980s, it added two law enforcement rangers, and the federal government deployed fewer than twenty Border Patrol agents to the vicinity. As late as 1997, the general management plan cast Quitobaquito as a pleasant place that tourists would want to frequent. By 2002, however, it took eighty Border Patrol officers and seven NPS law enforcement rangers to police the rising transborder movement of drugs and migrants through the park, and even that was not enough. Over the next decade, dozens of miles of vehicle fencing were constructed along the southern boundary of the park. The security ramp-up may have appeared sudden but was actually decades in the making, rooted in an old national affinity for borders. As soon as the United States and Mexico agreed on a boundary in 1848, they drew a line on maps, surveyed it on the ground, marked it physically, employed agents to monitor it, established legal ports of entry, and levied taxes on people, animals, and goods that crossed it. This is what modern nation-states do: manifest their authority by physically marking their borders. It was not much to see at first—only an occasional waist-high obelisk protruding from the sand to let the coyotes, pronghorns, rattlesnakes, and infrequent human passersby know where one great nation-state ended and another began. Long before the establishment of the national monument in 1937, however, the US government began defining what it wanted at Quitobaquito and what it did not, and it constructed borders to accomplish those preferences. At the same time, an eclectic and creative set of transgressors, including Apaches, O'odham, immigrants, filibusterers, cattle rustlers, seekers of forbidden pleasures, and many more for whom borders and ports of entry proved inconvenient, began to find ways around the barriers. Wherever a nation built a border, those impeded by it contested it, which spawned more and bigger borders, and so on. The dialectic continues to this day.[3]

Bordering, of course, was not the only way to conceptualize and manage space. As the local Native people are fond of saying, "There is no word for wall in the O'odham language." Although the O'odham do recognize the territoriality of peoples, they conceptualize boundaries primarily as permeable and impermanent rather than relying on maps depicting fixed boundaries. This is true, too, of Apaches. O'odham remembrances of the nineteenth and early twentieth centuries abound with stories of movement. In his autobiography, *A Papago Traveler*, James McCarthy recalled hearing tales of O'odham parents who left their children at their Arizona villages while the adults worked in Mexico.

Chona described to Underhill going to work "over the mountains where you call it Mexico," where some of "our" people lived. Her wording acknowledged that while Sonora was a different place from Arizona to Underhill, to Chona, it was essentially still part of the O'odham world. She had no separate name for it, and in her mind she had not crossed any borders. Verlon Jose, a longtime Tohono O'odham Nation tribal official, observed that "the international boundary's an invisible line to us." "Growing up," he remembered, it was like . . . we're just going down to grandma's house. Never did I know that I was going into a foreign country, as they call it." Beatrice Melvin also recalled that her people traveled regularly to Magdalena, Sonora, during the feast of St. Francis. For centuries, O'odham have made the pilgrimage for prayer, feasting, healing, and petitioning that saint. The fact that since 1848 it has been a journey across an international boundary has not dampened their enthusiasm, because for many it is constitutive of their religious identity as O'odham. The indigenous guides employed by Lumholtz six decades after the Treaty of Guadalupe Hidalgo still knew both Sonoran and southern Arizona geography equally well, undoubtedly a function of frequent crossings. And the Orozcos basically ignored the border. As Tohono O'odham vice chair Henry Ramon put it in 2002, "Our people do not recognize this imaginary line that is an international boundary."[4] In contrast to white people, for whom enclosed private property defined liberty and international boundaries established national sovereignty, the O'odham put freedom of movement at the core of their peoplehood. Their continued ability to move across borders for nearly a century after Mexico and the United States drew one was essential to their cohesion and autonomy as a people. It facilitated continuation of religious and other cultural practices, visitation of kin, and gathering of traditional foods. Crossing was an act of independence, of power.

Modern nation-states, however, understand space in terms of demarcation and restriction. During use by indigenous, Spanish, and Mexican peoples, exclusive borders were rare in the region. Starting in 1848, the United States and Mexico constructed one. In *Line in the Sand*, historian Rachel St. John traced the process into the 1930s. Construction began with a survey, but drawing a line was not the same as controlling it. In the second half of the nineteenth century, both nations used their militaries to enforce the line against filibusterers, rustlers, Apaches, O'odham, and others who crossed in and out of national jurisdictions as a way of shielding themselves from nation-states' authority. Military security enabled economic investment in the region and stimulated transborder trade. Both nations wished to regulate that trade to generate tax revenue and to protect the interests of political allies of the state. They established official ports of entry and customhouses, where duties could be levied, livestock inspected, and illegal importation forestalled. In the 1880s, the Mexican government established a customhouse across from Quitobaquito. The United States sent its first line rider, Jeff Milton, to Quitobaquito, making the oasis arguably the birthplace of the Border Patrol. In 1907, President Theodore Roosevelt reserved a sixty-foot strip north of the border, the Roosevelt Reservation, for enforcement activity and ordered it to be cleared of all structures. Ports of entry took on heightened strategic importance during the Mexican Revolution of 1910–1920, as government and rebel forces contested the space and the opportunity it provided to control the flow of arms and other supplies. In the 1920s and 1930s, the US government used nighttime border closures to try to compel moral behavior among its citizens, as Mexican urban vice districts attracted American pleasure seekers, who in turn brought smuggled goods, drunk driving, and scandal back across the boundary when they returned.[5] With agents, customs and immigration regulations, ports of entry, and nighttime closures, the countries tried to limit and direct the age-old pattern of people moving about, on which life in the Sonoran Desert had always been predicated.

Lines, consequently, invited transgressions. In the late nineteenth and early twentieth centuries, Americans hotly debated what to do about their southern border. Immigrants were streaming from Mexico in alarming numbers and without authorization. Avoiding the ports of entry, they resorted to desperate crossings at remote, dangerous locations, suffering and sometimes dying in the attempt. It provoked national soul-searching—would the nation welcome immigrants in the spirit of the words of poet Emma Lazarus inscribed at the base of the Statue of Liberty, or would it seal its border to people of foreign tongues and habits and the perceived threat of labor competition and environmental degradation they brought with them? Meanwhile, posturing American officials accused Mexico of encouraging foreign nationals to enter the country and doing nothing to prevent them from passing through to the United States, and they demanded, mostly unsuccessfully, to be allowed to send immigration police to work in Mexican territory. This dilemma, America's first problem with foreign nationals illegally entering the country, originated not in Mexico or Central America, however, but in Asia. Eager to enlarge the population of its northern provinces and to secure state power against unassimilated Indians, the Mexican government welcomed immigrants from China at the same time that the United States was excluding them. Some became Mexican citizens and entered the United States at ports of entry. Perplexed border officials scratched their heads and wondered whether to allow the migrants passage as Mexicans or to detain them as Chinese, their bewilderment the by-product of laws that failed to anticipate that one could be both.[6] Other sojourners, however, sought the dangerous path through the rugged desert. For them, Quitobaquito proved an attractive entry point. There, at least, they could obtain water and purchase supplies at Levy's store.

Over time, however, US immigration control increasingly targeted Mexicans. Thanks to vigorous lobbying by labor-hungry agribusiness interests, Congress had exempted Mexico from the 1920s immigration quotas it imposed on other nations. Still, the $18 per person fee (more than $300 in 2022 dollars), as well as the invasive personal inspection process at the ports of entry, increasingly encouraged Mexicans to cross at unauthorized locales, heightening Border Patrol efforts to find and deport them. Adding to this, rising antipathy to Mexicans and Mexican Americans during the Great Depression, with its surplus of cheap white labor, increasingly subjected even legal border crossers to detention and deportation. The category of "Mexican" became increasingly closely associated with the category of "illegal." In 1931, 28 percent of people expelled from the United States were Mexican nationals. By the end of the decade, they made up 52.7 percent.[7]

The transport of goods across the border proved as vexing as the movement of people. Ranchers moving animals to market found it inconvenient to drive the herds miles out of the way to ports of entry, where they had to pay duties and endure delays while officials inspected the livestock for disease. Other drovers, who merely wanted to rotate animals to different pastures north or south of the border, found the ports of entry equally inconvenient. Rustlers found a bonanza. They avoided the checkpoints, stealing livestock on one side and evading detection by selling them in a different jurisdiction on the other. The border and tariffs on goods also encouraged mom-and-pop smuggling operations that sneaked items across the border without paying import duties. Illicit drugs began to flow as well after Congress prohibited the importation of opium in 1909.[8]

By the 1930s, then, crossing the international boundary in southern Arizona had gotten harder, more expensive, more dangerous, and more humiliating, as both nations sought to curtail the movement on which life in the Sonoran Desert has always depended. The two nation-states had formed the habit of constructing and enforcing borders to exert sovereignty over people and space, while those for whom borders were inconvenient had grown used to circumventing them. It was in this context in 1937 that the United States established Organ Pipe Cactus National Monument with a thirty-mile southern boundary along the international border, ensuring that immigration, livestock, and drugs would disrupt management of the new preserve. It seemed at first, however, to be nothing that a good fence would not solve.

The First Fences

The concept of a national park implies effective boundaries. Parks are spaces set aside from the degraded world outside them, thus requiring clear legal demarcation between in and out. In the 1930s, it was still possible to step from Mexico to Quitobaquito without encountering any physical barriers. Not surprisingly, then, Organ Pipe's first custodian and lone full-time staff person, William Supernaugh, wanted to fence the perimeter of the monument. This ambition complemented the NPS's goal of freezing time. Among the outside things seeming to threaten to mar the park at the time were mining, roadbuilding, cactus collecting, and hunting. A press release at the park's founding touted its inside as "little changed from . . . 500 million years ago . . . the borderland between the habitable world and the uninhabitable." Preventing change and delimiting boundaries—freezing time and bordering space—went hand in hand from the outset. At first, World War II diverted resources away from fencing the new monument.[9] Later, however, the park allied with other federal agencies whose border goals did not hold environmental and archaeological preservation as priorities.

An outbreak of hoof-and-mouth disease south the border in the 1940s provided Supernaugh his opportunity. By the middle of the decade, about 1,000 head of Mexican stock—wild horses and burros along with stray cattle—foraged on monument vegetation. By comparison, the park's largest permitted rancher, the Gray family, grazed 1,050 head on the park's land. No matter who owned the stock, grazing impeded the park's conservation mandate. Livestock mowed down native vegetation, competed with wild animals for forage, and aggravated soil erosion. They were also an embarrassment, having reduced the popular picturesque Ajo Mountain Drive to a wasteland of dust, damaged vegetation, manure, and cattle carcasses and provoking complaints from visitors about the highly visible degradation. At a site slated for a campground, overgrazing had, in the estimation of one official, "ruined [it] as a public use spot." The associate director of the Park Service's Southwest Region considered controlling stock a matter of protecting "the basic values" of a "nationally important scenic and biological area." In other words, overgrazing in a national park threatened America's national heritage. In early 1947, an outbreak among Mexican cattle of *Aphtae epizooticae*, the virus that causes hoof-and-mouth disease, heightened the fence's importance to other federal agencies. The United States had eliminated the disease two decades before, and the US Bureau of Animal Industry feared its reintroduction. The Park Service lobbied for emergency funds by citing, with some exaggeration, the possibility of livestock spreading the disease to wildlife. By 1949—after months of bureaucratic false starts—the National Park Service, the International Boundary and Water Commission, and the Bureau of Animal Industry collaborated to string a livestock-proof fence along nearly all of the park's international border. Four strands of barbed wire ran past Quitobaquito all the way to Sonoyta, and three strands east of there. For the first time, Quitobaquito was severed from the rest of the Sonoran Desert. The bureau also established several line camps in the park, from which mounted riders patrolled the border.[10] To the Orozcos' consternation, one was at the oasis. In addition to pitching tents, the agents rerouted some of the ditches to secure a water supply. Thus, the Park Service harnessed its conservation ends to federal boundary-making initiatives and made Quitobaquito into a landscape that reflected the monument's expectation that the park stopped and started at its edges, was coterminous with the international border, and could exclude disruptions from the outside world.

Cattle and other troubles did not move into Quitobaquito only from Mexico. The oasis was also threatened by things that moved within the park. Neither the Grays nor José Juan Orozco made much effort to keep their animals away from sensitive areas like Quitobaquito. Just like wildlife and human beings, cattle in the Sonoran Desert tended to concentrate near water sources, which yielded an outsized impact on the environment at Quitobaquito, a fact laid bare during a series of midcentury droughts. According to one report, the cattle at Quitobaquito presented "problems in attempting to retain as much as possible of the natural vegetative condition and appearance." As part of a larger monument-wide program to preserve water sources, the park sprayed pesticides and rehabilitated water channels. A key component of the efforts were livestock exclosures. In 1961, at the same time it was clearing the remnants of the Orozco homestead, the park installed a quarter-mile, four-strand barbed wire fence at Quitobaquito to keep livestock out. The steep, rocky terrain around the lagoon made for grueling work as crews jackhammered into the caliche just below the topsoil. They also installed a pair of cattle guards along the newly constructed Puerto Blanco Drive, which passed between Quitobaquito and the border. A project report initially judged that the fence and cattle guard succeeded in "excluding all cattle from the Quitobaquito area," though the following year monument officials counted the efforts "not entirely successful" and lamented the continued damage from "trespass." In 1963, they added a second fence, this one south of Quitobaquito and paralleling the international border fence installed in the 1940s. This one prevented vehicles from entering the pond area and damaging the ditches. This work, along with pond dredging and vegetation removal, left Park Service naturalist Natt Dodge optimistic that "entirely natural conditions" would soon return to the oasis.[11] Thus by the early 1960s, the monument, operating from a set of aspirations that national park conditions must be permanent, had made Quitobaquito into a well-bordered landscape, preserved from the grazing, livestock disease, and automobiles that afflicted the world beyond monument boundaries. This departed significantly from the free-flowing movement that the O'odham had previously practiced. Borders that divided the out from the in, however, were essential to the park's larger objectives of freezing time and forestalling unwanted change at the oasis.

For the time being, border crossing by O'odham and other people was of considerably less concern than passage of livestock. Organ Pipe's law enforcement division, then called the Protection Division, had two permanent staff people assisted by a handful of seasonal employees. Among their tasks, since the park had no naturalist, was to provide interpretation services for visitors, which they performed "commendably," according to a 1957 report. Another duty was to patrol the only paved road in the park, the recently completed Arizona Highway 85, which ran from Ajo south to Sonoyta, bisecting the monument. Liquor being Sonoyta's primary attraction for Americans, the road saw numerous accidents among drivers returning to Ajo, especially late at night. Also, to the consternation of the division staff, motorists frequently picked up Mexican hitchhikers trying to enter the United States without authorization. Using the word "wetbacks," a particularly absurd term for crossers in the Sonoran Desert, the report described them as "generally docile" but added that "one can never be assured."[12]

In 1957, however, according to the report, it was "not at all difficult . . . to cross the International Boundary," and plenty of people did. Despite this and the overtaxed resources of the Protection Division, the superintendent ranked the hiring of a naturalist as his "first priority," ahead of law enforcement hires. Border crossers would remain nothing more than a minor distraction to the park for the next forty years. Notably, in the thousands of pages of documents the park produced between the 1960s and 1990s, transborder migration and drug-related violence were almost entirely absent. In 1983, park staff attributed some vehicle break-ins at Quitobaquito to thieves straying over from Sonora. A border crosser died on Puerto Blanco Drive in August 1991. And under a section titled "Constraints and Problems," the 1979 interim management plan for Quitobaquito listed many threatening things that might move in from Mexico: "effects of agricultural development, water depletion, pesticides, pollution, and feral animals." It did not, however, mention border-crossing people.[13] As late as the 1980s, immigration prevention and drug interdiction were simply not among park managers' most pressing concerns.

Nevertheless, the park's first half century laid the foundations for transforming Quitobaquito and the rest of the park's southern boundary into a bordered space, something it had never been in twelve thousand years of human habitation. From the sons and daughters of I'itoi to the fictional smugglers in Kent Nelson's novel, human well-being at Quitobaquito had always involved moving about. With barbed wire fences, line camps, and a small but growing number of federal patrollers and park law enforcement rangers, however, Quitobaquito in the 1990s reflected the American aspiration to limit passage through the area. Moreover, according to anthropologist Jessica Piekielek, the cooperation between the NPS and the Bureau of Animal Industry mirrored larger national projects to cast Mexico as an unmodern, dirty, diseased space and to create a thin layer of protection for the United States.[14] This was a discourse that would erupt in various forms down to the present day. As late as the 1990s, it was still simple to step through the barbed wire and over the border at Quitobaquito, but unhindered movement had generally given way to ports of entry and head taxes. The NPS had harnessed its conservation priorities to federal border control objectives. And a rhetoric that cast Indians and Mexicans as not belonging in the park had taken root. All this played out against the background of a deep, if not yet dramatically violent, history of smuggling and immigration.

America's Most Dangerous Park"

"We did believe that geography would be an ally to us," Doris Meissner told the *Arizona Republic* in 2000. Commissioner of the Immigration and Naturalization Service under President Bill Clinton, Meissner was reflecting on the wave of migrant deaths in the desert in the wake of the administration's clampdown

"Dying of Thirst in the Desert" appeared in the March 1891 volume of *Harper's*. It played on readers' anxieties about unauthorized Chinese entry into the United States. It also portrayed the desperate lengths to which would-be immigrants were willing to go during the era of Asian exclusion. Migrants crossing the US-Mexico desert border are nothing new. Public domain.

on urban crossing. "It was our sense," Meissner recalled, "that the number of people crossing the border through Arizona would go down to a trickle, once people realized what it's like." Shut off the flow at a few key points, the thinking went, and rugged terrain and high temperatures would take care of the rest. If she had seen the 1891 cartoon "Dying of Thirst in the Desert" or heard about the pitiful group of Japanese men that Hornaday encountered in 1907, she might have known that harsh desert conditions had rarely deterred resourceful migrants in the past. But she and Clinton were reading political tea leaves, not immigration history. It was the early 1990s. Both the United States and Mexico were in the throes of post–Cold War economic downturns, which elevated both Mexican immigration and American antipathy to it. Public pressure to reduce illegal immigration mounted. The resulting death tolls were enormous. By one count, more than five thousand people died crossing the border between 1994 and 2009, the actual tally probably being much higher. Thirty-six border agents also lost their lives in the line of duty.[15] In addition to domestic politics and the sluggish economy, dislocation from another Clinton policy, the North American Free Trade Agreement, drove people into the desert, as did the war on drugs. In the twenty-first century, international gang violence, the war on terror, climate change, and Mexico's slipping control of its drug cartels joined the growing list of things that emanated from afar and whose consequences spilled into Organ Pipe. Containment efforts were puny in comparison to the magnitude of the forces propelling people over the border. At Quitobaquito, bordering not only did not work, but it added another layer of exclusion to the landscape, jeopardizing many of the aims for which the monument was designated.

A small revolution in US border security practices began in 1994. Prior to that, agents and migrants had played hide-and-seek, much as Milton and his quarry had. People wanting to cross hired freelance guides called coyotes or contracted with family-run businesses. Some just made a break for it themselves, darting through arroyos and across dairy farms on the edges of border towns. Agents caught hundreds, sometimes thousands every night and sent them back across the border to try again another time. Even more, though, slipped through to the north. They met an increasingly hostile reception, as US politicians and ideologues blamed them for unemployment and wage stagnation during the economic transition following the end of the Cold War, and voters enthusiastically endorsed the scapegoating. In this context, Clinton's Border Patrol launched Operation Hold the Line in El Paso in 1993 and Operation Gatekeeper the following year in San Diego. The two measures and subsequent ones that expanded them deployed hundreds of agents and invested billions of dollars in concrete and steel walls, new patrol vehicles, seismic sensors, night-vision scopes, floodlighting, and high-tech fingerprinting. It worked. Crossing plummeted in urban areas. But there were unintended consequences. Now more difficult, border crossing fell to well-organized drug cartels, which eclipsed the small-scale operations by incorporating human smuggling with drug running. In addition, crossing moved away from the cities to the dangerous, remote desert. As the numbers fell in coastal California and Texas, the Border Patrol's Tucson sector saw a 591 percent surge in migrant apprehensions between 1992 and 2004.[16] Like squeezing a balloon, as Mexican novelist Carlos Fuentes and many others observed, obstructing the traffic in one place merely increased it elsewhere, geography notwithstanding. One of the elsewheres turned out to be Organ Pipe.

On May 19, 2001, twenty-six men and their guides crossed the border from a Sonoran truck stop at El Papalote to Quitobaquito. The men had come from varied points south, most of them from the state of Veracruz on the Gulf of Mexico. Several were coffee farmers, set in motion by a fall in global coffee prices.[17] NAFTA and the Mexican peso crisis hit people like these twenty-six hard. Meanwhile, after a sluggish start to the decade, the US economy boomed, whetting its appetite for cheap labor. And as inexorably as salt water diffuses across cell membranes from high concentration to low, they came—coffee farmers and other desperate people from Veracruz, Hidalgo, and elsewhere—funneling through a well-orchestrated system by which human smugglers conveyed them northward and deposited them in places like El Papalote to embark across the line. Four strands of barbed wire dividing Quitobaquito from the global south were not going to stop a cascade powered by free trade, two centuries of economic inequality between and within two modern nation-states, and the huge profits to be made from moving migrants and narcotics away from San Diego into the desert wilds.

In those days, people who knew where to look could easily find a cut in the fence or a spot where it had been mowed down by previous vehicles. Making it over the border was easy. Getting somewhere after you crossed was hard. A few minutes' walk brought the band near Quitobaquito, where a truck roared along a dusty road and picked them up. Get in, their nineteen-year-old guide told them. They got in. Possibly, it rattled up the rutted Pozo Nuevo Road, the main northbound track in the vicinity. Or maybe the driver headed overland, chewing up chollas and ocotillos to elude detection. Either way, they were roughly following the route along which Tom and Martha Childs had hauled their brood on trips between Bates Well and Quitobaquito. After about ninety minutes, the truck stopped. Get out, their guide said. They got out. Settling into the mottled shade under paloverde trees or mesquites, they rested through the heat of the day and marched at nightfall, keeping to high ground to avoid the Border Patrol.

Near the park's northern boundary, however, the nineteen-year-old guide lost his way. For days the party wandered under a blazing sun as the cells in their bodies gave up life-sustaining water. First came headaches and thirst. Moisture evaporated from their bodies as fast as they could sweat it out. Pasty spit dribbled between their bleeding lips. Their fevers burned. Desperate for moisture, they drank their own urine, licking their lips, sandpaper tongues scraping across open wounds. Blood vessels in their eyes burst. Confusion. They began to hallucinate—God, the devil, the lush greenery of Veracruz all paraded before their eyes. One man keeled over. Another. Some wandered off, delirious. One took off his clothes, which by this point rasped the raw nerve endings on his skin. He folded them neatly, lay down in the shade, and died. The others trudged on.[18] Fourteen of the walkers eventually perished. A massive Border Patrol rescue effort saved the other twelve. Death stalked Sonoran Desert travelers in the twenty-first century just as it had Melchior Díaz in 1541. The soulless exigencies of global capitalism started the coffee farmers' feet toward the border, but it was simply water diffusing across cell membranes that ended their journey.

Like Earth Maker, Tom Childs, Cipriano Ortega, Bill Supernaugh, and everybody else who had come to Quitobaquito, border crossers remade the landscape. More than a thousand people per day crossed the monument. Throughout the reserve and in the neighboring Barry M. Goldwater Air Force Range, Cabeza Prieta National Wildlife Refuge, and Tohono O'odham Nation, smugglers of narcotics and people built an infrastructure to facilitate their operations. Lookouts perched on hilltops with satellite phones and night-vision goggles. They drove modified high-speed vehicles off road through the vegetation. Drive twice in the same spot in the desert, and you have a road. They rested in camouflaged brush shelters and stashed gear. "It's like being in the midst of a guerrilla conflict," naturalist Douglas H. Chadwick wrote. Traffic in drugs and people led to development on the park's southern boundary at places like El Papalote, a wide

Vehicle barrier, 2019. This fence ran along the US-Mexico border crossing Organ Pipe Cactus National Monument. Built in the early 2000s to deter vehicle entry, it was replaced in 2019 with the current border wall by the Department of Homeland Security. This photo looks east, up Monument Hill, about ten miles east of Quitobaquito. Photo by Jerry Glaser, US Customs and Border Protection. Courtesy of Wikimedia Commons.

spot along Mexican Highway 2 with a truck stop and motel, whose primary purpose was to service the transborder movement. Development led to wood cutting on the monument, theft of native plants, windblown trash, incursion of feral dogs and livestock, disappearance of a $5,000 weather gauge (later recovered in Mexico), and removal of fence posts from historic structures for firewood. Parties of migrants wore trails into the ground, often following old wagon roads that had nearly revegetated after being closed when the park was designated as wilderness in 1978. Along the way, they discarded bottles, food containers, and clothing and set fires for warmth, cooking, and even rescue signals. In a 2002 study of the park, park staff and volunteers walked transects and recorded resource impact with GPS units. On an average five-kilometer east–west line, researchers found four vehicle tracks, two bicycle tracks, a horse track, seven pieces of trash, ten water bottles, three rest sites, a campfire, and five other cases of "major damage."[19]

The US government's response compounded the impact on the landscape. After the September 11, 2001, attacks on the World Trade Center and Pentagon, concern about saboteurs potentially entering the United States through its southern border linked Organ Pipe to an international war on terror. Between 2004 and 2006, the monument built a twenty-three-mile Normandy-style iron vehicle barrier along its southern border, replacing the barbed wire livestock fence at a cost of $18 million. Theoretically passable by wildlife, the fence created a wide swath of disturbance, coupled with the two roads paralleling the border, preventing pronghorns, jaguars, pygmy owls, and other animals from making the north–south migrations they depended on. And with fences came roads. The Border Patrol built new roads and improved old ones, which encouraged crossers to pioneer new thoroughfares. Agents drove off road in pursuit of fugitives, damaging wildlife habitat, tearing up fragile desert soils, and compacting the earth through which desert plant roots needed to bore in search of water. The number of roads in Organ Pipe proliferated until informal ones far outnumbered official ones. Off-road driving doubled in 2009 and tripled by 2010, with the Border Patrol making more of the new roads than migrants. Perhaps as many as 2,500 miles of illegal roads crisscrossed the monument. Agents tied old tires together, hitched them to vehicles, and dragged dirt roads smooth so that crossers would leave telltale footprints. Then they left the black rubber contraptions by the side of the road. Four-wheel-drive patrol trucks barreled back and forth along South Puerto Blanco Drive between Quitobaquito and Arizona Highway 85 just north of Sonoyta. Black Hawk helicopters buzzed overhead. Agents lugged boulders and debris into washes to discourage crossers from driving in them. They established rescue beacons, also called "panic poles," at which distressed walkers could summon the Border Patrol for assistance. They dug roadside trenches, installed metal aircraft landing strips, and erected concrete vehicle barriers. In 2003, a Border Patrol camp was opened at the remains of a historical ranch. In short, border-crossing countermeasures did everything possible to make the landscape inhospitable to movement by foot or automobile. Vehicle barriers and the rest brought a militarized atmosphere to the border and, in the words of park staff, "detract[ed] from wilderness aesthetics."[20]

Quitobaquito did not escape such impact. Topography determined migrant routes, and compared to other places in the park, Quitobaquito received a medium amount of traffic. Proximity to El Papalote made it appealing, as did a relatively straight shot north through Bluebird Pass (where the coffee farmers lost their way) down to Ajo, where water, services, and a ride awaited travelers. In 2013, I did field research at the oasis with my colleague Clarissa Trapp and a park archaeologist, Connie Gibson. Gibson initially thought we would need a law enforcement ranger escort, but that morning she learned that no illegal activity had been recently reported, so the three of us went on our own. To be on the safe side, she showed us how to use her two-way radio. As we drove out along South Puerto Blanco Drive, several Border Patrol vehicles roared by us, kicking up acrid dust and injecting into the soundscape more decibels than Beatrice Melvin, Father Kino, or Hohokam shell traders had ever heard there. Gibson pointed out vantage points from which *narcotraficantes* monitored the Border Patrol, and others from which the Border Patrol monitored the narcotraficantes. Six tires wired together lay by the side of the road. When we got to Quitobaquito, we saw no interpretive signage, learned nothing about pupfish, mud turtles, or ancient inhabitants. We did, however, see a warning to beware of illegal activity. We also passed by branches and rocks piled in washes to impede off-road vehicles. Trash lay everywhere, and I collected one of the many black water jugs—border crossers prefer them to clear ones, which are more easily spotted at night. They could be purchased at El Papalote and other points of departure. Being out there all day with no restrooms made relieving our bladders a tricky balance between seeking privacy and alerting each other to keep an eye out in case we did not return after temporarily disappearing into a ravine or behind a saguaro. We saw no border activity on our trek, but the possibility of it kept us on our guard all day. The 1997 master plan's vision to remake Quitobaquito as a wilderness subzone with trails for visitors and habitat protection had given way to a landscape that also reflected organized efforts to defeat and defend borders.[21]

The impact of transborder violations in the park mounted through the 1990s, but the impact did not fully sink in until a hot day in August 2002 when ranger Kris Eggle joined US Border Patrol agents in pursuit of a drug smuggler who had rumbled over the border from Sonoyta in a stolen SUV. Just a few months out of the Federal Law Enforcement Training Center, where he finished first in his class, Eggle found himself on the front lines of America's wars on immigrants, terror, and drugs, without the field training or mentorship period that officers in other border agencies routinely received. By all accounts, the twenty-eight-year-old was extremely well liked by his colleagues at Organ Pipe, his generous, upbeat spirit buoying staff morale. Perhaps the training honors or his friends' admiration or his widely acknowledged leadership skills and firm sense of duty gave him confidence beyond his experience that afternoon. Or perhaps it was the bullet-proof Kevlar vest he wore. Whatever the reason, Eggle had plenty of cause for self-assurance behind the wheel of an NPS vehicle hurtling down the dirt road that paralleled the international line. When the smuggler's SUV stalled, Eggle charged out into the 110° heat to chase him on foot through thorny tentacles of ocotillos. The smuggler crouched under a mesquite tree and waited for the ranger to catch up. He wore no shirt, and dirt caked on his sweaty body. Eggle spotted the fugitive and reached for his gun. Too late. A bullet from the smuggler's rifle hit the radio or some other metallic piece on Eggle's belt before veering under the vest and through his skin to pierce an artery.[22]

Eggle died defending a park perimeter that federal policy and national ideology required to be impermeable, but the bullet whizzing from a smuggler's rifle collided with the body of a spirited but ill-prepared ranger because of events that originated far from the park boundaries. The Clinton administration's urban border crackdown shifted the battle zone to remote and dangerous southwestern deserts. A globalizing economy displaced Latin America's poor and sent them over the US border. The lucrative transnational narcotics market brought the trafficker to the border, and the international war on drugs impelled him and his weapon into the mesquite shrubbery of Arizona. The federal budget battles that limited the number of law enforcement rangers in the park and stunted the length and scope of Eggle's training were fought and lost not in Arizona but in Washington. Even the endangered Sonoran Desert pronghorn and other wildlife, which Eggle was mandated as a park ranger to conserve, routinely crossed between Mexico and the United States. Nothing but American imagination actually stopped at the border. Eggle's death was partly the tragic result of expecting that boundaries could isolate pristine landscapes and keep them permanent.

In the aftermath of Eggle's murder, Organ Pipe closed most of its backcountry, some 60 percent of the monument, including Quitobaquito. The border had simply grown too violent. The Fraternal Order of Police labeled it "America's Most Dangerous Park." It was a landscape of exclusion, barring not only border crossers, but now the American public too. Scientists, park staff, and a few other classes of visitors could go there with a security detail, but most were forbidden. In 2012, when Gibson suggested improving interpretation at the pond in preparation for a possible reopening to tours in the winter, superintendent Lee Baiza supported the measures in principle but decided it was too dangerous for the time being. "I don't see visitors having access to this area and hanging out to have a picnic for quite some time," he wrote in an email. "In order to minimize risk if tours are re-established this winter it is better to get in and get out."[23] For the first time in twelve thousand years, Quitobaquito was closed to human beings.

What the Iron Wrought

Americans had been constructing the international boundary since the 1840s, marking it first with wooden obelisks, then barbed wire, and eventually iron rails. This border making threatened the cultural essence of the region's longest inhabitants. For millennia, the O'odham had thrived in the Sonoran Desert by moving about. It was part of their identity. As Tohono O'odham cultural resource specialist Joe Joaquin said, "We were brought into this world for a purpose, to be the caretakers of this land." This was their himdag, and it required unhindered movement throughout their territory to visit sacred sites, perform traditional ceremonies, gather essential plants, and tell the People's stories. The 1848 Treaty of Guadalupe Hidalgo had guaranteed the O'odham, as former Mexican citizens, "liberty and property, and . . . free exercise of their religion without restriction." They exercised this right, including its attendant border crossings, unfettered until the early twentieth century and with minimal interference for several more decades. By the 1990s, however, border enforcement threw up obstacles. Sonoran O'odham were sometimes denied entry to the United States. Border Patrol officers routinely stopped and harassed O'odham on the reservation. "Some of them were roughed up," tribal attorney Margo Cowan indicated, "dragged out of their cars, spoken to with profanity, and told they had to get documents." Agents made wrongful arrests and deportations and even unintentionally, though perhaps carelessly, killed a teenager with a vehicle. US customs officers confiscated feathers, leaves, sweetgrass, and other ceremonial property belonging to traveling O'odham, mistakenly believing the items to be illegal. The United States closed border crossings along traditional routes to sacred sites, and travel such as the Salt Pilgrimage, which had historically passed by Quitobaquito, became difficult, sometimes even impossible. And the rise in migrant deaths on the Tohono O'odham Nation after Operation Gatekeeper challenged the himdag of care. As a result of the increasing obstacles to movement through O'odham homeland, Joaquin observed, "ancestors' graves are unvisited; relatives go years without seeing family; fiestas, wakes, and ceremonial offerings go unattended. Elders, hampered from crossing for a number of reasons, fail to share traditional stories and to pass on knowledge about the past, about plants and animals, and about caring for their desert home."[24] In short, the border made it difficult for the O'odham to be caretakers—that is, to be O'odham.

Bordering had also made a mess at Quitobaquito. It had damaged vegetation and frightened away wildlife. It also spurred road making. Normandy-style vehicle barriers evoked images of World War II. Visitors could not go there. A ranger died. Veracruz coffee growers died. Too many people died. Since its founding, the monument had desired a border to advance its conservation goals of preserving a permanently pristine environment, safe from the devastation that loomed beyond park boundaries. Instead of protecting the park, however, border making repeatedly required the park to accept environmentally and archaeologically destructive imprints on the land and its people. By the end of the first decade of the twenty-first century, the bill for this devil's bargain came due. Quitobaquito was a landscape where many of the dominant features served to define who and what belonged or did not. Exclusion was just another in a long line of cultural aspirations manifested on the land, but it was an ugly one. It was not a place for sustaining life and community. Instead, it had become a place to get in and get out of as rapidly as possible. The "scenery and the natural and historic objects and the wild life therein" were poorly preserved and interpreted.[25] It was inaccessible to visitor enjoyment. And it was dangerous for people as well as plants and animals. Freezing time and making borders had produced a landscape that failed on both directives of the Organic Act and the implicit promise that national parks were good for human welfare. This was not America's best idea.

SIX | "Oasis of Hope"
Quitobaquito in the Twenty-First Century

A VIDEO SHOT A FEW MILES from Quitobaquito went viral in October 2019. Kevin Dahl of the National Parks Conservation Association, a private foundation, filmed a federal contractor driving an orange bulldozer over an old saguaro cactus. The contractor was clearing ground for construction of a four-hundred-mile steel-bollard wall that would tower thirty feet above the desert thornscrub and sport a crown of floodlighting. In the eighteen-second clip, the heavy machinery rattled into the saguaro, knocking it to the ground. The vehicle then reversed, kicking up dust and emitting shrill backup beeps, before lurching forward to push the downed cactus several feet forward over earth already imprinted with Caterpillar belt marks. The Border Patrol soon posted competing footage showing workers carefully cradling a saguaro, leaning it into a tilted truck bed, and lifting it out of the ground for replanting elsewhere in the park. Bulldozing, the agency video reassured viewers, happened only to saguaros that could not survive replanting.[1]

Depending on whom you asked, the project was either a bulwark against would-be border violators or a monstrosity that endangered immigrants, sacred indigenous sites, and ecological integrity. As they competed to depict wall construction according to rival aspirations, the dueling clips indicated that the international border through Organ Pipe had become a flashpoint for the nation's political divisions.

Amid the glare of national news, a series of new management challenges at Quitobaquito demanded park staff's attention in the first two decades of the twenty-first century. First an old cottonwood on the banks of the dam began to die. Had it toppled, it could have ruptured the historic dike, drained the pond, and altered the oasis irrevocably, damaging both its heritage and its future. Meanwhile, indigenous peoples demanded access to the park, sometimes with loud, brave voices and sometimes with soft insistence, but always articulating

Bulldozing a saguaro, 2019. Kevin Dahl's video of this saguaro being bulldozed went viral and helped consolidate opposition to construction of the border wall. Photo by Kevin Dahl, National Parks Conservation Association. Used with permission.

a basic right to land the United States had taken from them. Finally, the construction of the wall inched toward Quitobaquito, eliciting protests from environmental, indigenous, and immigrant advocates. By making national headlines and drawing management responses, these and other predicaments changed the landscape. In the first three decades of the twenty-first century, Quitobaquito lost the stately cottonwood and gained an imposing wall. The pond's water levels fluctuated unprecedentedly, generally shrinking, sometimes alarmingly, until in the summer of 2020 the pond nearly dried up. Quitobaquito and its vicinity attracted construction workers with heavy machinery, indigenous protestors, police to arrest them, international prayer observances, renewed but abridged Salt Pilgrimages, and a generous private donation for the Park Service to restructure the hydrology. Certainly, people making landscapes in service to their aspirations was old in the region. Doing so now, however, against the backdrop of climate change, boiling anti-immigration fervor, and the nation's reckoning with its colonial legacy embedded some of American society's most pressing twenty-first-century issues into the landscape at Quitobaquito.

The Leaning Cottonwood

Three years before Dahl's video, but with less fanfare, the park removed a different plant. Sometime around 1900, somebody had planted a cottonwood on the berm Dorsey had laid in the 1860s. Perhaps José Juan Orozco did it, or maybe

Leaning cottonwood, 2013. Planted in the early twentieth century, this tree began to die in the early 2000s. It threatened to rupture the dam as it leaned out over the pond. Photo by Clarissa Trapp. Used with permission.

it was Tom Childs. Maybe, since it was in an inauspicious spot, right at the edge of the dike, the sapling sprouted as a volunteer from an errant seed the wind had carried in a ball of white fluff one summer. Whatever the mechanism, it grew up over the century, one of several Fremont cottonwoods (*Populus fremontii*) at the oasis providing shade to the inhabitants as they worked the arrastras or ground corn on metates under a ramada. All of them are genetically the same, probably from a parent tree somewhere along the Río Sonoyta. Cottonwoods are native to the Sonoran Desert, but they are infrequent, growing only near streams and other water sources. They shoot up quickly, sometimes ten or more feet in a year, up to half an inch a day for short periods of the growing season. This one jutted out from the dam and leaned out over the pond almost horizontally. O'odham and other indigenous peoples of the Southwest and northern Mexico had long made good use of *Populus fremontii*, fashioning rakes, plows, and shovels for cultivating crops. They made fences and ramadas from the sturdy wood and chewed the bark as a vitamin C supplement. Cottonwood log drums with deerskin stretched taut across the top beat out a rhythm at harvest ceremonies and other occasions.[2] The leaning cottonwood was one of the landscape's few physical ties back to a world in which O'odham shared the pond with Mexicans, Anglo-Americans, Jewish Americans, French immigrants, and occasional Chinese border crossers. Fremont cottonwoods can live 130 years or more, but as this one neared its century mark, it began to die. Between 2003 and 2016, its demise demanded that conservation personnel balance the needs of wilderness, endangered species, historic resources, archaeological remains, tribal values, and tight park budgets, while wading through a tangle of regulatory mandates that did not exist when the pond had been dredged in 1962. The crisis forced the park to respond in ways that accepted impermanence at the site and integrated natural and cultural resource management to accommodate it.

Normally, the Park Service does not worry about the death of individual trees. This one, however, became an emergency in 2005 as water levels at the pond began a mysterious decline. The pond's surface level commonly fluctuated seasonally, usually dropping by two to four inches during spring and fall, rarely more than six inches. With the onset of long-term drought in the 1990s, the water level fell to the point that it ceased to flow through the outflow pipe at the southern end of the lagoon. In July 2005, the park recorded a then-record low of 11.5 inches below the pipe, an alarming drop, which quickly corrected to –4 inches with late-summer rains.[3] Over the next few years, however, such dips grew more frequent and severe, spawning the biggest management challenge at Quitobaquito since the NPS bought out Jim Orozco.

On July 11, 2007, the water level had fallen to –20.2 inches. Again, the late-summer rainy season partially refilled the pond, this time to –8.1 inches. Then, between September 6 and October 22, it fell to –23.25 inches. The unprecedented 15-inch drop led park staff to fear the "possibility the pond would be largely gone within weeks," and they began evacuating pupfish to temporary holding tanks. As the pond maintained that level and even rose a little with winter rains, conservation personnel began to suspect a leak.[4] Since 2005, resource management staff had taken numerous measures to stabilize the water supply at Quitobaquito, including renovating the northeastern spring, increasing the management of emergent plants, and repairing the stream channel. With the "imminent threats" to Quitobaquito's natural and cultural resources posed by plummeting pond levels in 2007, the park stepped up these efforts. In April 2008, park personnel inserted an impermeable diaphragm wall into the earthen berm. In 2009, they patched the pond's southeastern corner with bentonite to prevent water from seeping out there. In 2010, they tried to plug holes in the leaning cottonwood on the northwestern side of the lagoon.[5] Throughout, they removed tree roots that imperiled the structural integrity of the berm and bulrushes that encroached into the pond and evaporated water through their stems.

Such measures were taken with the hope of avoiding the wholesale dredging that had taken place in 1962, an approach that would be legally cumbersome in the twenty-first-century regulatory environment. Plus, the park was now more sensitive to the damaging impact on natural and cultural resources that such a draconian measure would impose. Instead, the park attempted to fix the suspected leaks by trial and error via smaller, less-intrusive means. Together they had a modest effect. From the lowest point of nearly 28 inches below the outflow pipe in April 2008, the stabilization measures raised the pond as high as –12 inches at times. A telling moment, however, came in March 2009, when the park trucked in water to fill the pond, only to watch the level quickly fall because of some unseen seep. Throughout this time, no telltale pools of water or soil saturation adjacent to the pond hinted at the source of the leak, but somewhere, around the level of –12 inches, water was escaping from the pond.[6]

Park resource managers turned their attention to the cottonwood. A century of photographs documented the tree's gradual tilt over the pond until part of its trunk leaned slightly below horizontal, dipping into the water and providing a possible conduit from the pond into the berm. A 2010 investigation revealed two basketball-sized holes in the decaying base of the tree and "yielded strong evidence, perhaps final proof, that the cottonwood and/or the immediately adjacent retaining berm" were the source of a significant leak. The monument's wildlife biologist Tim Tibbitts poured twelve cans of polyurethane foam into the cavity to drive out the Africanized bees that had nested in the tree. They moved to another and harassed him as he worked to keep the bulrushes down. Meanwhile, the cottonwood's eventual death—or worse, an untimely premature collapse—threatened to rupture the retaining berm. The park called such a prospect "catastrophic." A breach could drain the pond and kill the pupfish, which lived nowhere else in the United States. It might also destroy habitat for the mud turtle and other species that depended on the pond, as well as damage Dorsey's 150-year-old dam, the historic orchard area downstream from the berm, and any extant subsurface archaeological resources. In short, the tree's collapse could destroy Quitobaquito's value as an ecological setting and historic resource.[7]

Removing the leaning cottonwood, however, was not easy. It would require operating heavy machinery in a designated wilderness area and temporarily implanting a cofferdam in the pond to protect endangered species while work was done on the tree. Moreover, the tree was itself of historical value. It recalled an era when the pond hosted a living, working community, a time when people like José Juan Orozco, Tom Childs, M. G. Levy, and Beatrice Melvin came to Quitobaquito to find water, raise crops, exchange news, and purchase supplies. Since then, the cottonwood had graced countless photographs and enchanted visitors. It still held considerable cultural value to the O'odham. According to park staff, Tohono O'odham elders remembered jumping into the pond from the cottonwood as children. In order to remove such an iconic tree, one park document acknowledged, "the NPS would need strong evidence the tree is in fact the problem."[8]

With water levels dropping in spring 2016 and the cottonwood continuing its demise, however, doing nothing seemed equally inadvisable. "Quitobaquito pond is experiencing the lowest water level since 2012," a park document observed in June. "The cottonwood tree is near the point of breaking apart near the base. . . . Temporary fixes have been exhausted." One resource, the tree, was now endangering all the others. The park decided to intervene on behalf of the pupfish, turtles, remnant orchard, archaeological remains, historic dam, and eco-logical and historical character of Quitobaquito. It removed the tree on June 16, 2016. Doing so, however, required deft and conscientious maneuvering through the legal environment that had arisen since the early 1960s. In compliance with the 1964 Wilderness Act, the park completed the *Minimum Requirements Decision Guide Workbook*, under which staff compared alternatives, including doing nothing. Through a series of questions, rating tables, and justifications, monument personnel considered Quitobaquito's wilderness characteristics such as "untrammeled," "undeveloped," and "natural." Resource management staff also examined solitude, primitive recreation, historic resources, habitat, and worker safety. After twenty-nine pages of careful documentation following the Wilderness Act rubric, the ironic but inescapable conclusion was that using heavy machinery to cut down a tree in the wilderness was an appropriate course of action. "The positive impacts to the natural quality," the worksheet stated, "outweigh the negative impacts in the long term."[9]

Following the guidelines of the Endangered Species Act, the park obtained permission from the US Fish and Wildlife Service for its emergency plan to relo-cate the endangered pupfish. It also consulted with eleven federally recognized tribes, including the Tohono O'odham Nation, and two additional ones not recognized by the US government. Initially, indigenous people were hesitant to have it cut down, so in deference, the park nurtured it along. By 2016, however, the Tohono O'odham agreed that the tree needed to be removed. The park made wood from the tree and cuttings available to the tribe. In compliance with the National Historic Preservation Act, the park assessed the impact of the tree's removal on cultural resources and consulted with the Arizona State Historic Preservation Office before commencing the action. In addition, an archaeologist was present prior to and during tree removal to ensure proper care of any cultural resources work crews might unearth (they found none). In the months after the action, the park felt confident that "water levels have stabilized."[10]

The park removed the cottonwood in a manner that stewarded both the human and environmental histories of Quitobaquito. As the *Minimum Require-ments Decision Guide* attested, the pond was not a natural resource only: "Though in wilderness, Quitobaquito Pond is NOT a natural feature but entirely a man-made contrivance . . . that relies on human intervention to be maintained."[11] Although percolating in park thinking for three decades, such a frank acknowl-edgment of the pond's hybrid character and the need for active management of it went beyond previous statements. Translation of that thinking into action at the pond was even more of a novelty. So, too, was the care the park took to remove the cottonwood in a way that respected the tree's context and minimized damage to other things around it. This contrasted with the Department of Homeland Security's rough treatment of vegetation in the way of the border wall three years later. Instead of operating under a waiver of forty-one laws, the park scrupulously followed existing regulations. In particular, it engaged tribes in the process. In the national context of growing Native power and demands for a share in the management of their traditional lands, the park took seriously the cultural heritage value the tree embodied for Native people. This was part of larger park efforts to engage the O'odham in Quitobaquito management, efforts that have yielded mixed results.

Quitobaquito as a Twenty-First-Century Indigenous Landscape

Fifteen hundred people were incarcerated at the high-security federal penitentiary on Alcatraz Island in San Francisco Bay between 1934 and 1963. In 1969, indigenous people representing a group called Indians of All Tribes (IAT) occupied the by-then-decommissioned prison. Upon departing for the rocky twenty-two-acre prominence, IAT spokesperson Richard Oakes held up some cloth and beads before media cameras and announced he was going to purchase Alcatraz from the United States. The occupation, which lasted nineteen months before the federal government forced them off the island, helped ignite a pan-Indian movement in the United States. Since then, Alcatraz has become part of the Golden Gate National Recreation Area, managed by the National Park Service. In 2019, the NPS sponsored a celebration of the occupation's fiftieth anniversary. The dramatic protest at Alcatraz and the Park Service's subsequent commemoration of it mirror a larger process of indigenous empowerment that came to influence landscapes as small and remote as Quitobaquito. Although the federal government did its best to thwart the occupation in 1969, today, the national recreation area features the takeover prominently on its website, ranking it among the most important moments in the island's history and crediting the event with not only benefiting the tribes but preserving the historic site itself. Notably, Alcatraz's other interpretive emphasis is the history of mass incarceration in America, making the site a place that doubly challenges the nation's conscience.[12] The O'odham, who had been dispossessed of much of their lands in the nineteenth and twentieth centuries, occasionally managed to collaborate in stewarding them by the 2010s. This was a local manifestation of broader social and political trends in the United States and globally, as indigenous peoples grew more insistent in claiming a role in decisions that affected them, and as the federal government and non-Native people in general grew somewhat more sympathetic to those claims, a shift manifested at both Alcatraz and Quitobaquito. Although halting, the genuine progress in the relationship between the O'odham and Park Service between the 1970s and the 2010s set up the possibility for even more innovative management at the oasis later.

The colonialism that Indians of All Tribes was exposing and resisting at Alcatraz had also characterized the O'odham experience since the late nineteenth century. Between the 1860s and 1900, O'odham access to resources dwindled as the American and Mexican governments privatized lands they wrongly believed to be unused. In the 1890s, the United States allotted plots of land to individual

O'odham under the Dawes Act, most parcels too small to yield a living in the desert. The Tohono O'odham were further hemmed in by the creation of the Papago Indian Reservation in 1916. Also that year, Mexico began preventing O'odham from crossing the border, and shortly after, the United States fenced its side of the boundary.[13] Shortly after, the Office of Indian Affairs began sending O'odham children to boarding schools.

For the first third of its existence, Organ Pipe Cactus National Monument continued this colonial relationship with the O'odham. Although the park allowed some O'odham grazing and other activities, monument staff negotiated these agreements paternalistically with white officials from the Office of Indian Affairs who represented what they defined as O'odham interests. Not once in these early years did Organ Pipe documents record the monument discussing park access directly with O'odham people themselves. Similar to the proponents of nineteenth-century ideas surrounding Manifest Destiny and westward expansion, park management initially presupposed the land was mostly peopleless and believed it legitimate to move the people who were there, such as the Orozcos, off the land. Like westering settlers of earlier generations, the Park Service believed that indigenous peoples did not use the land properly and that federal rangers could do better in protecting cactus, wildlife, and scenery. Park staff never doubted their freedom to modify the land—to knock down buildings, drain ponds, build parking lots, and string barbed wire—without consulting the historical inhabitants. These things can be described as colonial in that they mirrored the actions of Spanish missionaries and conquistadors and subsequent Mexican and American settler-colonists. The waiving of environmental and religious freedom rules and the bulldozing of saguaros signaled that colonialism had endured well into the twenty-first century. It has, however, become more difficult to ignore.

The impossibility of ignoring colonialism any longer is largely a result of the amplification of Native voices in the public sphere over the last fifty years. The Alcatraz occupation shined a spotlight on colonial injustice and helped launch the Red Power movement, through which indigenous peoples reasserted their claims to land, artifacts, and self-determination. Over the middle decades of the twentieth century, the government of the Tohono O'odham Nation, for example, evolved from an institution that largely did the bidding of the Bureau of Indian Affairs into a powerful advocate for its members' interests and an intermediary between the tribe and the federal government. Ironically, since centralized authority had not been part of O'odham tradition since I'itoi and his followers toppled the priestly sivanyi class, the rising power of the tribal government simultaneously entailed a departure from decentralized O'odham political structures. For example, in the 1950s, the tribal government won the right to control royalties from mineral leases on reservation land. In the 1960s, it funneled the benefits of federal job training, Head Start, and other Great Society programs to the tribe. In 1970 it won a $26 million land claim settlement from the US government as compensation for territory lost during the 1916 establishment of the reservation. It distributed much of that settlement to tribal members in the 1980s, which inspired many O'odham to officially join the tribe in order to claim their payments and other benefits of belonging. Swelling numbers of enrolled members, in turn, strengthened the tribal government in its dealings with outside interests.[14]

Empowerment at the tribal level coincided with rising individual awareness among descendants of Quitobaquito residents of their indigenous roots and connections to the pond. Among those who joined the Tohono O'odham Nation's rolls in the 1980s were Lorraine Marquez Eiler and her Hia C'ed O'odham family. Eiler had grown up on Bureau of Land Management land at Darby Well, just south of Ajo. Her friends and relatives had lived on Cabeza Prieta National Wildlife Refuge at Chico Suni, on Organ Pipe Cactus National Monument at Bates Well, and in the old "huge village" at Quitobaquito. As a nurse living in Phoenix from the 1960s to the 1980s, Eiler began to question why her people could no longer live at these places. She started looking into Hia C'ed O'odham history and found very little written on it. What she did find was only an occasional paragraph here and there, often stating that they were extinct. She also developed an interest in environmental and social issues as they affected the O'odham. Technically, at the time, only enrolled tribal members could receive health services, but enforcement was lax. But in the early 1980s, rumors circulated that the tribe would do away with care for nonmembers. Eiler's mother had cancer and could not afford to risk losing care. The complicated enrollment process took four years, but Eiler, her mother, and other family members joined the Tohono O'odham Nation along with 150 other Hia C'ed O'odham. Eiler expanded her growing interest in politics in the late 1980s, getting elected to the Tohono O'odham legislative council, serving in advisory capacities to various federal land management agencies, and facilitating conversations among an initially loosely knit group of O'odham, Mexicans, and Americans about cultural and environmental concerns that would ultimately have a big impact at Quitobaquito. Like many women of her era (and Chona before them), Eiler translated traditional female O'odham responsibilities of mother, household matriarch, and healer into public leadership roles.[15]

Although sometimes thought to have vanished with the Orozcos, the Hia C'ed O'odham continued visiting Quitobaquito, as did Tohono O'odham. Verlon Jose, who has held many official positions as a public servant in the Tohono O'odham Nation, recalled going to Quitobaquito once or twice a year while growing up in the 1960s and 1970s. His mother worked for tribal senior services, and many elders wanted to go there. She took Verlon and her family on these trips. Like many others who remember Quitobaquito today, Jose recalls Quitobaquito as green and lush, a "hidden treasure" in the "middle of the desert." The elders told stories of even earlier times when the water used to flow onto the fields on the Mexican side. "God, it probably was beautiful," he exclaimed in a 2022 interview. "A'al Waipia"—he used the Tohono O'odham word, with a *W*—

"is a sacred place. It's a holy place. It's a place where people call home. It's a place where we go to nourish our body, to ask for blessings, to pray and give thanks. . . . It's a place that provides precious water." At places like Quitobaquito, where water bubbles from the ground, the water comes up from Mother Earth, he said, comparing it to "holy water in the churches."[16]

Rising indigenous claims began to have an impact on Quitobaquito management. When Rijk Moräwe started as Organ Pipe's chief of natural and cultural resources in 2012, he approached the position with serious commitment to engaging with indigenous peoples. He had participated in Park Service initiatives in the 1990s that trained him to manage natural and cultural resources together and to value both. He and his staff met with various tribal representatives and, as needed, attended the monthly meetings of the Four Southern Tribes Cultural Resources Working Group, a consortium made up of cultural resources staff from the Ak-Chin Indian Community, the Gila River Indian Community, the Salt River Pima-Maricopa Indian Community, and the Tohono O'odham Nation. At the meetings, they updated the tribes about park activities and received input. Moräwe twice presented about the leaning cottonwood to the group. He also invited tribal representatives to Quitobaquito to discuss the plans. "It's alive," they told him. Cutting it down would remove an important piece of their heritage. Others said removing it made sense to them once Organ Pipe staff explained the damage the tree was doing to the site and how it would change Quitobaquito if it collapsed. In response to these conversations, Moräwe suggested taking cuttings to keep portions of the tree alive. One person suggested keeping the wood so carvers could fashion artistic objects from it. The park implemented all these ideas.[17]

The renewal of salt runs has especially strengthened the relationship between the Park Service and the O'odham. One day sometime around 2015 or 2016, Moräwe got a call from some Tohono O'odham men who wanted to rejuvenate the pilgrimages.[18] This was the ritual in which Chona's first husband had met Coyote on the beach and received his calling as a healer.[19] The twenty-first-century renewal of the event reflected the broader rise in O'odham interest in their heritage, and the organizers wanted their run to pass by Quitobaquito, a traditional route. Moräwe helped them by alerting the Border Patrol and park law enforcement about the itineraries and campsites. The Border Patrol is required by law to pursue unauthorized desert crossers, and Moräwe wanted to make sure officers did not detain or disturb the runners. For subsequent salt runs, he served as a communications liaison between law enforcement, the tribe, and the runners, ensuring safety while minimizing disturbance.[20] Thus, in response to O'odham requests, the park cooperated to restore Quitobaquito to its place as an important stop in a sacred ceremony.

Organ Pipe's responsiveness to the O'odham requests regarding the salt runs and the cottonwood reflected not only local indigenous insistence but changing sensibilities among non-Natives as well. In the 1990s and 2000s, civil rights movement narratives about the long-awaited triumph of American values of equality and democracy over bigotry and discrimination gave way to uncomfortable questions about why racialized poverty, injustice, and inequality persisted so long after the sit-ins, bus boycotts, marches on Washington, and occupations of Alcatraz. Historic advances like the election of a Black president in 2008 were tempered by backlashes among white "birthers" who denied the legitimacy of his presidency. In the 2010s, a series of flashpoints gave pause to white confidence in the civil rights–era progress. The ongoing national debate over immigration and the vicious rhetoric and brutality it spawned, the US Supreme Court's 2013 rejection of portions of the transformative 1965 Voting Rights Act, the continued murder of Black people by law enforcement, the protests on the Standing Rock Reservation over construction of the Dakota Access Pipeline, and the appalling white supremacist violence in Charlottesville over the removal of Confederate statues were only a few of the dramatic incidents that persuaded at least some people that white-dominated society, especially government, needed to do more to address historical injustices. In this context, the National Park Service began to engage more seriously with indigenous concerns at Alcatraz and many other places. Still, as late as the removal of the cottonwood in 2016, O'odham influence at Quitobaquito was mostly only aspirational. Soon, however, a further environmental crisis at the pond would open the door to more substantive and innovative engagement.

Maintaining the Pond in an Impermanent World

In the summer of 2020, the pond at Quitobaquito dried up. Monsoon rains failed that year, and where several feet of water usually stood, red-brown sludge coated the exposed bottom, and cracked mudflats poked above the surface. "I've been going to Quitobaquito . . . for 32 years," ethnobotanist Gary Paul Nabhan observed, "and have never seen it in worse condition." Amber Ortega, an O'odham woman whose ancestors had once lived there, lamented that Quitobaquito was "extremely different, and it's happened extremely fast." Depending on whom you asked, possible culprits included climate change, border wall construction, Mexican groundwater pumping, or changing groundwater flow, and these explanations were not mutually exclusive. Likely, the most immediate cause was the decay of the aging clay pond liner, but because it occurred in the hothouse of border wall construction, climate change, and immigration debate, many found it easy to link the dry-up to these contested issues. Regardless of its cause, this latest crisis forced the park yet again to confront challenges that stemmed from impermanence and originated well beyond the reach of its management decisions. Calling it "the greatest oasis of hope in the entire borderlands," twenty-five prominent scientists wrote to the Department of Homeland Security requesting that wall construction halt within ten miles of Quitobaquito to protect its groundwater source.[21] Debates about the impact of the wall turned on some of the most polarizing divides in

American society. Meanwhile, an innovative and highly pragmatic solution came from a partnership with a local nonprofit organization. The project took into account Native voices, and it involved bridging differences.

Bridging differences has been a rare and difficult thing in early twenty-first-century America. After the economic crash in 2008, border crossing declined. Incentive for politicians to manufacture an immigration crisis to build political support among Americans struggling with job loss and other economic woes as well as perceptions of cultural marginalization during the slow and uneven recovery, however, did not decline. Nor did political supporters of immigration shy away from using divisions over immigration to stoke the fervor of their political bases. Presidents Clinton, Bush, Obama, and Biden all, at times, touted themselves as tough on immigration and postured about border security, taking various, mostly feckless steps. Meanwhile, Congress has failed to pass meaningful immigration reform. As a result, the issue has festered.

In 2015 and 2016, presidential candidate Donald Trump campaigned by stirring up antipathy to immigrants, especially Mexicans, painting them as rapists and drug dealers, and he promised to build an enormous wall to keep them out. Not only that, he vowed, Mexico would pay for it. Trump rode a wave of xenophobia to the White House. To his supporters, among all his promises, the wall symbolized his presidency and persona, and by 2019, with stinging losses by Republicans in the midterm elections and the 2020 presidential campaign looming, it had become a signature issue on which he felt compelled to deliver. Mexico, of course, did not pay for it, so after a protracted congressional budget battle that temporarily shut down the federal government in early 2019, Trump declared a national state of emergency. This allowed him to secure funds, which the House of Representatives would not appropriate, by dipping into already-allocated Defense Department monies and build his monument to American chauvinism across land sacred to the O'odham. To expedite construction and spur his reelection campaign, Trump issued executive orders waiving forty-one laws, including the National Environmental Policy Act, the Endangered Species Act, the National Historic Preservation Act, the American Indian Religious Freedom Act, and the Native American Graves Protection and Repatriation Act. In building the wall across environmentally and culturally sensitive territory, the Department of Homeland Security would not have to comply with any of the laws set in place during the previous half century designed to protect such spaces.

In 2019, contractors for Homeland Security began removing saguaros and other obstacles, clearing the way for construction of a four-hundred-mile wall. The following year, the wall ran along Organ Pipe Cactus National Monument's entire southern border and right past Quitobaquito. On social media, Trump's supporters reacted with vitriol to Dahl's post that showed the bulldozing of the cactus. "The saguaro is fine, it can be replanted by at a nursery with just a phone call. get over your hate for trump," one commented. "Nice. That cactus will be deported. GET OUT OF THE WAY WE ARE GOING TO BUILD THE WALL," said another.

Another dismissed the video as "fake news." And from a fourth: "Who gives a crap about a single cactus. FFS."[22] From their perspective, the nation was under siege from undesirable foreigners, and the border was the front line of a war in which landscapes must be modified to fend off the invaders. Sacrifice of saguaros and other obstacles was a small price to pay.

The landscape of exclusion that wall supporters felt was necessary simultaneously jeopardized the O'odham himdag, renewing an assault that had been going on for centuries. In the eighteenth century, Spaniards had entered the vastness of the Papaguería, and Mexican and American immigrants had crowded in during the nineteenth. Federal agencies had chased the O'odham from Quitobaquito, Bates Well, Chico Suni, and other homes in the twentieth. The twenty-first brought further insults, this time from the Border Patrol. O'odham movement and care for people and places were under siege just as much as the saguaro. As the number of Border Patrol agents operating on the Tohono O'odham Nation increased, so did the abuses. Agents left trash and drove trucks across sacred ground near I'itoi's cave on Baboquivari Peak. Tohono O'odham travelers reported being questioned at gunpoint while moving about on their reservation, and the Border Patrol wrongly deported a couple en route to the Sells clinic to seek care for their seven-year-old grandson with a heart condition. Since Operation Gatekeeper and Operation Hold the Line have diverted border crossers from cities into the desert, thousands of migrants have died on Tohono O'odham lands. It "stains our land with the blood of our neighbors," the nation's vice chair Henry Ramon said in 2002, "and pierces the hearts of our people." Construction of border infrastructure regularly damages cultural artifacts and ancestral O'odham graves.[23] Having to choose between being terrorized by narco-traffickers or harassed by Border Patrol agents has evoked a diversity of sentiments among tribal members, searing bitter divides into the tribe over how much if at all to cooperate in border security. Social division adds another wound on top of the other disruptions of border security measures the Tohono O'odham have borne.

The new wall also disrupts cultural life in more subtle ways. Although the O'odham are no longer nomadic, movement is built into the fabric of their lives. Hia C'ed O'odham elder Marlene Vazquez, for example, recalled visiting relatives at the Quitobaquito cemetery with her grandmother as a child. The family would travel from Bates Well to Sonoyta to purchase or trade for crepe paper for making flowers to decorate the graves. The family also acquired other goods in Sonoyta because they were cheaper there, mining having driven up prices in Ajo. Eiler, too, recalled the importance of crossing the border during childhood. Her mother frequently carried food and old clothing to relatives in Sonora, even though her own family was barely getting by. For a long time, Eiler continued the practice as an adult. As border crossing rules and physical barriers grew more restrictive, she began detouring to official checkpoints. In addition to taking her well out of her way, this subjected her to harassment by Mexican customs personnel and the *morditas*, or bribes, as high as $200, they extracted to let her bring the goods into the country. She discontinued the journeys in 2019 because they became too difficult. Meanwhile, Sonoran O'odham have found it extremely difficult to enter the United States for pilgrimages to Baboquivari Peak, and salt runs into Sonora and trips to Magdalena have become harder for US O'odham too. As one former tribal council member observed of the detention and harassment that often attend O'odham border crossings for religious and other reasons, "To be detained for hours disrupts the whole ceremony." A wall in addition to all this, tribal member Thomasa Rivas said, "is going to change our lives. It is going to change who we are. The world will change too."[24]

As the wall became a certainty in the second half of Trump's presidency, these two visions—exclusion and caretaking—competed for predominance at Quitobaquito. Although monument staff were powerless to stop the wall, they departed from the park's history of Indian removal and fence building and supported caretaking. Early in the process, for example, resource chief Rijk Moräwe advocated for installing a gate in the wall near Quitobaquito. Years of working with salt runners had familiarized him with the border-crossing needs of the people, and he urged the Department of Homeland Security to place a gate near the parking lot. Among other things, this would allow ready access for elders who could not walk long distances over rugged terrain. At first, the department assented and told Moräwe to assure the O'odham there would be a gate there. Installation of gates to mitigate the offense of walls is a tried-and-true method the federal government has used at the oasis to pacify locals. It had placated Orozco and Senator Hayden, after all, but this time the department reneged even on this minimal promise. As construction neared Quitobaquito, apparently with no gate in the plans, Moräwe protested and received word that there was already a gate a half mile away. The O'odham could walk to it. No further explanation was forthcoming.[25]

In addition, the park conducted an archaeological survey in the Roosevelt Reservation, the sixty-foot right-of-way along the border that President Theodore Roosevelt had designated in 1907. Realizing that wall construction would surely unearth artifacts and possibly even unknown graves, the Park Service conducted a hasty surface investigation, calling in help from regional NPS archaeologists to examine a ribbon of border twenty-five miles long and one hundred feet wide. Customs and Border Protection said the survey was not necessary, citing a 2002 report that covered much of the terrain. Park Service staff, however, deemed that the earlier investigation inadequately and unclearly documented the area. "We thought it was important to know about the area before the wall," said Organ Pipe cultural resources manager Lauren Kingston. It was a chaotic time, Kingston recalled. Staff did not know when construction would begin exactly, and "it was not clear when things would happen." As it was, the survey found human bone fragments within two sites near Quitobaquito. The chips were small—they would fit in the palm of your hand—but after the team consulted with Arizona State Museum bioarchaeologists, it became inescapably clear that the remains were human and looked to be very old, at least hundreds of years. Likely Huhugam, Moräwe believed. Carefully, the archaeologists wrapped the bones in linen, following the O'odham request to use natural cloth.[26] The park kept the pieces during the repatriation process and then gave them to the Tohono O'odham Nation for reburial.

Under the Native American Graves Protection and Repatriation Act (NAGPRA), such a find would ordinarily have triggered a tribal consultation to determine the origins of the bone fragments and ensure proper repatriation. This occurred for some of the remains, which came from outside the Roosevelt Reservation. Other bits, however, were discovered inside the Roosevelt Reservation, where Trump had waived NAGPRA. So Organ Pipe conducted what Kingston called a "NAGPRA-like process," which was approved by the NPS, the Department of the Interior, and the Department of Homeland Security and involved consulting with the tribe and following NAGPRA exactly, without calling it that. The park kept the pieces while the procedures ensued and then gave them to the Tohono O'odham Nation. Reburial waited more than a year because of tribal restrictions on gatherings during the COVID-19 pandemic. When the time came, Moräwe alerted park staff and the Border Patrol that roughly a dozen O'odham would be at Quitobaquito for the ceremony. Early on a spring morning in 2021, park law enforcement came out to Quitobaquito to unlock the gate on the west side of the pond and then made themselves scarce. When they returned at nightfall to lock the gate, the O'odham had come and gone and performed the rituals to lay the remains in a proper burial place in one of the arroyos snaking down from the Quitobaquito Hills.[27] In caring for artifacts and human remains and engaging the tribe in salvaging what it could from the wall construction, park staff intervened not only on behalf of natural resources, but for cultural resources and O'odham interests as well, a significant departure from the park's history of removing the Orozcos and building fences. Even in the shadow of the border wall, park staff and O'odham cooperated to ensure that the sons and daughters of I'itoi could still rest at A'al Vaipia.

Meanwhile, 2019 monsoons had moistened the desert generously, and water levels remained stable in the pond. Park staff were feeling good about the health of the oasis. Then in December 2019, almost two months before wall construction reached Quitobaquito or its groundwater recharge area, the pond dropped dramatically. Winter rains usually maintained pond levels, so park officials feared the water level was too low to sustain the pond through to the summer monsoon season.[28] As summer monsoons failed in 2020, the pond reached its lowest point since 2008. Back then, Quitobaquito had been a remote, little-known location. By 2020, however, Dahl's video and publicity from the Center for Biological Diversity and other coverage of the controversial wall had riveted the nation's eyes on the dwindling oasis. Mixing concrete for the wall and dampening dusty roads and construction sites gulped eighty-four thousand gallons of groundwater per day. Moreover, trucks rumbled along the border road and heavy machinery pounded the earth, shaking that had the potential to damage the fragile labyrinth of underground fissures that conducted water from La Abra Plain to Quitobaquito Springs.

Although not in a position to demand anything, the park took steps to mitigate the worst effects of construction. In one early meeting, a Department of Homeland Security contractor had asked Moräwe whether contractors could take water straight from Quitobaquito. Moräwe explained that the pond was a limited resource, home to two endangered species and a third that was under consideration. The contractor then proposed drilling a new well adjacent to Quitobaquito, and Moräwe urged them not to pump within five miles of the springs. Moräwe did succeed in getting the contractors to post fifteen-mile-per-hour speed limit signs east and west of the pond to limit ground vibrations, though many drivers did not comply.[29]

Photographs of a contractor well eight miles east of Quitobaquito and another seven miles west led many to believe groundwater pumping was damaging the oasis. An exposé conducted by investigative reporters for the website Bellingcat correlated the decline to the advent of wall construction. Many, including the twenty-five desert scientists who signed the letter to the secretary of homeland security, believed the wall might be to blame. The Center for Biological Diversity, an environmental organization, and some other opponents of the project felt certain. Local and then national and international media pilloried the park and the wall in general, sometimes ignoring data such as the water level declines that predated the wall.[30]

There were other potential explanations as well. One possible culprit was climate change. After holding steady for most of the twentieth century, spring flow at the oasis began to fall in the early 2000s. In 1917, hydrologist Kirk Bryan had estimated the spring flow at 43 gallons per minute. Measurements between the 1950s and 1970s pegged it at 30 to 35 gallons per minute. After the US Geological Survey installed continuous monitoring devices in 1981, records fluctuated between 15 and 40, with an average of 28. By the 2010s, however, the flow declined to 10 to 15 gallons per minute, and by the 2020s, the spring was trickling at only 8.4 gallons per minute, with one August 2020 outlier reading only 5.5. Something longer term than wall construction was required to explain this. Detailed temperature records for the park and surrounding areas since the 1940s indicated unprecedented heat. Hundred-degree days were starting earlier in the season and occurring later. Although not unmatched in the long-term precipitation record, a prolonged drought has affected Quitobaquito and the park since the 1990s, with the result that the groundwater capture area for the springs is not being adequately replenished.[31]

Moreover, park staff suspected more leakage from the pond, as the gains in water level from cutting down the leaning cottonwood in 2016 did not seem to have stuck. Ironically, by compacting soil, cattle had made the pond more impermeable and better able to retain water. With the end of grazing at the pond, it leaked more.[32] Declining groundwater recharge and pond leakage were not necessarily incompatible with groundwater pumping and subterranean geologic alteration from wall construction, though there appears to be no direct evidence that the wall was at fault. University of Arizona hydrologist Thomas Meixner doubted that wall construction could explain all of the dry-up so quickly, but he said that the pumping would eventually register an impact on Quitobaquito. "You could do things today," he indicated, "and you might not see the effect of it for 20, 30, 50, 100 years."[33]

With the dry-up, the Park Service had to confront the reality that even with an end to pumping for wall construction, the wet conditions that had attracted generations of Garcías, Childses, and Orozcos to the pond were impermanent. With climate change models projecting that by 2040 spring flow might dip as low as 4.5 gallons per minute,[34] an organization structured to preserve yesterday's status quo faced the possibility that there was no longer enough water to support the pond as it had existed for the previous century and a half.

Even though the data imputing the water decline to wall construction were unclear at best, the disappearing pond was a tipping point for many. On September 9, 2020, Amber Ortega and a handful O'odham activists occupied the construction site visible from Quitobaquito. She climbed into the backhoe bucket. Others blocked operation of machinery, halting construction for more than an hour. One demonstrator posted a video from the scene, saying "This is a live call out to all O'odham, we need you here on the front line to stand for our sacred site." At a larger protest on September 21, two dozen people sang and prayed for several hours, stopping construction again, this time for most of the day. They displayed an enormous banner, as tall as the people carrying it, that read "Borders = Genocide, No Wall on O'odham Land." Speakers cast the wall as the last straw in a string of abuses. "We had a land, we had a history. We had farms. We were able to live right here. Our ancestors are buried in that mountain. We have a children's shrine where you're desecrating," one speaker said. "That water aquifer that you're draining helped us survive and helped every traveler that came through survive, that water didn't discriminate." Another said, "We cannot move without you all over us, we cannot walk through our desert without these cameras filming everything we do, you don't have that in your community. But then you come here, thinking you can take whatever you want." And a third: "We want our ancestors' bones back, we want all of our artifacts back, we want everything you've stolen back." Twice, Park Service and Border Patrol law enforcement tried to breach the line of protestors. The wall was not yet finished, and the weight of the protestors leaning on it could have toppled it, with fatal results. But the activists linked arms, forming a human chain, both times resulting in skirmishes as demonstrators fell to the ground while law enforcement tried to pry them away.[35]

A week later, O'odham elders organized a different sort of gathering at Quitobaquito. Fifteen youth prayer runners ran all weekend from the Tohono O'odham Nation to the border at Quitobaquito. There they met a similar group of Sonoran

O'odham runners coming from Mexico. The Arizonans handed a gourd full of sacred pond water over a cement barrier to the Sonorans, the panels of the nearly complete wall standing sentinel. Runners and observers, including Lorraine Eiler, then gathered to pray at Quitobaquito for the rest of the morning. Protests all along the border had erupted the previous month, and among the participants at Quitobaquito were members of other tribes who came to Quitobaquito in solidarity with the O'odham. Eiler, one of the organizers of the event, said its purpose was to highlight the ongoing connection between O'odham north and south of the border. "The barriers they put up are not going to stop us from continuing on with understanding our relatives across [the border]."[36]

Meanwhile, coinciding with the protests, Organ Pipe drew on an innovative and pragmatic relationship with a multiracial community organization, the International Sonoran Desert Alliance. As Eiler and other Hia C'ed O'odham were enrolling members in the Tohono O'odham Nation in the 1980s, the Ajo copper industry was dying. After the mines shut down, the economy tanked. Unemployment soared to 25 percent, and up to a third of the population lived below the poverty line. Ajo would have to reinvent itself. Part of the reinvention came in the 1990s and early 2000s with the arrival of border personnel, giving the town a new federal economic base. But, as Eiler recalled, something else was happening too. "Open-minded people" were moving in. Many of the newcomers were interested in the arts, the environment, and historic preservation. They were concerned about immigrants, sustainability, and the impact of border infrastructure on the desert. Eiler was a skilled networker. Measured, thoughtful, and smart, with a compelling personal story, she developed relationships and served in advisory capacities to the Bureau of Land Management, the National Park Service, the Fish and Wildlife Service, and even the Reserva de la Biosfera El Pinacate y Gran Desierto de Altar across the border. She was also widely respected in both the Hia C'ed O'odham and Tohono O'odham communities.[37]

She and other stakeholders joined in informal conversations and started building an organization that could make Ajo and the surrounding area into a vibrant community. They held meetings in town, but also in Hermosillo and Puerto Peñasco in Sonora and on the Tohono O'odham Nation. At one point, they consulted with the Sonoran Institute, which empowers communities to balance environmental and community concerns. The institute facilitated conversations that eventually led to the founding of the International Sonoran Desert Alliance (ISDA) in 1993. ISDA was a self-consciously trinational organization, representing and serving the interests of people from the American, Mexican, and indigenous nations. It sought to give voice to people not traditionally at the table in shaping their local community, and it committed to ensuring indigenous involvement. Its bylaws encoded this principle by designating minimum numbers of Mexican and indigenous members and stipulating that at least one board member should be appointed by the Tohono O'odham Nation.[38] Eiler, who had attended segregated schools in Ajo, was now a cofounder of a multiracial organization designed to build a vibrant and just community. Three decades later, ISDA would find its way to the home of her forebears, A'al Vaipia.

ISDA held meetings to listen to community concerns. To the surprise of some listeners, many informants talked not about sustainability or cultural issues, but about economic opportunity, food security, and safety. "We realized," said future ISDA executive director Aaron Cooper, "if we wanted to move the needle [on culture and the environment], we needed to address people's immediate needs." Helping people meet such needs through job training, apprenticeships, youth programs, support for entrepreneurs, and other workforce development activities, then, formed the core of ISDA's work by the early 2000s.[39]

Along with these efforts, which Cooper called "small footprint work" because it served individuals and families at an intimate level, ISDA undertook "big footprint work" to improve the quality of life in Ajo and southern Arizona for everybody. In many cases, this involved (re)making landscapes. Over the course of the first two decades of the twenty-first century, ISDA purchased dilapidated properties, rehabilitated them while retaining their historical character, and adapted them to new uses for community benefit. For example, the historic campus of the Curley School, built at the height of the copper mining boom between the 1910s and 1940s, was remade to house an artist-in-residence program, ISDA's Registered Apprentice program, a youth agriculture group called Get Going, Get Growing, and the nonprofit Sonoran Desert Inn and Conference Center, which provided affordable lodging in a town almost entirely lacking business and vacation accommodations. ISDA also rehabilitated Ajo's downtown plaza. Built between 1916 and 1947 in a Spanish colonial revival style, the plaza consisted of a central grassy open space surrounded by buildings whose red-tiled roofs covered arched walkways. At the time ISDA purchased it in 2008, two-thirds of the ninety thousand square feet in its buildings was vacant. In a multiyear project that is still ongoing, ISDA has upgraded the spaces, taking care to maintain the historical atmosphere. Retail and food establishments have moved in. The chamber of commerce occupies the old train depot at the east end, and the plaza hosts numerous festivals and other events that gather the community.[40]

ISDA calls its big footprint work "creative placekeeping." Creative placekeeping, in the words of Oakland, California, mayor Libby Schaaf, "is about engaging the residents who already live in a space and allowing them to preserve the stories and culture of where they live."[41] As a way of making landscapes, it is notably distinct from the freezing of places in time that characterized the historic preservation and wilderness protection movements of the 1960s and 1970s. It also departs from the urban renewal of the same period, which sought to tear down and replace landscapes, often making them incompatible with the lives of people who lived there and driving them away. Instead, ISDA has sought to repurpose spaces so that they can anchor existing communities more effectively. It has also sought to honor people's heritage while empowering them to thrive in the face of economic and social change. Thus, ISDA's creative placekeeping has acknowledged change, accepted responsibility for making places, and used them to gather people across cultural distinctions, refusing to exclude. In the words of one guide to placekeeping, "By rooting ourselves in our communities and weaving the connections among us, we strengthen our base and build a platform from which we can face and withstand disruption.[42] In 2019 and 2020, as protests, anti-immigrant rhetoric, border wall panels, and declining water levels shook the earth, Quitobaquito, too, was in need of an approach that could endure impermanence.

That was not an impossibility. ISDA had partnered with Organ Pipe from the beginning. Lorraine Eiler got to know superintendent Harold Smith in the 1980s and interested him in the founding of ISDA. Although staff turnover required Eiler and other ISDA leaders to constantly renew ties to the park, Organ Pipe personnel were heavily involved in ISDA's early years, providing environmental expertise and sitting on an advisory council. When Lee Baiza retired as monument superintendent in 2014, he joined the ISDA board. Organ Pipe sent rangers to speak at events in Ajo, and ISDA brought locals down to camp overnight and learn how to harvest saguaro fruit. Lorraine Eiler served as one of the speakers.[43]

In 2016, Organ Pipe's designation as a UNESCO Biosphere Reserve was up for its ten-year renewal. The program had begun in the 1970s, with an emphasis on scientific study of undisturbed areas. Organ Pipe was named a reserve in 1976 in the first phase of designations. Over time, however, the program's concern for cultural sustainability grew, with a key moment coming in 1995 with the adoption of the Seville Strategy, which called for conservation of both natural and cultural diversity. Organ Pipe had long been primarily a nature park, and new resource chief Rijk Moräwe felt uncertain about how to justify a renewal of the monument's status. There was even talk among Park Service personnel of letting the designation go, something other parks in the United States had already done. Instead, Moräwe reached out to Aaron Cooper, who drew on ISDA's creative placekeeping experience with combining stewardship of culture and nature and helped the park redraft its ten-year review, which UNESCO recently approved.[44]

With this partnership cemented, creative placekeeping came to Quitobaquito in 2020. O'odham people had long expressed concern for accessibility and sustainability at the oasis, but the drying of the pond in summer 2020 greatly intensified that. Cooper described the indigenous response to the dry-up as "visceral." While organizations like the Center for Biological Diversity and the O'odham Anti Border Collective tried to stop the wall or block groundwater pumping, ISDA, whose mission focused on bringing people together, occupied a different niche in the struggle. On behalf of its O'odham constituency, ISDA leadership reached out to Moräwe and superintendent Scott Stonum to discuss the oasis. Park staff were already committed to redesigning the pond to make it more sustainable, but they needed more funds. At the time, ISDA leadership had been talking to an individual who was interested in funding a project to support indigenous communities. Eiler suggested Quitobaquito as a possibility, and the pieces began to fall into place. The generous donor pledged $100,000 to launch a Quitobaquito redesign project. While not enough to cover the entire needs of the oasis, the gift was enough to advance it up the ladder of National Park Service priorities. With the support of a community organization and private donor, Organ Pipe leadership was able to persuade the National Park Service to put in another $250,000.[45]

Embracing the uncertainty of future water levels at Quitobaquito in the face of climate change and other disruptions, the project planned for the oasis to be resilient and able to endure as both a cultural and natural resource amid a range of potential hydrological scenarios. It would be made smaller, so it could still fill even if modest spring flow, low precipitation, and high temperatures continued. It would have a stair-step bottom design, allowing for both deep-water and shallow habitats. The depths would reduce evaporation and could endure even when the shallows dried up. A sediment trap pond at the north end would slow the water entering the pond and capture infilling sediment from major storms. This in turn would keep the area marshy and protect habitat for pupfish and mud turtles by providing a refugium during construction and future low water levels in the pond. When there is enough water to fill the pond, it will flow back through the traps and infiltrate the ground, allowing vegetation growth for wildlife habitat. A full pond could also flow out the overflow pipe into the old orchard downstream of the dam and possibly enable the replanting of fruit trees. The park may also replant cottonwoods and willows along the north shore to enhance the historical ambience. Still regretting that he had not invited O'odham observers to be present at the downing of the cottonwood, Moräwe invited O'odham visitors to Quitobaquito to discuss the changes envisioned and was pleased by their positive response. The park also posted information in newspapers and sent official letters to all tribes with cultural affiliations with the park. Meanwhile, ISDA convened several community meetings in fall 2020 to publicize the plan and receive input. One was dedicated specifically for O'odham participants. In response to indigenous feedback, the park selected a Native-owned contractor to design and build the project.[46]

In spring 2022, park staff and volunteers began to remove pupfish and mud turtles in buckets to safe pools on-site. They temporarily diverted the spring water and pumped the pond water into a natural wash. A new liner was laid on the bottom of the pond to keep it from leaking. Hia C'ed O'odham observers during the reconstruction were cautiously optimistic. Future work calls for the possibility of enhanced interpretation at the site, restrooms and shade structures, and other infrastructure to support O'odham visits for reburials and other events. The memorandum of understanding between ISDA and Organ Pipe also stipulated opportunity for continued indigenous engagement in future phases, which reinforces the legal requirements for consultation that federal law already mandates.[47]

The challenges of early twenty-first-century America were being imprinted on the landscape at Quitobaquito. Climate change, immigration debates, and national reckoning with the legacy of colonialism each in one way or another, sometimes in combination, influenced the removal of the cottonwood, the O'odham requests for involvement in the site, the park's general responsiveness to those pleas, the wall, the dry pond, the protests, the ceremonies, and the redesign of the oasis. While grappling with the enormous scale of these kinds of issues, the Park Service suffered from inadequate resources for doing the difficult work now demanded of it. These challenges inspired some significant management innovations, but the treads of federal bureaucracy grind slowly. Many of the steps the Park Service has taken to embrace its role as not just a preserver of landscapes at Quitobaquito but a maker of them are still ad hoc rather than habitual or built into the institution's structure. But perhaps the arrest of O'odham protestors and the steamrolling of saguaros are, for now, a thing of the past.

Caretaking

Early in 2020, before the novel coronavirus precluded such gatherings, NPS staff led a diverse group to Quitobaquito. We were scientists, activists, journalists, and historians, children, adults, and elders, interns and senior park personnel. We were white, Latinx, Mexican, and indigenous, locals and out-of-towners, first-timers and repeat visitors. Quitobaquito was looking unusually shabby that day. The water level was in decline, turning the emerald bulrushes brown and leaving a muddy bathtub ring about the edges of the pond. Several Hia C'ed O'odham on the field trip recalled visiting Quitobaquito in their youth. It was green and lush then, a pleasant, well-tended place where they enjoyed the company of relatives living there. Now it was brown, and everybody was gone. "It's not cared for anymore," one lamented. Later, a monument staff person described the park's wilderness preservation efforts as a kind of caretaking.

The National Park Service is the ultimate American steward. Caretaking is rooted deeply in its mission and self-conception. More than a century after its birth, the agency still prominently proclaims the dual mission in its enabling legislation, the 1916 Organic Act. In fact, Organ Pipe's handout to the group that day began with that founding mission: "To conserve the scenery and the natural and historic objects and wild life therein and to provide for the enjoyment of the same in such manner and by such means as will leave them unimpaired for the enjoyment of future generations."[48] No institution invests more time, sweat, or heart in taking care of America's natural and cultural heritage. And yet a Native woman, in full sincerity, standing a few feet from Organ Pipe personnel, could not see any caretaking at Quitobaquito. This gap of perceptions between peoples who take care of the land by living on it and those who take care of it by not living on it can be bridged. Quitobaquito is a good place to try.

CONCLUSION | # Designs for an Impermanent World
Blue Sky Recommendations for Quitobaquito

IN ITS INFANCY, THE EARTH SHOOK. I'itoi tuned into a spider, spun a web, and finally stilled the trembling. At Quitobaquito/A'al Vaipia, however, stasis turned out to be a temporary condition. Change has been the rule. Corn taught the People how to farm. They cultivated the wet places and built grass huts. Invaders came from afar, bringing diseases, new religion, and livestock. Somebody built a dam. Someone introduced new crops. Someone planted a cottonwood. For a moment, O'odham, Americans, Mexicans, and European immigrants lived and worked together at the pond. And then they did not. The Park Service prevented anyone from living or working there but encouraged study and play. It bulldozed previous residents' compounds and later wrote National Historic Register nominations to preserve the memory of what it had removed. Federal agencies built fences to keep cattle out, and then, as federal immigration deterrence practices hardened, they built stronger ones to keep vehicles out. The park removed the leaning cottonwood and helped O'odham runners resume Salt Pilgrimages. Trump built a wall. Today, Organ Pipe is trying to remake the landscape yet again to sustain it through hotter, drier conditions of climate change. It is a truism to say of any place that the only constant is change. Still, it is worth noting that the people who have endured there the longest, the O'odham, have persisted by adapting to ever-evolving conditions and developing a tolerance for impermanence.

For much of the twentieth century, the NPS did the opposite of tolerating impermanence. It reserved a bounded parcel of space, imagined a pristine time in the past, and attempted to prevent change from those conditions. Although Quitobaquito is badly imperiled, decades of protecting it from environmental deterioration have accomplished some things of great value. The roar of Carretera Federal 2 and the glower of the border wall have damaged the ecology and ambience of the site, but national monument and wilderness designations have prevented additional damage from prospecting, overgrazing, groundwater pumping, and the like. The park has not paved South Puerto Blanco Drive or encouraged hordes of tourists to descend on the oasis. The Endangered Species Act requires habitat protection for pupfish and mud turtles, and so the park cannot ignore golden shiners, pond leaks, and other threats. For visitors who tune out the highway and turn their backs on the wall, Quitobaquito remains a quiet place that refreshes the spirit. Despite climate change and border walls, the oasis still evokes something of what people experienced there in the past and retains some measure of ecological integrity. Without protective laws and dedicated management by park staff, the oasis would not be much good for anyone—the O'odham, visitors, scientists, monument personnel, or pupfish. Still, Quitobaquito could be even more.

It could also be a place that honors the indigenous past and helps sustain its present, stretches visitors by challenging their assumptions about nature, history, and cultural difference, and models how the NPS can abandon its colonial legacy. Right now, because of the erasures and exclusions, the oasis reflects the nation's past as a colonizing power: the dispossession of early Native people and the subsequent development and degradation of their lands; then, the romanticization of past landscapes and people; and finally, the erasure of real people and their pasts as well as the denial of their continued presence. While the NPS should by no means stop trying to protect the site's nonhuman nature, it can complement that by preserving and making visible other layers of the landscape. Here, it is helpful to adopt the O'odham idea of continuous becoming.[1] Instead of managing Quitobaquito as a static place that once was, then was not, and now must be restored, Organ Pipe could treat the oasis as a place that is continuously becoming something else. Rather than preserving some arbitrary state of the oasis, the goal would be to steward the process of becoming and ensure that A'al Vaipia remains a place of value in an impermanent world.

Some Blue Sky Recommendations

Here is what it might look like to manage Quitobaquito in an impermanent world. First, it would take brave, creative, innovative thinking to envision alternative futures for the oasis. The tensions between conservation and indigenous claims at Quitobaquito are also manifest all around the world. Other places have begun to work out some solutions. Organ Pipe can look to those contexts for guidance in how to manage its own challenges. Second, the Park Service could actively design the site for the ends it wants to achieve. In partnering with ISDA and O'odham peoples to build a Quitobaquito more resistant to climate change, the Park Service is already engaged in design. So entrenched in our thinking is the idea of re-creating an imagined pristine past that the project is commonly mislabeled as an act of "restoration," even though it envisions something highly engineered that has never existed at the site before. Messy language aside, it is design, not preservation, that anthropologist Arturo Escobar argues can fulfill aspirations toward justice for indigenous and other marginalized peoples around the world in a time of transitions.[2]

In the spirit of innovative thinking and just design, here are some blue sky recommendations based on the research for this book. Blue sky thinking means thinking beyond limits. If there were no political, financial, physical, or other constraints on what Quitobaquito could be, how would we remake it? Blue sky thinking is not necessarily intended to provide immediately workable actions, though that can sometimes be one outcome. More often and more importantly, its primary value is to open possibilities and expand the range of options before us. As one idea generates others, blue sky thinking converges on practicable approaches previously thought impossible, or not even thought of before at all. Nor does blue sky thinking aim to supplant pragmatic approaches that try to achieve the possible. Both are needed. With this in mind, I offer three blue sky recommendations below. If implemented, they would reveal and challenge the colonial legacy currently embedded in the Quitobaquito landscape. I am, of course, aware of the obstacles to what I propose, the good reasons why these things have not been implemented before, yet I also believe they are not far beyond the realm of possibility if thinking and other limitations opened even a bit. It is also possible that not all of these specific suggestions will prove workable, but consideration of them might lead to other good ideas that accomplish similar benefits by different means.

Replant the Orchard

Although not without challenges, one medium-term goal should be to replant the orchard of figs and pomegranates that many different peoples tended in the late nineteenth and early twentieth centuries. This would be a logical subsequent phase once the Quitobaquito redesign project stabilizes the hydrology. One philosophical barrier is the traditional understanding of preservation. All the fruit trees at the oasis have died, so restoring the orchard would not be about preserving something old but rather about planting something new, which might be perceived as conflicting with the Park Service's historical goal of freezing a moment in time and keeping things as they were. And yet this book, and other literature such as Laura Alice Watt's *Paradox of Preservation*, has argued for broadening the concept of preservation to include things such as replanting orchards. Other NPS units, including Tumacácori National Historical Park in Arizona, have initiated orchard restorations. In fact, according to one Park Service website, as many as 30 percent of units have orchards or historic trees within their boundaries. These plants, the site points out, "are often the only remnants of former subsistence or agricultural uses of land by indigenous people or later settlers. Fruit trees give us clues about how people used to live, and tell us a lot about the history of local cultures, environments, and socioeconomics. . . . Additionally, fruit orchards are repositories of genetic diversity of heirloom and rare varieties that may not be found anywhere else."[3] From a practical standpoint, the park made cuttings of the trees before they died, so genetic descendants of the historic plants tended by Dorsey, the Childses, and the Orozcos could once again grow at Quitobaquito. Perhaps a new acequia could be installed to carry water through the grove as far as the border wall. Pristine nature is only one aspect of A'al Vaipia's past. Garden is another. Replanting the orchard would make that visible.

The name of this kind of multilayered landscape is "palimpsest." Physical geographers use the term to describe a landscape in which evidence of many different geophysical processes is apparent, some that are no longer happening as well as some that are still taking place. A simple way to conceptualize this is to imagine a series of layers in a cake, one atop the other, each layer being formed by a different process yet each integral to the whole dessert. Human impact through agriculture, deforestation, roadbuilding, or other activities may be among these geophysical agents. Most cases, however, are more complicated. The layers are not always distinct, more like a lasagna than a cake. They were formed at different times, but with baking, slicing, and serving, they come to overlap and bleed into one another so that different processes from different periods and operating on different temporal scales may be jumbled up and visible all at once in the same landscape. Both history and geology work this way. Applying the concept of a palimpsest to a cultural landscape like Quitobaquito implies preserving evidence of the many different social processes that have taken place over the years.

For example, at Castlereagh, a suburb some forty miles northwest of Sydney, Australia, developers began digging a quarry in the 1960s to supply materials to the metropolis's building boom. Then, decades later, the gravel extracted, they rehabilitated the acreage for subdivisions nestled among lakes and native plants.[4] The quarry and housing development wiped out a historical white farming settlement that in turn had supplanted an Aboriginal landscape that itself had modified previous nature. As historian Grace Karskens has observed, each group's displacement of the previous one brought "appalling loss." At each stage, "people fought for their country; they still mourn for it."[5]

Several landscapes of human use lay atop each other, but like the early monument managers at Quitobaquito, the Australian developers ignored this palimpsest. Instead, they argued that the area could be rehabilitated with native fauna to enhance biodiversity. Housing tracts that returned the countryside to pristine conditions, not unlike the dredging of Quitobaquito two decades earlier, were seen as better for local plants and animals, and thus an improvement over the disruptions that Aboriginal Australians and settlers had worked on the landscape. Bulldozing made way for an aesthetic wetland and a development dotted with lakes. The new landscape enriched developers and attracted wealthy Sydney home buyers weary of urban chaos and eager to get back to nature. Karskens, in contrast, called the erasure an act of "historical amnesia" and critiqued the way that cultural landscapes were "re-interpreted as 'disturbance.'" Only by "historicizing" such landscapes, she argued, and by preserving evidence of the palimpsest can we see the ways that "powerful ideas like 'wilderness' and 'restoration' can be harnessed by dominant groups to justify environmental and social destruction."[6]

We have inherited a similar landscape of erasure at Quitobaquito. Replanting the orchard, however, could help recast the oasis as a palimpsest of many layers. With interpretation, perhaps a brochure or some signs at the parking lot to minimize the need for construction in wilderness, the orchard would give visitors a sense of both the scale of change Quitobaquito has experienced in the last two centuries and the colonial processes by which newcomers imposed crops and methods of production that disrupted Native lifeways. It would also demonstrate the highly adaptive inventiveness with which the O'odham have persisted as a people over the long haul in an impermanent world.

Because nearly everyone who has come to the oasis practiced it, agriculture is the most tangible example of multicultural human thriving over the long term at Quitobaquito; therefore, replanting the orchard could symbolize and help interpret many other elements of the palimpsest. Interpretation would tell of O'odham corn and creation stories, the first transportation of maize into the Southwest (and the extensive trade networks that accompanied it), the arrival of Kino and his remarking about the agricultural potential of the "good place" and its surroundings. It might recall the entrepreneurial Dorsey's construction of the dam that created the pond and that visitors walk on today. It would recall Beatrice Melvin's childhood fascination with the food can labels, donkeys, arrastras, and melons. It would evoke the store owned by the son of Jewish immigrants tended by a Frenchman that sold goods to Americans, Mexicans, O'odham, and Asians. It would substantiate the memories of living O'odham who recall A'al Vaipia as a lush place, where crops grew and children jumped from boughs into the pond. And it could narrate the history of the park's role there, too, and maybe even foretell the transformation of the Park Service from an institution that once reinforced colonialism into one that preserves many worlds at once at the oasis of hope. A few trees in the orchard, and maybe a cutting of the leaning cottonwood, could evoke all these layers of the palimpsest. It would remind visitors that they are not the first to walk here; rather, they do so in a long parade of people who came to Quitobaquito (and valued it) before them. It would honor those ancestors' role in creating our world today, while also acknowledging the uniqueness of their himdags and difference from us.

Preserve the Trash

Border crossers have left mountains of material behind as they have traversed the backcountry of Organ Pipe Cactus National Monument. Shoes, clothing, sleeping bags, Bibles, blankets, rosaries, hats, backpacks, water bottles, photographs, diaries, all manner of things. Particularly heart wrenching are many of the accoutrements pertaining to children. Strewn across Organ Pipe and other protected areas, the debris stains otherwise magnificent land. Massive cleanup efforts cart much of it away, but with subsequent waves of crossers, it accumulates again, a Sisyphean struggle between landscape making and erasure. The objects, however, constitute yet another layer of the palimpsest. They tell stories of people with aspirations who passed through the area at a moment in time. They left their mark on it like all others. The debris reveals the travails of its owners—the carriers' ties to home and dreams for the future, their mechanisms for crossing difficult terrain, the traumas that caused them to abandon still useful objects, and the suffering and death that resulted for some. If we think of Quitobaquito as a place continuously becoming, we realize that at some point in the future, it will be something else, and then we will want some way of remembering the people who left the trash. Someday, Americans may value these personal effects as artifacts, much as we value the belongings, say, of people who passed through Ellis Island or the names carved into rock along pioneer trails. As Gabriella Soto, an archaeologist of the contemporary, contends, the line between garbage and heritage often blurs.[7]

Organ Pipe has an opportunity to preserve those stories and Quitobaquito's role in them. A roadside interpretive exhibit on South Puerto Blanco Drive, just steps from the border and the wall, would be a powerful juxtaposition for such a display. It might feature photos of some spot in the monument previously strewn with garbage, to give a sense of the scale of waste. It could also help visitors form a human connection to migrants, by showing personal items, especially ones associated with children—perhaps a stuffed animal or a tiny pink backpack. The text could describe the global forces behind migration and drug trafficking, linking these modern manifestations with long-term movement through the region, including historical smuggling. One sign might teach readers about the homemade so-called carpet shoes that border crossers made for their sojourn across the desert and display a photo of a manufactured pair. The text could explain that border crossing has developed its own economy, leading to market innovations such as selling to migrants goods they once made themselves. Another sign could interpret the cleanups, exploring the tension between the act of beautifying the desert as a public service and imposing yet another erasure in a long and belittling line of them. The visitor center back on Highway 85 could supplement this cluster of markers by displaying some actual artifacts, making the interpretation accessible to visitors who stop only there and do not make the forty-five-minute drive out to Quitobaquito. Additional objects could be stored at the Western Archeological and Conservation Center, within the constraints of the facility's storage capacity, so that professional archaeological and anthropological study of them could reveal what we can learn of the migrants. The Tohono O'odham Solid Waste Management program hosts such an exhibit of nearly one hundred objects, so it seems theoretically feasible for Organ Pipe to do something similar.[8]

None of this would be an easy message to swallow, and the Park Service would have to assemble the interpretation sensitively, but it might be one with which many visitors would be willing to engage. In her research on border trash, Soto has participated in migrant garbage cleanups and interviewed others who have as well. She has noticed patterns in the reactions to abandoned objects. "Look at this!" starts many conversations, as a volunteer lifts some poignant object from the ground. From there, she observes, people develop extraordinary attachments to the artifacts. Sometimes they want to take them home. The point is that the people Soto has observed show interest in the objects. Freud called this phenomenon "the uncanny"—that is, people's habit of seeing themselves in another person or object. Theater scholar Michael Shanks used the term "suture" to describe a similar relationship between the audience and characters in a play. People can form bonds of care, curiosity, and empathy for others unlike themselves through engagement with objects. By preserving the belongings of border crossers, the Park Service could bridge part of the gap between materially comfortable, mostly white visitors and disadvantaged, brown migrants. Admittedly, border security is a divisive topic, and such interpretation would stretch some visitors beyond their comfort zone. Such an exhibit could embroil the monument in controversy. But displaying objects humanizes their carriers and forces observers to consider the real possibility that the former owners suffered greatly or even perished in the desert. This creates openings, as Soto argued, for audiences to relate to the objects and their human owners apart from the racialized and politicized context of current border debates. With such an exhibit, the park could move beyond merely catering to visitor expectations and instead provide them the kind of genuinely "transformative experience" that the 2012 NPS report *Revisiting Leopold* said should be the "overarching goal of NPS resource management."[9]

Empower the O'odham as Landscape Makers

Organ Pipe could start this by embracing some or all of the items on a list it received from ISDA cofounder Lorraine Marquez Eiler. In 2021, as the Quitobaquito pond redesign was getting underway, Eiler and others in the ISDA and O'odham communities hoped the project would be the first phase of a long-term partnership for sustaining Quitobaquito as an ecological and cultural asset. In conversation with others, including fellow O'odham as well as renowned ethnobotanist Gary Paul Nabhan, Eiler drew up a list of actions that would enhance Quitobaquito. She submitted it to the Park Service and Tohono O'odham Nation.[10] Much of it is consistent with projects the monument has underway or has expressed interest in undertaking. Launching these actions soon and systematically would enable Eiler and other O'odham to make landscape at A'al Vaipia, as their ancestors did for generations before.

Eiler's list begins by requesting O'odham involvement in the pond redesign. O'odham should review the request for proposals distributed to design firms. The park should select an indigenous-owned firm and notify the tribes when a plan is in place and when construction starts. Some O'odham workers should be hired for the project, and O'odham should also participate in monitoring the construction on-site. The park has already agreed to and implemented much of this, but the list does not stop with the reconstruction itself. When the pond liner work is complete, the park should clean up damage done by the summer 2021 flooding and mitigate the devastation of the border wall construction. Eiler went on to ask for a bathroom to be built at the oasis to ease the burden of multihour and all-day visits, and for a traditional ramada and more benches so that O'odham elders and others can sit in the shade. She recommended replanting pomegranate trees and medicinal plants—park staff should consult O'odham specialists on this latter item—and obtaining authorization for O'odham to assist in maintaining the cemetery and other burial sites. The park should install interpretative signage to inform visitors in O'odham, Spanish, and English of the place's rich history and culture. O'odham artists should be invited to help design the signage. There should be summer youth programs and adult employment programs. Although indigenous peoples are already allowed to gather wild plants, camp overnight, and perform ceremonies, when, where, and how they are allowed to access Quitobaquito is not always clear. Such requirements should be made explicit in a memorandum of understanding. Finally, a gate in the border wall should be installed near the pond to facilitate Salt Pilgrimages and other transborder ceremonies.[11]

As with this chapter's other recommendations, there are obstacles to Eiler's requests. Quitobaquito's wilderness designation is one of them. The construction necessary for bathrooms, ramadas, and interpretive signs, for example, would require exemptions, which are time consuming to obtain and thus expensive. Even if granted, there may be restrictions on the design of the facilities, their construction methods, their location, and how elaborate they can be. Exemptions could be requested, though—or, because the oasis lies at the edge of the wilderness boundary, some facilities could be located on nonwilderness land adjacent to the oasis. Less specific but equally constraining is the question of sovereignty. Under federal law, agreements between parks and tribes require formal government-to-government relations. Park staff cannot simply make an arrangement with Eiler or other concerned individuals; they must engage the Tohono O'odham Nation in formal conversation. Complicating this is the fact that the Hia C'ed O'odham are not a federally recognized tribe. Conversations can take place informally, of course, and more explicitly through the Tohono O'odham Nation, of which Eiler and many other Hia C'ed O'odham are enrolled members. But the procedures for discussing agreements among a federal agency, a federally recognized tribe, and a cultural group without official recognition will be cumbersome. The parties should start with what they can accomplish informally on their own.

That still leaves plenty of room for progress. The park and tribes have already accomplished much in terms of opening A'al Vaipia to indigenous access. They have begun substantial collaborations through the Quitobaquito redesign project. Implementing many of the items on Eiler's list, perhaps even all, is a matter primarily of developing the will to build on the practices that are already underway.

Other parks provide precedents for cocreating and comanaging park spaces, and the NPS is open to such initiatives. A book in the works, titled *Native Americans and National Parks* and edited by Christina Gish Hill, Matthew Hill, and Brooke Neely, chronicles several parks where staff and indigenous peoples have collaborated successfully. On an even larger scale, the Bureau of Land Management and the Forest Service at Bears Ears National Monument in Utah along with five tribes—the Hopi, Navajo, Ute Mountain Ute, Ute Indian Tribe of the Uintah and Ouray Reservation, and the Pueblo of Zuni—committed in June 2022 to an ambitious comanagement plan for the monument that will protect an entire area around the archaeological treasures. Presidential Proclamation 10285 in October 2021 called for "meaningful engagement" between the two federal agencies and the Bears Ears Commission, to be composed of representatives appointed by the five stakeholder tribes. A memorandum of understanding will spell out the parameters by which the commission will make recommendations about "the development and implementation of the monument management plan" and on how "to integrate the [indigenous] traditional and historical knowledge and special expertise" into functional management of the monument. Although Eiler has been involved with park leadership since 1988, she appreciates that the Quitobaquito redesign has "opened more dialogue." Late in 2021 she and a few representatives from the Tohono O'odham Nation attended a meeting at Organ Pipe headquarters with superintendent Scott Stonum, chief of resources Rijk Moräwe, and several NPS superintendents from around the country. Convened by Jaqueline Lavelle, the recently appointed superintendent of Grant-Kohrs Ranch National Historic Site, the meeting was to discuss ways to address indigenous claims in and around national parks. Eiler was gratified not only by the involvement of Organ Pipe's leadership but also by the interest in the question shown by so many superintendents over such a wide geographic space and variety of park units.[12] The possibility of the O'odham once again shaping landscapes at A'al Vaipia does not seem so far-fetched.

Landscapes and Belonging

If Organ Pipe replanted the orchard, preserved the trash, reempowered the O'odham as landscape makers, and took other, similar steps, it could decolonize a little corner of the National Park Service. The Park Service is an artifact of America's colonial past. Not only was it complicit in the dispossession of indigenous peoples' lands, but by embracing and perpetuating the idea of an original uninhabited wilderness, it has contributed to the ongoing erasure of those people in cultural representations. Quitobaquito, however, could be—and may already be becoming—a place that challenges America's colonial past instead of one that reinforces it.

Both dispossession and erasure can be countered by reestablishing belonging. The institution of private property presupposes that land belongs to somebody, but the O'odham imagine themselves belonging to the land. Recasting Quitobaquito as a palimpsest with a richly layered human history can convey that many peoples have belonged and still belong there. In recent oral histories, Marlene Vazquez and Lorraine Eiler both indicated that many O'odham do not feel welcome at Quitobaquito or elsewhere in the monument. During border wall construction, for example, when the park closed the road to the oasis, many interpreted the move as blocking access to sacred space. In practice, that closure was temporary. Moreover, it applied to everybody, not just O'odham. And the park soon reopened access for ceremonial and other purposes. What seemed to park staff a simple bureaucratic action, however, appeared to some people to be yet another example of exclusion. It was not clear to Native people when or whether they would be allowed back. This is the kind of miscommunication that construction of a palimpsest landscape, devoted at least partly to explicitly welcoming the O'odham, can avoid in the future. In the context of a colonial legacy, there is an enormous difference between being allowed access according to some piece of paper in a park superintendent's drawer and being actively welcomed by a landscape deliberately constructed to signal a valuing of the Native past and current presence.[13]

Essentially, the lost landscapes of Quitobaquito are part of something that scholars and indigenous activists around the world describe as a pluriverse. In the 1990s, the Mexican peasant and worker liberation group Ejército Zapatista de Liberación Nacional envisioned a world in which many worlds would fit. The *zapatistas* believed humanity is big enough to contain, tolerate, and give life to many smaller but nevertheless whole worlds, each complete unto itself. In the nation the zapatistas wanted to construct, "all communities and languages fit, [and] all steps may walk."[14] For a long time, the Park Service insisted that Quitobaquito contain only one world—pristine, untouched nature—and excluded all others. At a national scale, the border wall similarly aims to exclude. Preserved, however, as a palimpsest that records twelve thousand years of human habitation, Quitobaquito can accommodate and make visible many worlds, even ones as seemingly antithetical to each other as wilderness, agriculture, and migrant trash deposits. In combination with palimpsest, the concept of pluriverse might serve as an aspirational goal for Quitobaquito's caretakers. A palimpsest landscape makes visible the many layers of historical human presence at a particular spot. Thinking of it as a pluriverse brings those past layers into the present and recognizes that the many different heirs of those many pasts can coexist and collaborate in the present day.

In her research on Indonesian conservation and mountain peoples, anthropologist Anna Tsing argued that recognizing a multitude of worlds and their variation does not diminish the value or wholeness of any one of them. She embraced what she calls the creative "friction" that sparks when distinctive worlds confront their differences. To illustrate this, Tsing recounted a day when she and Uma Adang, her indigenous mentor and informant, sat down to try to name every species they knew. As the list swelled into the thousands, the stories about each multiplied, the classification of the organisms grew more elaborate, and Tsing realized that the joint endeavor was a negotiation. The Western scholar and the Indonesian forest dweller each contributed different perspectives, and the list reflected both views. But neither woman could have produced that particular list on her own. It was a creative outgrowth of their relationship that could come into being only because of the difference—creative friction—between the worlds the two women inhabited. Plus, it was fun![15]

This is consistent with the O'odham expectation of being a people constantly in the state of becoming. While Western thought, including conservation (especially conservation), has long tended toward erasing indigenous people from wild environments or essentializing them as primitive and leaving scant impression on landscapes, the O'odham have not disappeared. Rather, they adapted and persisted, became something new. Scholars, conservationists, and indigenous activists around the world commonly use the concept of interdependency to describe the way that relationships mutually reshape their participants.[16] Although certain important cultural characteristics persist, the O'odham are not the same people who toppled the sivanyi with I'itoi or whom Kino met at Quitobaquito in 1698. Nor are they the same people who watered their crops from Dorsey's little reservoir, who intermarried with American newcomers like Childs, or who left Quitobaquito to work for mines and railroads. As they have continually become new people, they have developed new aspirations and built new landscapes in response. If given the chance, they would make yet another landscape at Quitobaquito in the twenty-first century. Like Tsing and Adang, the O'odham today are a people shaped by interactions with other peoples, and they are no less O'odham as a result.

Nor would the Park Service or its visitors be diminished through engagement with the O'odham. As Escobar put it, "Only privileged groups can afford to . . . act as if the entire world were, or should be, as they see it."[17] Confronting their difference with the O'odham himdag and realizing that it fits within their own world might help them see this. This is why interpretation of migrant garbage, the O'odham cultural past, and other evidence of the oasis's ongoing human history is so important. Visitors, who are predominantly white and comparatively well off, will be shaped by confronting the history of people largely unknown to them. Learning that migrant children carry backpacks, that Tom Childs and Jim Orozco were friends, or that indigenous youngsters flung themselves into the lagoon may establish new interhuman connections that are much harder to make in the arenas of economics and politics, where debates over border security, race, and the nation's colonial past most often arise and seem intractable and threatening. National parks, in contrast, where people recreate and play, and where encounters with cultural difference are perhaps less frightening, may prove more fruitful for establishing a sense of interdependency. As Albert Einstein allegedly said of American racism, "If the majority knew of the root of this evil, then the road to its cure would not be long."[18]

This is what Quitobaquito—A'al Vaipia—could be. It could be a place where rich human histories are visible, a place that remembers many peoples and tells their stories, a place where indigenous peoples once again play a meaningful role in making landscapes, a small world that fits with many others into a larger one. This is a different Quitobaquito from the one the Park Service built in the twentieth century. It replaces dispossession with belonging, erasure with recovery of lost landscapes. It contains ecological integrity and also preserves the stories of indigenous peoples, colonizers of all races and nationalities, settlers, migrants, border patrollers, the National Park Service itself, and even smugglers. It casts all these people as being in a continuous state of becoming even as the place itself does the same. Stewarding the process of becoming is a way to endure in an impermanent world. In this, A'al Vaipia can be a model for the rest of the Park Service and the world.

GLOSSARY OF O'ODHAM AND SPANISH TERMS

A'al Vaipia	Hia C'ed O'odham name for Quitobaquito
A'al Waipia	Tohono O'odham name for Quitobaquito
Akimel O'odham	River People; sometimes called Pimas or One-Villagers
Baboquivari	Mountain in southern Arizona and home of I'itoi, according to Tohono O'odham; Hia C'ed O'odham believe his home is in the Sierra Pinacate
Hia C'ed O'odham	Sand People; sometimes called Sand Papagos, Areneños, or No-Villagers
himdag	Traditional way of living
Huhugam	O'odham word for a group archaeologists call Hohokam; means ancestors who are no longer here but did not disappear
I'itoi	A creator deity who brought the O'odham people out from inside the earth; sometimes called Elder Brother
Papaguería (Spanish)	Land of the Papagos, roughly northwestern Sonora and southern Arizona
sivanyi	A class of Hohokam priests believed to control the wind and rain
Siwani	Influential man overthrown by I'itoi and followers in the O'odham creation story
tinaja (Spanish)	Natural rock tank that captures and holds water perennially or seasonally
Tjuni Ka:ak	O'odham village near the modern site of Bates Well in Organ Pipe Cactus National Monument
Tohono O'odham	Desert People, sometimes called Papagos or Two-Villagers

NOTES

ABBREVIATIONS

AF NARAMD Administrative Files, 1949–1971, 79.570.81.1.7, Record Group 79, National Archives and Records Administration, College Park, Maryland

AF1 NARARMR Southwest Regional Office, Administrative Files, 1959–1972, 8NS-79–95–040, Record Group 79, National Archives and Records Administration, Rocky Mountain Region, Broomfield, Colorado

AR NARAMD Superintendent's Annual Narrative Reports, 1980–2001, 79.150.55.32, Record Group 79, National Archives and Records Administration, College Park, Maryland

AZHS Arizona Historical Society, Tucson

C1 NARARMR Southwest Regional Office, Correspondence Relating to the National Parks, Monuments, and Recreational Areas, 1927–1953, 8NS-079–94–143, Record Group 79, National Archives and Records Administration, Rocky Mountain Region, Broomfield, Colorado

CCF NARAMD Central Classified Files, 1907–1949, 79.150.34.11.6, Record Group 79, National Archives and Records Administration, College Park, Maryland

CH Carl Hayden Papers, Arizona State University Libraries, Department of Archives and Special Collections, Tempe

CSF NARAMD Correspondence and Subject Files, 1928–1959, 70.570.81.33.4, Record Group 79, National Archives and Records Administration, College Park, Maryland

DBL Desert Botanical Laboratory of the Carnegie Institution Records, 1903–1985, University of Arizona Special Collections, Tucson

GC 53–58 NARARMR Southwest Regional Office, General Correspondence Files, 1953–1958, 8NS-79–93–273, Record Group 79, National Archives and Records Administration, Rocky Mountain Region, Broomfield, Colorado

GC 53–61 NARARMR Southwest Regional Office, General Correspondence Files, 1953–1961, 8NS-79–93–279, Record Group 79, National Archives and Records Administration, Rocky Mountain Region, Broomfield, Colorado

GCPPR NARARMR Southwest Regional Office, General Correspondence and Planning Program Records, 1953–1961, 8NS-79–93–280, Record Group 79, National Archives and Records Administration, Rocky Mountain Region, Broomfield, Colorado

GP John Campbell and Isabella Greenway Papers, Arizona Historical Society, Tucson

HFD Henry F. Dobyns Papers, University of Arizona Special Collections, Tucson

HOHP Bill Hoy Oral History Project, University of Arizona Special Collections, Tucson

MKU Morris K. Udall Papers, University of Arizona Special Collections, Tucson

NARAPCR Bureau of Indian Affairs Records, National Archives and Records Administration, Pacific Coast Region, Riverside, California

NARARMR National Archives and Records Administration, Rocky Mountain Region, Broomfield, Colorado

NPS National Park Service

ORPI Organ Pipe Cactus National Monument Library

ORPI CONS Documents currently in the possession of park conservation personnel, Organ Pipe Cactus National Monument

ORPI CRM Documents currently in the possession of park cultural resource management personnel, Organ Pipe Cactus National Monument

SPOHP Sand Papago Oral History Project, University of Arizona Special Collections, Tucson

SWRO Miscellaneous administrative history documents provided to the author by the staff of the National Park Service Southwest Regional Office, Santa Fe, New Mexico

UAZ University of Arizona Special Collections, Tucson

USMBS US Congress, House of Representatives, *United States and Mexican Boundary Survey*

WACC Western Archeological and Conservation Center, Tucson

WACC CRR Organ Pipe Cactus National Monument Cultural Resources Records, CAT ORPI 15916, Western Archeology and Conservation Center Natural Resource Records, Tucson

WACC NRR Organ Pipe Cactus National Monument Natural Resources Records, ACC ORPI 00445, CAT ORPI 15915, Western Archeological and Conservation Center Natural Resource Records, Tucson

WACC RMR Organ Pipe Cactus National Monument Resource Management Records, ACC ORPI 00354, CAT ORPI 15917, Western Archeological and Conservation Center Natural Resource Records, Tucson

INTRODUCTION

1. Carruth, "Hydrogeology."
2. Jose, oral history, 7; Rankin, Eiler, and Joaquin, "Water and the Human Spirit," 598.
3. Rankin, Eiler, and Joaquin, "Water and the Human Spirit," 508.
4. McEvoy, "Toward an Interactive Theory"; Alanen and Melnick, eds., *Preserving Cultural Landscapes*; Longstreth, ed., *Cultural Landscapes*; UNESCO, "Cultural Landscapes," accessed January 28, 2022, https://whc.unesco.org/en

/culturallandscape/; Jackson, *Discovering the Vernacular Landscape*; Jackson, *Sense of Place*; Watt, *Paradox of Preservation*, 14–17.

5. John Washington and Sophia Diez-Zhang, "Why Is the Biden Administration Trying to Jail an Indigenous Woman for Protesting Trump's Border Wall?," *New Republic*, November 15, 2021, accessed December 3, 2021, https://newrepublic.com/article/164404/amber-ortega-indigenous-protest-border-wall; Alisa Reznick, "Indigenous Activists Arrested in Demonstration against Border Wall Construction near Quitobaquito Springs," Arizona Public Media, September 10, 2020, accessed December 3, 2021, https://news.azpm.org/s/80016-indigenous-activists-arrested-in-demonstration-against-border-wall-construction-near-quitobaquito-springs/; Paul Ingram, "Native Activist Found Not Guilty in Border Protest after New Arguments on Religious Freedom Defense," *Tucson Sentinel*, January 19, 2022, accessed June 13, 2022, https://www.tucsonsentinel.com/local/report/011922_ortega_hearing/native-activist-found-not-guilty-border-protest-after-new-arguments-religious-freedom-defense/.

6. An Act to Establish a National Park Service, and for Other Purposes, Approved August 25, 1916 (39 Stat. 53), accessed November 19, 2021, https://www.nps.gov/parkhistory/online_books/anps/anps_1i.htm; Presidential Proclamation 2232, April 13, 1937, in *Foundation Document: Organ Pipe Cactus National Park*, May 2016, accessed November 19, 2021, https://www.nps.gov/orpi/getinvolved/upload/ORPI_FD_SP.pdf.

7. Spence, *Dispossessing the Wilderness*.

CHAPTER 1

1. Saxton and Saxton, *O'othham*, 1–2; Bahr, ed., *O'odham Creation*, 5–9; Underhill, *Papago Indian Religion*, 9.

2. Saxton and Saxton, *O'othham*, 3–9, 37, 147; Bahr, ed., *O'odham Creation*, 6–11; Underhill, *Papago Indian Religion*, 9.

3. Saxton and Saxton, *O'othham*, 147–68; Underhill, *Papago Indian Religion*, 11; Bahr et al., *Short, Swift Time*, 4, 229.

4. For a full description of the major informants and a comparison and synthesis of their versions, see Hill, *From Huhugam*, 65–88; Di Peso, "Prehistory," 92–99; Saxton and Saxton, *O'othham*, xvii; Bahr, ed., *O'odham Creation*, 3–4; Bahr et al., *Short, Swift Time*, 7.

5. Hill, *From Huhugam*, 66, 75–76.

6. Flores, *Coyote America*, 3, 8–10.

7. Kresan, "Geologic Tour," 40–44; Scarborough, "Geologic Origins," 74–77; Brown et al., *Inventory of Surface Water*, 4.

8. Van Devender, "Deep History," 61–67; Dimmitt, "Biomes and Communities," 4, 10–11, 12; Ingram, "Desert Storms," 42.

9. Felger et al., "Botanical Diversity," 202–3; Dimmitt, "Biomes and Communities," 11, 13; Ingram, "Desert Storms," 41–46; Hackenberg, "Pima and Papago," 162; Brown et al., *Inventory of Surface Water*, 6.

10. Nabhan, "Welcome to the Sonoran Desert," 1–2; Ingram, "Desert Storms," 48; Felger, "Vascular Plants," 1.

11. Rankin, *Archeological Survey*, 44, 47; Altschul and Rankin, introduction to *Fragile Patterns*, 9–18.

12. Hill, *From Huhugam*, xiii, 5; Dean, "Thoughts on Hohokam Chronology," 61–149; Gumerman and Haury, "Prehistory," 76; Rankin, *Archeological Survey*, 52–55; Malakoff, "Hohokam Hybrid?," 27–33; Bahr et al., *Short, Swift Time*, 2.

13. Gibson, "Class II Archeological Reconnaissance," iv; Rankin, *Archeological Survey*, 55–58, 105, 370.

14. Gibson, "Class II Archeological Reconnaissance," ii, iii; Rankin, *Archeological Survey*, 105, 370–72; Merrill et al., "Diffusion of Maize," 21019.

15. Hill et al., "Prehistoric Demography," 689–716; Bahr, ed., *O'odham Creation*, 3, 46; Font, "Diary of an Expedition," 35; Underhill, *Papago Indian Religion*, 13; Bahr et al., *Short, Swift Time*, 2, 9.

16. Mason, "Papago Migration Legend," 267.

17. Fontana, "Pima and Papago," 133; Bahr, "Pima and Papago," 187; Hackenberg, "Pima and Papago," 163–65.

18. Fontana, "History of the Papago," 131; Bahr, "Pima and Papago," 187, 189; Erickson, *Sharing the Desert*, 8–10; Saxton and Saxton, *O'othham*, 37; Hackenberg, "Pima and Papago," 163–64.

19. Anderson, Bell, and Stewart, "Quitobaquito," 222; Fontana, "History of the Papago," 127–31; Rankin, *Archeological Survey*, 65; Hackenberg, "Pima and Papago," 161; William R. Supernaugh, "Memorandum for Interpretational Staff," February 18, 1940, folder 13, series 3, WACC RMR; Erickson, *Sharing the Desert*, 10; Vazquez, oral history, 3.

20. Erickson, *Sharing the Desert*, 34, 48; Burrus, ed., *Kino and Manje*, 37; Truett, *Fugitive Landscapes*, 21; Ezell, "History of the Pima," 150–51.

21. Font, "Diary of an Expedition," 34–41; Coues, ed. and trans., *On the Trail*, 96.

22. Kino, *Kino's Historical Memoir*, 188; Kino, "Relación Diaria," 21–25; Manje, *Luz de Tierra*, 110.

23. Kino, *Kino's Historical Memoir*, 193–94, 255–56, 279–80, 288–89, 310; Manje, *Luz de Tierra*, 110, 158 (Manje put the cattle figure at fifty).

24. Truett, *Fugitive Landscapes*, 24–26, 39–40; Sheridan, *Landscapes of Fraud*, 53–54; Manje, *Luz de Tierra*, 110; Kino, *Kino's Historical Memoir*, 279–80, 357–60.

25. This phenomenon of peoples migrating into what is now southern Arizona and northern Sonora is quite old. For example, Merrill et al. posited a migration of Proto Uto-Aztecan speakers from the Great Basin into the Gila and Colorado river drainages approximately 6,600 years ago. Merrill et al., "Diffusion of Maize," 21022–23; Zepeda, "Quitobaquito Oral History Project," 12, and "Miguel Velasco," 24, both in SPOHP; Hackenberg, "Pima and Papago"; Jacoby, *Shadows at Dawn*, 21–30; Blyth, *Chiricahua and Janos*, 44; Kino, *Kino's Historical Memoir*, 175–83.

26. Rosen et al., "Ecology," 4; Kino, "Relación Diaria," 21; Kino, *Kino's Historical Memoir*, 255.

27. Broyles et al., eds., *Last Water*, 93; Martínez, "Hiding in the Shadows," 135, 137; Manje, *Luz de Tierra*, 30, 111.

28. Truett, *Fugitive Landscapes*, 23.

29. Truett, 27, 39–40; Jacoby, *Shadows at Dawn*, 28–29.

30. Font, "Diary of an Expedition," 506.

31. Hill, *From Huhugam*, 55.

32. Chona, "Autobiography of Chona," in Underhill, *Papago Woman*, 36, 66–69, 73, 74. The space between "any" and "more" is in the original.

33. Chona, 34–35, 43–47.

34. Chona, 34, 36.

35. Chona, 53–54, 64, 67–68, 74.

36. Chona, 35, 54, 56.

37. Chona, 36, 39–40, 51, 81.

38. Font, "Diary of an Expedition," 41.

CHAPTER 2

1. Zepeda, "Beatrice Melvin," 32–40, SPOHP. Melvin's syntax here is unconventional, but rather than smooth it over, I have chosen to render it exactly as the transcript recorded it. It conveys the exuberance of her childhood memory. Just as the spring itself gushed water, she, too, gushed—unable to get the words out fast enough or in quite the right order—as she remembered the marvelous water of her childhood.

2. Anderson, Bell, and Stewart, "Quitobaquito," 222; Zepeda, "Sand Papago Oral History Project," 9; Vazquez, research interview with the author, July 26, 2022.

3. West, *Sonora*, 83–91; Sheridan and Broyles, "First Europeans," 73–101; Childs, "History of Quitobaquito," in Hoy, "Organ Pipe Cactus Historical Research," ORPI, 148.

4. Santiago Redondo to José Urrea, April 28, 1838, in McCarty, ed., *Frontier Documentary*, 61.

5. Childs, "Sketch of the 'Sand Indians,'" 33–36; Fontana, "History of the Papago," 139; Joseph et al., *Desert People*, 22.

6. Broyles et al., eds., *Last Water*, 99–103, 105–13; Forbes, *Crabb's Filibustering Expedition*; Wyllys, "Henry A. Crabb"; Santiago Redondo, Altar, to José Urrea, May 12, 1838, in McCarty, ed., *Frontier Documentary*, 62; Childs, "History of Quitobaquito," in Hoy, "Organ Pipe Cactus Historical Research," ORPI, 148; Childs, "Sketch of the 'Sand Indians,'" 29; Childs to *Desert Magazine*, October 1949, 27 (the September issue of *Desert Magazine* attributed the family's deaths to dehydration); Lumholtz, *New Trails in Mexico*, 329; Van Valkenburgh, "Tom Childs," 6.

7. Childs, "History of Quitobaquito," in Hoy, "Organ Pipe Cactus Historical Research," ORPI, 148; Dobyns, "Sketch of the 'Sand Indians,'" 29–30; Childs to *Desert Magazine*, October 1949, 27; Lumholtz, *New Trails in Mexico*, 329; Martínez, "Hiding in the Shadows," 149; Erickson, *Sharing the Desert*, 85; Hoy, "Don Tomás," 10.

8. Hoy, "Don Tomás," 2–7; Van Valkenburgh, "Tom Childs," 5–6.

9. Martínez, "Hiding in the Shadows," 145; Gray, "Report of A. B. Gray," 88.

10. Gray, "Report of A. B. Gray," 90–91; US Congress, Senate, "Report of the Secretary of the Interior," 29–34.

11. Michler, "Report of Lieut. Michler," 120–23, USMBS.

12. Michler, "Report of Lieut. Michler," 115, USMBS; Schott, "Geological Observations," 74, USMBS; Emory, "Sketch of Territory," 93–94, USMBS.

13. Emory, "Sketch of Territory," 95–96, USMBS; Michler, "Report of Lieut. Michler," 117, USMBS ("guarantied" is in the original).

14. Michler, "Report of Lieut. Michler," 117, 118, USMBS; Emory, "Sketch of Territory," 95–96, USMBS.

15. Michler, "Report of Lieut. Michler," 123, USMBS; US Congress, Senate, "Report of the Boundary Commission," 2:174, 192.

16. Dorsey is referred to in some documents as Andres or, probably incorrectly, as Adolph. Alden W. Jones, Sells, AZ, to Morris Burge, June 26, 1945, 3, ORPI; Hoy, "Organ Pipe Cactus Historical Research," ORPI, 34; Stiles, "Quitobaquito," Ephemera Files, AZHS; Anderson, Bell, and Stewart, "Quitobaquito"; Michler, "Report of Lieut. Michler," 115, 123, USMBS; Schott, "Geological Observations," 74, USMBS.

17. Childs, "History of Quitobaquito," in Hoy, "Organ Pipe Cactus Historical Research," ORPI, 148; Anderson, Bell, and Stewart, "Quitobaquito," 217–18; Celaya, Ezell, and Dobyns, "Interview with Alberto Celaya," 439, 477.

18. Gibson, "Class II Archeological Reconnaissance," ii, iv, 8; excerpts from Kirk Bryan, "Relief Map of the Western Part of the Papago Country, Arizona" and "Relief Map of the Central Part of the Papago Country, Arizona," both in Bryan, *Papago Country*; Childs, "Sketch of the 'Sand Indians,'" 31; Anderson, Bell, and Stewart, "Quitobaquito," 217, 219.

19. Childs, "Sketch of the 'Sand Indians,'" 31, 33; Lumholtz and Dracopoli, "Sonora Desert," 516; Van Valkenburgh, "Tom Childs," 5–6.

20. Celaya, Ezell, and Dobyns, "Interview with Alberto Celaya," 437, 439, 453–54, 477; Anderson, Bell, and Stewart, "Quitobaquito," 231, 233.

21. Celaya Ezell, and Dobyns, "Interview with Alberto Celaya," 466; Childs, "Sketch of the 'Sand Indians,'" 31; Childs, "History of Quitobaquito," in Hoy, "Organ Pipe Cactus Historical Research," ORPI, 148; Lumholtz, *New Trails in Mexico*, 291; Vazquez, oral history, 1, 3; Vazquez, research interview with the author, July 26, 2022.

22. Anderson, Bell, and Stewart, "Quitobaquito," 217–25; Childs to Dobyns, February 9, 1950, box 7, folder 18, HFD; Childs, "History of Quitobaquito," in Hoy, "Organ Pipe Cactus Historical Research," ORPI, 148.

23. Alden W. Jones, Sells, AZ, to Morris Burge, June 26, 1945, 2–3, ORPI; "Aged Indian Dies; Fled Massacre," Ephemera Files, AZHS; Childs, "History of Quitobaquito," in Hoy, "Organ Pipe Cactus Historical Research," ORPI, 148. Although "Orosco" is the more common spelling in Park Service and other documents, I am using "Orozco" for all family members. Anderson, Bell, and Stewart indicate that this is the preferred spelling of Luis's descendants ("Quitobaquito," 220).

24. Anderson, Bell, and Stewart, "Quitobaquito," 220; Lumholtz and Dracopoli, "Sonora Desert," 503, 505.
25. Rose, *Ancient Mines*, 21–25; Rickard, "Copper Ores," 1–3; Hoy, "Don Tomás," 9.
26. US Congress, Senate, "Report of the Boundary Commission," 2:8; Mearns, *Mammals of the Mexican Boundary*, 2.
27. Mearns, *Mammals of the Mexican Boundary*, 118; US Congress, Senate, "Report of the Boundary Commission," 2:23; McGee, "Old Yuma Trail," 107.
28. Hornaday, *Camp-Fires*, 99; Haley, *Jeff Milton*, 345–46.
29. Hoy, "Interview with Binion," CD 4, 36:26, HOHP.
30. Documents sometimes refer to him as "M.G.," "Manuel," "Michael," and "Miguel." According to former park archaeologist Connie Gibson, his great-granddaughter said that his name was Emanuel García. Hoy, "Organ Pipe Cactus Historical Research," 173, ORPI; Childs, "History of Quitobaquito," in Hoy, "Organ Pipe Cactus Historical Research," ORPI, 148; Celaya, Ezell, and Dobyns, "Interview with Alberto Celaya," 475; Hoy, "Interview with Binion," CD 4, 36:26, HOHP.
31. Hoy, "Organ Pipe Cactus Historical Research," 174, ORPI; Childs, "History of Quitobaquito," in Hoy, "Organ Pipe Cactus Historical Research," ORPI, 148; "Hike to Victoria Mine," National Park Service, accessed January 9, 2023, https://www.nps.gov/thingstodo/hike-to-victoria-mine.htm; Celaya, Ezell, and Dobyns, "Interview with Alberto Celaya," 450; McGee, "Old Yuma Trail," 131; Hoy, "Interview with Binion," CD 4, 28:50, HOHP.
32. Alden W. Jones, Sells, AZ, to Morris Burge, June 26, 1945, 3, ORPI; Childs, "History of Quitobaquito," in Hoy, "Organ Pipe Cactus Historical Research," ORPI, 148; Anderson, Bell, and Stewart, "Quitobaquito," 220; Hoy, "Don Tomás," 12, 19.
33. Hoy, "Don Tomás," 11, 24.
34. Anderson, Bell, and Stewart, "Quitobaquito," 220; Hoy, "Don Tomás," 10.
35. Anderson, Bell, and Stewart, "Quitobaquito," 222–23; Alden W. Jones, Sells, AZ, to Morris Burge, June 26, 1945, 3, ORPI; Hoy, "Organ Pipe Cactus Historical Research," 13–14, ORPI; Bill Hoy, "Interview with Binion," CD 4, 44:05, HOHP; Haley, *Jeff Milton*; Hornaday, *Camp-Fires*, 122–29.
36. Anderson, Bell, and Stewart, "Quitobaquito," 223, 229–34; Celaya, Ezell, and Dobyns, "Interview with Alberto Celaya," 436–37, 454, 468.
37. Celaya, Ezell, and Dobyns, "Interview with Alberto Celaya," 479–80; Chona, "Autobiography of Chona," in Underhill, *Papago Woman*, 77–80; Alden W. Jones, Sells, AZ, to Morris Burge, June 26, 1945, 6, ORPI.
38. McGee, "Old Yuma Trail," 103, 140–42. The spelling of "forbears" is in the original.
39. McGee, "Old Yuma Trail," 143; Hays, *Conservation and the Gospel*; Tyrrell, *Crisis of the Wasteful Nation*.
40. Antiquities Act, 16 U.S.C. 431–43, June 8, 1906, accessed January 9, 2023, https://uscode.house.gov/view.xhtml?req=gran; Organic Act, 39 Stat. 535, 16 U.S.C., accessed January 9, 2023, https://www.govinfo.gov/content/pkg/COMPS-1725/pdf/COMPS-1725.pdf.

CHAPTER 3

1. Hornaday, *Camp-Fires*, vii.

2. Hornaday, vii, ix.

3. Whisnant et al., *Imperiled Promise*, 99; Watt, *Paradox of Preservation*, 4–5, 13–22.

4. Van Dyke, *The Desert*; Wild, *John C. Van Dyke*, 5–11.

5. Chona, "Autobiography of Chona," in Underhill, *Papago Woman*, 37–40, 53, 56, 64–66, 69–71.

6. Hornaday, *Camp-Fires*; MacDougal, "Across Papaguería," 705–25; Lumholtz, *New Trails in Mexico*; Clotts, *Report on Nomadic Papago*; Bryan, *Routes to Desert Watering Places*, 2, 4.

7. Sykes, "Camino Del Diablo," 71–72.

8. Nichols and Broyles, "Afield with Desert Scientists," 353–70; Shreve, "Problems of the Desert," 199.

9. Greene, *Historic Resource Study*, 58–59.

10. Bennett and Kunzmann, *History of the Quitobaquito*, 15; Lissoway, "Administrative History," 16; Greene, *Historic Resource Study*, 44–46, 52; "Greenway Said to Have New R. R. Funds," *Weekly Journal-Miner* (Prescott, AZ), December 10, 1919, 2, SWRO; Wilton E. Hoy, "Organ Pipe Cactus National Monument Historical Research: Administrative," unpublished manuscript, October 1970, 140, SWRO; "Ajo District Is Booming, *Bisbee Daily Review*, October 23, 1909, 6, SWRO; William Supernaugh to General Superintendent, Southwestern National Monuments, January 25, 1953, folder L1425, box 1759, AF NARAMD.

11. Andrew A. Nichol, "Special Report: Organ Pipe Cactus National Monument," July 5, 1939, folder 000, box 2318, CCF NARAMD; [Charles Budge], "Fish and Wildlife of Organ Pipe Cactus National Monument," 1960, folder N16 ORPI, box 62, GC 53–61 NARARMR.

12. Wilton Hoy, "Organ Pipe Cactus Historical Research," 1970, 204, ORPI; Bennett and Kunzmann, *History of the Quitobaquito*, 24.

13. Dilsaver, *Preserving the Desert*, 111; McKee, Grand Canyon, to Forrest Shreve, Tucson, May 11, 1931, and Shreve to McKee, Grand Canyon, May 16, 1931, folder 1, box 16, DBL; Roger Toll, Denver, to Director of the National Park Service, March 31, 1932, folder 000, box 2318, CCF NARAMD ("sahuaro" is the original spelling in the document); Greenway to Cammerer, Washington, DC, February 27, 1934, folder 432, box 34, GP; Gladstone McKenzie to Lawrence C. Meriam, San Francisco, February 7, 1934, folder History General, 1934–42, box 2319, CCF NARAMD; Pima County Supervisors to Whom It May Concern, January 9, 1934, folder History General, 1934–42, box 2319, CCF NARAMD; Hoy, "Organ Pipe Cactus Historical Research," 1970, 209, ORPI; J. H. Davis, "Organ Pipe Cactus National Monument: A Study of Conservation Objectives Relating to Its Establishment, Boundary Adjustments, and Private Interest in the Area," unpublished manuscript, 3, ORPI; Arno B. Cammerer, Washington, DC, to Isabella Greenway, December 30, 1935, folder 432, box 34, GP.

14. Roger Toll, Denver, to Director of the National Park Service, March 31, 1932, 1, 33–34, 49, E. R. Pohl to Mr. Traeger, Washington, DC, August 25, 1936, Roger Toll, Yellowstone National Park, to Director, National Park Service, Washington, DC [1935?], A. E. Demaray, Washington, DC, "Memorandum for the Commissioner," July 7, 1939, all in folder 000, box 2318, CCF NARAMD.

15. Shreve, "Problems of the Desert," 208; Shreve, "Plant Life," 205, 213; W. B. McDougall, "Special Report: The Organ Pipe Cactus National Monument," February 10, 1938, folder 000–02, box 215, C1 NARARMR.

16. Frank Pinkley, "Memorandum for the Director," June 21, 1939, folder 000, box 2318, CCF NARAMD; Frank Pinkley, "Memorandum for the Files," May 31, 1939, folder 000, box 2318, CCF NARAMD; W. B. McDougall, "Statement Concerning Status of Vegetation in Organ-Pipe Cactus National Monument," October 18, 1937, folder 000–02, box 215, C1 NARARMR; A. E. Demaray, Washington, DC, "Memorandum for the Commissioner," July 7, 1939, folder 000, box 2318, CCF NARAMD.

17. E. R. Pohl to Mr. Traeger, Washington, DC, August 25, 1936, folder 000, box 2318, CCF NARAMD; US Department of the Interior, "Memorandum for the Press," April 17, 1937, folder 1, box 215, C1 NARARMR; W. B. McDougall, "Statement Concerning Status of Vegetation in Organ-Pipe Cactus National Monument," October 18, 1937, folder 000–02, box 215, C1 NARARMR.

18. John Collier to Arno B. Cammerer, May 22, 1939; A. E. Demaray, Washington, DC, to Commissioner Office of Indian Affairs, Washington, DC, n.d.; John Collier, Washington, DC, to Arno B. Cammerer, Washington, DC, [1939?]; A. E. Demaray, Washington, DC, "Memorandum for the Commissioner," July 7, 1939; Frank Pinkley, "Memorandum for the Director," June 21, 1939, all in folder 000, box 2318, CCF NARAMD; "Field Agreement between Superintendent Southwestern National Monuments, Coolidge, Arizona, and Superintendent, Papago Indian Reservation, Sells, Arizona Relative to the Work Necessary to Consummate the Agreement on the Use of National Monument Lands for Use by the Papago Indians," [1940], folder Grazing, 1946–59, box 172, CSF NARAMD; John Collier, Washington, DC, to Director, National Park Service, Washington, DC, June 2, 1936, folder 000, box 2318, CCF NARAMD. The bureau also asked the NPS to adjust the reserve's eastern boundary, which abutted the reservation, to accommodate Indian historical grazing use of the land. Demaray wrote: "Regarding the Indians' use of the cactus fruits within the monument, I see no reason for attempting to prescribe regulations for such practices at this time. So far as we know, they have picked these fruits for an indefinite period of time and there is still an abundance of cactus." Similar reasoning appeared in the US Department of the Interior's press release announcing the monument's creation. US Department of the Interior, "Memorandum for the Press," April 17, 1937, folder 1, box 215, C1 NARARMR.

19. Vazquez, research interview, 1–2; Vazquez, oral history, 1–2; Cato Sells to T. F. McCormick, ca. December 28, 1920, folder 820.2 Fort Yuma, box 80,

Central Classified Files, 1919–1950, Phoenix Area Office Papago Agency, RG 75, NARAPCR; John Collier to Mira DeRoades, n.d., folder 824, Incorrigible Students, box 83, Central Classified Files, 1919–1950, Phoenix Area Office Papago Agency, RG 75, NARAPCR; Harold Ickes to Superintendents, Principals, and Secretaries in the Indian Service, August 16, 1934, folder 824, Incorrigible Students, box 83, Central Classified Files, 1919–1950, Phoenix Area Office Papago Agency, RG 75, NARAPCR; John Collier to Field Supervisors of Education and Superintendents, ca. September 1, 1934, folder 824, Incorrigible Students, box 83, Central Classified Files, 1919–1950, Phoenix Area Office Papago Agency, RG 75, NARAPCR.

20. Vazquez to the author, May 20, 2022; Vazquez, research interview with the author, July 26, 2022.

21. "Baboquivari Is Taken," [Happy Days, February 25, 1939], folder 010 General and Statistical—CCCID, Publications, 1939–1940, box 10, Central Classified Files 1924–1951, Sells Indian Agency, RG 75, Pacific Region, NARA, Riverside, CA; J. C. McCaskill, "Report of Investigation into Problems of Misbehavior at Pima Day School, at Sacaton," July 29, 1935, folder 824, Incorrigible Students, box 83, Central Classified Files, 1919–1950, Phoenix Area Office Papago Agency, RG 75, NARAPCR; Department of the Interior, Office of Indian Affairs, Industrial Section, "Indian Boys and Girls Club News," June 1925, folder 013 General and Statistical—Publications, Other Governments 1930–1938, box 10, Central Classified Files, 1919–1950, Phoenix Area Office Papago Agency, RG 75, NARAPCR.

22. Proclamation No. 2232, 2 Fed. Reg. 827 (April 16, 1937), folder 000–01, box 215, C1 NARARMR; Andrew A. Nichol, "Special Report: Organ Pipe Cactus National Monument," July 5, 1939, folder 000, box 2318, CCF NARAMD.

23. "Descriptive Statement for Organ Pipe Cactus National Monument, Arizona," [1940], folder 600–01, box 218, C1 NARARMR; "The Interpretational Development Plan for Organ Pipe Cactus National Monument," n.d., folder 600–01, box 218, C1 NARARMR. For one sample of the many documents that emphasize this, see W. B. McDougall, "Special Report: Roads and Wildlife at Organ Pipe Cactus National Monument," November 1940, folder Reports General, box 2319, NARAMD.

24. For documentation of opposition to the mining in the monument, see, for example, Stephen Tripp, "Memorandum for Mr. Drury," October 29, 1941, folder Mining Claims, box 2320, CCF NARAMD, and the numerous other documents in this folder. See also W. B. McDougall, "Special Report: The Organ Pipe Cactus National Monument," February 10, 1938, folder 000–02, box 215, C1 NARARMR; John Collier, "Memorandum to Director," July 28, 1938, transcript in John H. Davis, "Organ Pipe Cactus National Monument: A Study of Conservation Objectives Relating to Its Establishment, Boundary Adjustments and Private Interest in the Area," November 1957, 6, 13–14, folder H 14, box 1, GC 53–58 NARARMR; A. E. Demaray, Washington, DC, "Memorandum for the Commissioner," July 7, 1939, 14, folder 000, box 2318, CCF NARAMD.

25. Dunn, "Report on Orosco Interests," August 1, 1951, 3, 6–8, folder L54, box 1982, AF NARAMD; Vazquez, oral history, 6; Hoy, "Organ Pipe Cactus National Monument Historical Research: Administrative," unpublished manuscript, October 1970, 140, SWRO; Miller and Fuiman, "Description and Conservation Status," 601–2; Rankin, Eiler, and Joaquin, "Water," 599; P. P. Patraw, Santa Fe, to the Director, December 21, 1950, folder L1425 ORPI, box 1759, AF NARAMD; National Park Service, *Cultural Landscapes Inventory*, 58.
26. Hoy, "Organ Pipe Cactus National Monument Historical Research: Administrative," unpublished manuscript, October 1970, 141, SWRO; William Supernaugh, Ajo, to Superintendent, Southwestern National Monuments, Coolidge, May 10, 1941, copy in Hoy, "Organ Pipe Cactus National Monument Historical Research: Administrative," 142, SWRO.
27. Wade Head to Commissioner of Indian Affairs, August 1, 1941, folder 339 Forestry and Grazing, 1941, box 56, Central Classified Files, 1919–1950, Phoenix Area Office, RG 75, NARAPCR.
28. John M. Davis, "Memorandum for the Custodian, Organ Pipe Cactus," October 22, 1947, folder 611–01, box 218, C1 NARARMR.
29. Hoy, "Organ Pipe Cactus National Monument Historical Research: Administrative," unpublished manuscript, October 1970, 141, 145, SWRO; John M. Davis, "Memorandum for the Custodian, Organ Pipe Cactus," October 22, 1947, folder 611–01, box 218, C1 NARARMR; Thomas Childs, Rowood, AZ, to Carl Hayden, Washington, DC, March 23, 1948, folder 611–01, box 218, C1 NARARMR (note: spelling as in the original); Carl Hayden to Newton B. Drury, March 30, 1948, folder 611–01, box 218, C1 NARARMR.
30. Newton B. Drury, Washington, DC, to Carl Hayden, April 15, 1948, folder 611–01, box 218, C1 NARARMR; Hoy, "Organ Pipe Cactus National Monument Historical Research: Administrative," unpublished manuscript, October 1970, 140, SWRO; L. M. Lawson, El Paso, to John M. Davis, Santa Fe, October 17, 1947, folder 611–01, box 218, C1 NARARMR; John M. Davis, Santa Fe, to L. M. Lawson, El Paso, October 12, 1948, folder 611–01, box 218, C1 NARARMR.
31. Dunn, "Report on Orosco Interests," August 1, 1951, 6, folder L54, box 1982, AF NARAMD; P. P. Patraw, Santa Fe, to Director, August 10, 1950, folder L54, box 1982, AF NARAMD.
32. The legal story of the monument's acquisition of the Orozco interests between 1950 and 1957 can be traced in minute detail in the following materials: folders L1425 ORPI, ORPI 2, and Orosco, box 1759; folders L54 ORPI, 1954 ORPI, and ORPI 1/1/62–12/31/63, box 1982, AF NARAMD; and folders 600–03, 611–01, 611–02, box 218, C1 NARARMR. It is summarized in Hoy, "Organ Pipe Cactus National Monument Historical Research: Administrative," unpublished manuscript, October 1970, SWRO; Lissoway, "Administrative History"; and Greene, *Historic Resource Study*.
33. National Park Service, *Cultural Landscapes Inventory*, 71; James M. Eden, Organ Pipe Cactus National Monument, to Hugh M. Miller, Santa Fe, October 28, 1957, folder D5039a ORPI, box 45, GCPPR NARARMR; James M. Eden, Organ Pipe Cactus National Monument, to Regional Director,

September 22, 1958, folder H30, May 1953–1958 ORPI, box 5, GC 53–58 NARARMR; Monte Fitch, Ajo, to Regional Director, November 13, 1959, folder A915, box 123, AF1 NARARMR; "Development Schedule 'B,'" 4, folder A915, box 123, AF1 NARARMR.

34. Natt N. Dodge, Santa Fe, to Regional Chief, Division of Interpretation, March 23, 1962, folder K1817, box 46, AF1 NARARMR; Bennett and Kunzmann, *History of the Quitobaquito*, 36; Vazquez, oral history, 2.

35. E. Donald Kaye, Scottsdale, to Stewart Udall, Washington, DC, June 2, 1962, folder A36156, box 131, AF1 NARARMR; Dave Rees, "U.S. Squeezes Ajo: Citizens Wonder Why Uncle Sam Needs More Land," [*Arizona Republic* (Phoenix), May 31, 1932], folder A36156, box 131, AF1 NARARMR; John A. Carver to E. Donald Kaye, [July 1962], folder H30, box 41, AF1 NARARMR. Future Park Service documents would claim the buildings dated to the 1880s. I have seen no evidence to confirm or deny this, and Park Service documents assert this without citations of original documents or archaeological study.

36. Wilderness Act, Pub. L. No. 88–577, 16 U.S.C. 1131–1136, 88th Cong., 78 Stat. 890 (1964), section 2; Jose, oral history, 7.

CHAPTER 4

1. Dowie, *Conservation Refugees*; NPS, "Raze," ORPI CRM.

2. Lawrence F. Van Horn, "National Register of Historic Places Registration Form," October 10, 1994, 4, 19–20, ORPI CRM.

3. Peter S. Bennett, Tucson, to Regional Chief Scientist, Western Regional Office, March 19, 1981, folder 10, series 14, WACC NRR.

4. Stegner, "Best Idea," 4; US Department of the Interior, National Park Service, "Mission 66 for Organ Pipe Cactus National Monument," n.d., folder A98 Prospectus ORPI, box 735, AF NARAMD.

5. US Department of the Interior, National Park Service, "Mission 66 for Organ Pipe Cactus National Monument," n.d., 1, folder A98 Prospectus ORPI, box 735, AF NARAMD; Harthon L. Bill, Santa Fe, to Director, April 18, 1956; James M. Eden, Ajo, to Director, April 22, 1956; and James M. Eden, Ajo, to Chief, Western Office, Division of D&C, April 8, 1958, all in folder D18a ORPI, 1956–1958, box 30, GCPPR NARARMR; Jerome C. Miller, Santa Fe, to Regional Chief of Operations, March 22, 1956, D22a ORPI, 1956–1958, box 34, GCPPR NARARMR; Bennett and Kunzmann, *History of the Quitobaquito*, 36–38, 59; James B. Felton, Ajo, to Southwest Regional Director, May 27, 1964, folder 54, series 2, WACC RMR.

6. Baird and Girard, "Descriptions of New Species," 387–90; Bennett and Kunzmann, *History of the Quitobaquito*, 35–37; W. L. Minckley, "The Desert Pupfish of Organ Pipe Cactus National Monument," unpublished manuscript, October 28, 1965, 2, ORPI; Miller and Fuiman, "Description and Conservation Status," 593–609; Cox, "Behavioral and Ecological Study"; NPS, "Raze," ORPI CRM.

7. Bennett and Kunzmann, *History of the Quitobaquito*, 35–37.

8. Bennett and Kunzmann, 35–37; Peter S. Bennett, "Preliminary Proposal: Natural Resource Evaluation of Quitobaquito Springs, Organ Pipe Cactus

National Monument," [ca. 1981], folder 10, series 14, WACC NRR; Minckley, *Fishes of Arizona.*

9. Sam Henderson, Coolidge, AZ, to Chief, Arizona Archeological Group, June 27, 1974, folder 16.1, series 3, WACC RMR; Bennett and Kunzmann, *History of the Quitobaquito*, 36–39; Organ Pipe Cactus National Monument, *Water Resources*, 28; Pearson and Conner, "Quitobaquito Desert Pupfish," 384; National Parks and Recreation Act, Pub. L. No. 95–625, 95th Cong., 92 Stat. 3467 (1978), 3490. The efforts to get Organ Pipe designated first as a national park and then as a wilderness area are well chronicled in the Morris K. Udall Papers, University of Arizona Department of Special Collections; see especially box 183/folders 1–2, box 190/folder 23, box 203/folder 1, and box 275/folder 12.

10. Peter S. Bennett, "Preliminary Proposal: Natural Resource Evaluation of Quitobaquito Springs, Organ Pipe Cactus National Monument," [ca. 1981], folder 10, series 14, WACC NRR. Evidently, the Park Service was coming to the conclusion that Quitobaquito was both natural and artificial in this era because other documents from the era make similar comments; see, for example, the handwritten notes on an untitled lined yellow sheet of paper in folder 16.1, series 3, WACC RMR, probably from 1978, in which superintendent Ray G. Martinez scribbled, "Quitobaquito is not a natural resource." Another writer referred to Quitobaquito as a "'man-made' ecosystem." Acting Leader, Cooperative National Park Resources Studies Unit/University of Arizona, Tucson, to Chief, Park Planning, Western Region, October 26, 1978, folder 16.1, series 3, WACC RMR; Pearson and Connor, "Quitobaquito Desert Pupfish," 385.

11. National Park Service Western Regional Office, "Interim Management Plan," ORPI CRM; Peter S. Bennett, "Preliminary Proposal: Natural Resource Evaluation of Quitobaquito Springs, Organ Pipe Cactus National Monument," [ca. 1981], folder 10, series 14, WACC NRR.

12. Connie Gibson to the author, June 11, 2015; Peter S. Bennett, "Preliminary Proposal: Natural Resource Evaluation of Quitobaquito Springs, Organ Pipe Cactus National Monument," [ca. 1981], folder 10, series 14, WACC NRR.

13. Peter S. Bennett, "Preliminary Proposal: Natural Resource Evaluation of Quitobaquito Springs, Organ Pipe Cactus National Monument," [ca. 1981], folder 10, series 14, WACC NRR.

14. "Aged Indian Dies; Fled Massacre," *Arizona Republic* (Phoenix), January 19, 1977, Ephemera Collection, AZHS; Eiler, research interview, 1, 3; Zepeda, "Sand Papago Oral History Project," 4; Broyles, Bell, and Bell, "Accidental Anthropologists," 680; Piekielek, "Creating a Park," 13; Vazquez, oral history, 3–4; Western Regional Office, "Interim Management Plan," 2, ORPI CRM. Although the report specifically named the Hia C'ed O'odham, many groups past and present, including all other O'odham peoples, also have cultural and religious traditions associated with Quitobaquito. It may be possible for Quitobaquito Springs to be nominated as a Tribal Cultural Place by tribal leaders in the future.

15. Proclamation No. 2232, 2 Fed. Reg. 827 (April 16, 1937), folder 000–01, box 215, C1 NARARMR; National Historic Preservation Act, Pub. L.

No. 89–665, accessed January 20, 2023, https://www.govinfo.gov/content/pkg/STATUTE-80/pdf/STATUTE-80-Pg915.pdf.

16. Brown and Hoy, "Historic Sites and Structures," 1967, 6, 7, 16–20, SWRO.

17. Sam Henderson, Coolidge, AZ, to Chief, Arizona Archeological Center, June 27, 1974, folder 16.1, series 3, WACC RMR; Blanche P. Henderson, Tucson, to Superintendent, Organ Pipe, July 8, 1974, folder 1, series 01.012, WACC CRR; Bennett and Kunzmann, *History of the Quitobaquito*, 39.

18. Keith M. Anderson to Superintendent, Organ Pipe, October 14, 1976, folder 1, series 01.015, WACC CRR; Nancy Curriden to Chief, Division of Internal Archeological Studies, October 13, 1976, folder 1, series 01.015, WACC CRR; Nancy S. Hammack to Chief, Division of Internal Archeological Studies, July 27, 1977, folder 1, series 01.015, WACC CRR.

19. Lynn S. Teague, Tucson, to Keith Anderson, October 28, 1977, 1–7, ORPI CRM.

20. Zepeda, "Sand Papago Oral History Project," 3, 20; Blansett, *Journey to Freedom*, 3–8; Eiler, research interview, 1; Eiler, email to the author, July 27, 2022.

21. Howard H. Chapman, San Francisco, to Dorothy Hall, Phoenix, April 20, 1979, folder 5, series 9, WACC RMR; George J. Chambers, "The Quitobaquito Graves Project," November 24, 1980, ORPI CRM. The meeting and ensuing collaboration are chronicled extensively in folder 16.02, series 3; folder 5, series 9; folder 14, series 3, and other WACC RMR folders. See also "Sand Papagos Approve Plans for Quito-baquito Burial Ground," *Ajo Copper News*, August 18, 1977, 3, folder 14, series 3, WACC RMR; Ray G. Martinez Jr. to Files, June 28, 1977, folder 16.02, series 3, WACC RMR; Anderson, Bell, and Stewart, "Quitobaquito," 215–37; Bell, Anderson, and Stewart, *Quitobaquito Cemetery*, 1; Fillman C. Bell to Keith Anderson, Tucson, March 10, 1980, folder 16.02, series 3, WACC RMR; Ray G. Martinez, Ajo, to Regional Director, WRO, February 12, 1979, folder 16.02, series 3, WACC RMR; "Assessment of Effects," February 1979, folder 5, series 9, WACC RMR; Harold H. Chapman, San Francisco, to Louis S. Wall, Denver, June 12, 1979, folder 16.02, series 3, WACC RMR; Dorothy H. Hall, Phoenix, to Harold H. Chapman, San Francisco, May 23, 1979, folder 16.02, series 3, WACC RMR.

22. Howard H. Chapman, San Francisco, to Dorothy Hall, Phoenix, April 20, 1979, folder 5, series 9, WACC RMR; "Aged Indian Dies; Fled Massacre," *Arizona Republic* (Phoenix), January 19, 1977, Ephemera Collection, AZHS; Zepeda, "Sand Papago Oral History Project," 4.

23. Rankin, *Archeological Survey*, v, xxiv–xxv, 665–67; National Park Service Intermountain Region, "Organ Pipe Cactus National Monument Cultural Resources Records Archeological Project Records Series I Finding Aid," 2010, 143, WACC CRR; Rankin, "Scope of Work," 1, ORPI CRM.

24. [Adrianne Rankin], "Quitobaquito National Register Review Notes," 1992, folder 2, series 1.073.1, WACC CRR.

25. Edward C. Rodriguez Jr. to General Superintendent, January 11, 1974, ORPI CRM ("loosing" is in the original); Jerome A. Greene, "National Register of Historic Places Inventory—Nomination Form," April 15, 1977, folder

29.01, series 3, WACC RMR; Ray G. Martinez Jr. "Superintendent's Annual Report," March 21, 1979, 4, ORPI; Alanen and Melnick, eds., *Preserving Cultural Landscapes*, vii–ix, 6–7.

26. Dolores Hayden, foreword to *Preserving Cultural Landscapes*, eds. Alanen and Melnick, vii–ix; Alanen and Melnick, eds., *Preserving Cultural Landscapes*, 7–8.

27. The State Historic Preservation Office had raised this concern before the nomination went to the National Register; Shereen Lerner, Phoenix, to Stanley T. Albright, San Francisco, August 27, 1991, folder 1, series 01.073.1, WACC CRR. The fragmentary record of the nomination can be partially traced in Harold Smith, Ajo, to Joseph Joaquin, Sells, June 2, 1993, folder 3, series 01.073.1, WACC CRR; Lawrence F. Van Horn, "National Register of Historic Places Registration Form," October 10, 1994, 6, 9–10, 16–18, 21, 24, 32, ORPI CRM; Adrianne [Rankin] to George [Teague], February 24, 1993, folder 3, series 01.073.1, WACC CRR; Adrianne G. Rankin to Chief, Division of Archeology, July 14, 1992, folder 3, series 01.073.1, WACC CRR; [Rankin], "Quitobaquito National Register Review Notes," 1992, folder 2, series 1.073.1, WACC CRR; Raymond Murray Jr., San Francisco, to James Garrison, Phoenix, folder 3, series 01.073.1, WACC CRR; Patrick A. Flemming, Denver, to Regional Director, December 7, 1994, ORPI CRM.

28. Organ Pipe Cactus National Monument, *Natural and Cultural Resources Management Plan, Organ Pipe Cactus National Monument*, December 1994; National Park Service, *Organ Pipe Cactus National Monument: Final General Management Plan*, [1996], iii, 16, 17, 51, 69–179, accessed January 21, 2023, http://www.nps.gov/orpi/learn/management/upload/fingmp.pdf.

29. Miller and Fuiman, "Description and Conservation Status,"593–609; Rijk Moräwe, email to the author, February 23, 2016; Rosen and Lowe, "Population Ecology of the Sonoran Mud Turtle," 3, 6, 32–33, 38–41; Bennett and Kunzmann, *History of the Quitobaquito*, 37, 53.

30. National Park Service, *Organ Pipe Cactus National Monument: Final General Management Plan*, 20, 21, 23, 37, 48. Although the document specifically named the two O'odham groups, it might well have also mentioned that many peoples past and present have cultural ties to the park.

31. National Park Service, *Organ Pipe Cactus National Monument: Final General Management Plan*, ii, 49, 56, 115.

CHAPTER 5

1. Nelson, *Language in the Blood*.

2. Organ Pipe Cactus National Monument, "Border-Related Impacts," 36; Clynes, "Arizona Park."

3. Organ Pipe Cactus National Monument, "Border-Related Impacts," 91; Vanderpool, "Amid Cactuses"; Maier, "Consigning the Twentieth Century," 807–9; Truett and Young, "Making Transnational History," 2; Orsi, "Construction and Contestation."

4. Leza, *Divided Peoples*, 57, 65, 67; Zepeda, "Sand Papago Oral History," 9, 85; St. John, *Line in the Sand*, 51; McCarthy, *Papago Traveler*, 9; Chona,

"Papago Woman," in Underhill, *Papago Woman*, 68; Verlon Jose, oral history, 3; Schermerhorn, *Walking to Magdalena*, 2, 5; Piekielek, "Creating a Park," 10.

5. St. John, *Line in the Sand*, 96, 98; Haley, *Jeff Milton*.

6. Lee, *At America's Gates*, 179–87; St. John, *Line in the Sand*, 103–7; Delgado, "At Exclusion's Southern Gate," 183–208.

7. Hernández, *Migra!*, 70–82.

8. St. John, *Line in the Sand*, 98–102.

9. Lissoway, "Administrative History," 40–43; Piekielek, "Creating a Park," 4; Newton B. Drury, "Memorandum for the Solicitor," December 23, 1947, folder "Repairs and Improvements, Fences," box 2320, CCF NARAMD.

10. E. Harold M. Ratcliff, "Memorandum for the Regional Director, Region Three," July 2, 1946, folder "Grazing, 1946–1959," box 172, CSF NARAMD; Drury, "Memorandum for the Solicitor," December 23, 1947, folder "Repairs and Improvements, Fences," box 2320, CCF NARAMD; R. Martell, Lafayette, Ind., to Conrad L. Wirth, Washington, DC, May 2, 1955, folder "Grazing, 1946–1959," box 172, CSF NARAMD; John M. Davis, Santa Fe, to L. M. Lawson, El Paso, September 6, 1946; William Supernaugh, "Memorandum for the Regional Director, Region Three, January 24, 1947; E. T. Scoyen, Santa Fe, to L. M. Lawson, El Paso, February, 4, 1947; E. T. Scoyen to F. L. Schneider, Albuquerque, February 4, 1947; E. T. Scoyen, "Memorandum for the Director, February 4, 1947; E. T. Scoyen, Santa Fe, to Lawrence M. Lawson, El Paso, April 1, 1947, all in folder "Repairs and Improvements, Fences," box 2320, CCF NARAMD; L. M. Lawson, El Paso, to E. T. Scoyen, Santa Fe, February 6, 1947, folder 611–01, box 218, C1 NARARMR; Piekielek, "Creating a Park,"6–7. The interagency conversation leading to the fence construction is well chronicled in the Park Service papers at the National Archives branches in College Park, MD, and Denver, CO. See, for example, M. R. Tillotson, "Memorandum for the Files," November 15, 1946, file 611–01, box 218, C1 NARARMR; E. T. Scoyen, Santa Fe, to John C. Pace, El Centro, CA, June 26, 1947; L. M. Lawson, El Paso, to E. T. Scoyen, Santa Fe, August 1, 1947; E. T. Scoyen, Santa Fe, to the Director, August 5, 1947, all in folder "Repairs and Improvements, Fences," box 2320, CCF NARAMD; C. M. Aldous, "Special Report: International Boundry [*sic*] Animal Migration Investigation, Organ Pipe Cactus National Monument and Cabeza Prieta Game Refuge, Arizona," 1949, folder "Organ Pipe Rules," box 2319, NARAMD.

11. E. T. Scoyen, Santa Fe, to L. M. Lawson, El Paso, August 7, 1946; Thomas J. Allen to E. R. Martell, Lafayette, Ind., n.d.; Ran Bone, C. F. Dierking, and Volney M. Doublas, "Organ Pipe Cactus National Monument: Report on Land Use Conditions," November 30, 1946, all in folder "Grazing, 1946–1959," box 172, CSF NARAMD; National Park Service Region 3, "Area Management Study: Organ Pipe Cactus National Monument," January 1957, folder A6435, 1956–1958, box 107, p. Prot 1, AF1 NARARMR; "Report of Soil and Moisture Conservation Activities, Fiscal Year 1961, Organ Pipe Cactus National Monument," June 22, 1961, folder D54A, box 25, AF1 NARARMR; "Report of

Soil and Moisture Conservation Activities, Fiscal Year 1962," August 20, 1963, folder D54A, box 25, AF1 NARARMR; "Report of Soil and Moisture Conservation Activities, Fiscal Year 1963," August 10, 1963, folder D54A, box 25, AF1 NARARMR; Natt N. Dodge to Division of Interpretation Regional Chief, March 23, 1962, folder K 1817, 1962–1964, box 46, AF1 NARARMR.

12. National Park Service Region 3, "Area Management Study: Organ Pipe Cactus National Monument," January 1957, folder A6435, 1956–1958, box 107, pp. Prot 1–3, AF1 NARARMR.

13. National Park Service Region 3, "Area Management Study: Organ Pipe Cactus National Monument," January 1957, folder A6435, 1956–1958, box 107, pp. Prot 1–3, AF1 NARARMR; Harold J. Smith, "Superintendent's Annual Report, 1983 Calendar Year," February 23, 1984, 20, ORPI; Harold J. Smith, "Superintendent's Annual Narrative Report for 1991 Calendar Year," March 12, 1992, 8, ORPI; Western Regional Office, "Interim Management Program," ORPI CRM.

14. Piekielek, "Creating a Park," 7.

15. Regan, *Death of Josseline*, xxii–xxiii; Annerino, *Dead in Their Tracks*, 169, 172–83; Robin Reinke labels the deaths as "accidental" but nevertheless "violent" and a "structured result of U.S. border and immigration policies" ("Naming the Dead," 10) .

16. Kristina Davis, "Operation Gatekeeper at 25," *Los Angeles Times*, September 30, 2019.

17. Urrea, *Devil's Highway*, 143–49.

18. Urrea, 103–14, 120–29.

19. Vanderpool, "Parks under Siege," 24; Nielsen, "Illegal Immigrants"; Chadwick, "Songs of the Sonoran"; Organ Pipe Cactus National Monument, "Border-Related Impacts," 12–15, 30, 38, 43, 72–77, 112–36.

20. Nielsen, "Illegal Immigrants"; Organ Pipe Cactus National Monument, "International Border Vehicle Barrier," https://www.nps.gov/orpi/planyourvisit /barrier.htm; Ring, "Border out of Control," 17; Organ Pipe Cactus National Monument, *Border-Related Impacts*, 65, 77, 82–86, 94, 95–96.

21. Organ Pipe Cactus National Monument, *Border-Related Impacts*, 9, 27–28; National Park Service, *Organ Pipe Cactus National Monument: Final General Management Plan, Development Concept Plans, Environmental Impact Statement*, 1997, 40–46, accessed July 30, 2022, http://www.nps.gov/orpi /learn/management/upload/fingmp.pdf.

22. Organ Pipe Cactus National Monument, "Park Statistics," accessed May 25, 2012, http://www.nps.gov/orpi/parkmgmt/statistics.htm; Clynes, "Arizona Park."

23. Lee Baiza to Connie Gibson, August 1, 2012, email in author's possession, originally in cultural resource manager's files at Organ Pipe Cactus National Monument.

24. Leza, *Divided Peoples*, 56, 58, 72; Austin, "Culture Divided," 98–102.

25. An Act to Establish a National Park Service, and for Other Purposes, Approved August 25, 1916 (39 Stat. 535).

CHAPTER 6

1. Kevin Dahl, "The Border Wall Is Destroying What This Park Was Created to Protect," October 16, 2019, accessed August 12, 2021, https://www.npca .org/articles/2325-the-border-wall-is-destroying-what-this-park-was-created -to-protect; Rafael Carranza and Curt Prendergast, "Feds Explain Conservation Measures after Viral Video Shows Bulldozed Saguaro at Arizona Border," AZ Central, October 14, 2019, accessed January 26, 2022, https://www .azcentral.com/story/news/local/arizona/2019/10/14/u-s-border-officials-push -back-against-video-shows-contractor-bulldozing-saguaros/3949020002/.

2. Moräwe, email to the author, July 21, 2022; Taylor, "Populus fremontii"; Castetter and Bell, *Pima and Papago*, 131, 137–39, 228.

3. Organ Pipe Cactus National Monument, *Biological Assessment*, 6, ORPI CONS.

4. Organ Pipe Cactus National Monument, *Biological Assessment*, 6.

5. Organ Pipe Cactus National Monument, *Emergency Actions*, 5, 23, ORPI CONS; Organ Pipe Cactus National Monument, *Biological Assessment*, 1; Organ Pipe Cactus National Monument, *Project Summary*, ORPI CONS.

6. Organ Pipe Cactus National Monument, *Biological Assessment*, 7–9; Organ Pipe Cactus National Monument, *Project Summary*, 1.

7. Organ Pipe Cactus National Monument, *Biological Assessment*, 15; Organ Pipe Cactus National Monument, *Project Summary*, 1, 4; Tim Tibbitts to Connie Gibson, Rijk Moräwe, and Lee Baiza, August 2, 2012, email in author's possession, originally in cultural resource manager's files at ORPI; Moräwe, email to the author, July 21, 2022; Organ Pipe Cactus National Monument, *Minimum Requirements*, 1, 3, 4, 7, 13, 27, ORPI CONS.

8. Organ Pipe Cactus National Monument, *Repair Quitobaquito Pond*, 1, ORPI CONS; Organ Pipe Cactus National Monument, *Project Summary*, 4–5; Moräwe, phone conversation with the author, November 18, 2016.

9. Organ Pipe Cactus National Monument, *Minimum Requirements*, 7, 19.

10. Moräwe, email to the author, July 21, 2022; Organ Pipe Cactus National Monument, *Repair Quitobaquito Pond*, 2, 5, 22; Tyler Coleman, Lauren Kingston, and Rijk Moräwe, "Quitobaquito Cottonwood Tree Removal, Pond Retention Dam Repair, Organ Pipe Cactus National Monument," August 2016, ORPI. The tribal consultation took place by phone and email. The email communication is documented in park files. My understanding of the tribe's response is based on email communications from park personnel Lauren Kingston (February 13 and 22, 2017) and Rijk Moräwe (February 16 and 23, 2017).

11. Organ Pipe Cactus National Monument, *Minimum Requirements*, 25, 27; Moräwe, email to the author, February 23, 2017.

12. Blansett, *Journey to Freedom*, 1–2; "Alcatraz Island," National Park Service, accessed July 31, 2022, https://www.nps.gov/alca/index.htm.

13. Schulze, *Are We Not Foreigners*, 51–56.

14. Meeks, *Border Citizens*, 215, 217, 221–23.

15. Eiler, research interview, August 16, 2021; Meeks, *Border Citizens*, 218.

16. Jose, oral history, 6–7.

17. Moräwe, research interview, October 2021, 1, 2, 4; Moräwe, email to the author, July 21, 2022.
18. Moräwe, email to the author, July 21, 2022.
19. Moräwe, email to the author, July 21, 2022.
20. Moräwe, research interview, 20; Chona, "Autobiography of Chona," in Underhill, *Papago Woman*, 71.
21. Alisa Reznick, "Experts: Border Wall Construction May Imperil Sacred Source of Water in the Desert," Cronkite News, August 10, 2020, https://cronkitenews.azpbs.org/2020/08/10/border-wall-construction-quitobaquito-springs-desert/; Gary Nabhan, "Halt the Border Wall Construction's Desiccation and Desecration of Quitobaquito Springs, the Greatest Oasis of Hope in the Borderlands," July 29, 2020, accessed September 24, 2021, https://www.healingtheborderdisorder.org/2020/07/29/25-prominent-desert-scientists-speak-out/.
22. "Saguaro Cactus Bulldozed to Build Border Wall at Organ Pipe National Monument," accessed January 29, 2022, https://www.youtube.com/watch?v=ALyHmZPjooo ("by at" is in the original, as is the unconventional capitalization).
23. Leza, *Divided Peoples*, 5, 57–58.
24. Vazquez, research interview, 2–3; Eiler, oral history, December 13, 2021, 2–4; Leza, *Divided Peoples*, 60–61.
25. Moräwe, research interview, 7.
26. Kingston, research interview; Moräwe, research interview, 6a; Kingston to the author, July 8, 2022.
27. Kingston, research interview; Moräwe, research interview, 6b.
28. Moräwe, research interview, 11; Moräwe, email to the author, July 21, 2022.
29. Moräwe, research interview, 15; Moräwe, email to the author, July 21, 2022.
30. Moräwe, email to the author, July 21, 2022.
31. Moräwe, research interview, 15; Williams, "Disappearance of Quitobaquito"; Moräwe, email to the author, July 21, 2022.
32. Moräwe, email to the author, July 21, 2022.
33. Moräwe, research interview, 10b; Alisa Reznick, "Experts: Border Wall Construction May Imperil Sacred Source of Water in the Desert," Cronkite News, August 10, 2020, https://cronkitenews.azpbs.org/2020/08/10/border-wall-construction-quitobaquito-springs-desert/.
34. Moräwe, research interview, 10a.
35. Reznick, "Indigenous Activists Arrested"; Moräwe, email to the author, July 21, 2022; Reznick, "Stand Off."
36. Reznick, "NPS Closes Route."
37. International Sonoran Desert Alliance, "Creative Placekeeping"; Eiler, research interview; Cooper, research interview, October 19, 2021, 1–2, 5.
38. Cooper, research interview, 1–2, 5.
39. Cooper, research interview, 1–2.
40. International Sonoran Desert Alliance, "Creative Placekeeping."
41. International Sonoran Desert Alliance, "Creative Placekeeping."

42. Schamess, "Toward Placekeeping"; Schwartzman, *Cultural Placekeeping Guide*.

43. Eiler, research interview, 4–5; Cooper, research interview, 10b; "ISDA Has New Board Members and Officers," *Ajo Copper News*, February 26, 2014, http://ajo.stparchive.com/Archive/AJO/AJO02262014P07.php?tags=isda |has|new|board|members|and|officers; "Plaza Will See Living History Show This Thursday," *Ajo Copper News*, February 22, 2012, http://ajo.stparchive .com/Archive/AJO/AJO02222012p01.php?tags=plaza|will|see|living|history |show|this|thursday; "Saguaro Harvest Is Next in Series of Desert Evenings," *Ajo Copper News*, June 22, 2011, http://ajo.stparchive.com/Archive/AJO /AJO06222011p06.php?tags=saguaro|harvest|is|next|in|series|of|desert|evenings.

44. UNESCO, *Biosphere Reserves*; Cooper, research interview, 6.

45. Cooper, research interview, 4; Moräwe, email to the author, July 21, 2022.

46. Moräwe, research interview, 4b, 10b; Moräwe, email to the author, July 21, 2022; Cooper, research interview, 4.

47. Reznick, "In Southern Arizona's Organ Pipe"; Moräwe, email to the author, July 21, 2022.

48. "Organ Pipe Cactus National Monument," handout to registrants of the 6th Tri-National Sonoran Desert Symposium, March 2020; copy in author's possession.

CONCLUSION

1. Hill, *From Huhugam*, 66.

2. Neumann, *Imposing Wilderness*; Brockington and Duff, *Capitalism and Conservation*; Dowie, *Conservation Refugees*; Escobar, *Designs for the Pluriverse*, ix–xi.

3. "Orchard," Tumacácori National Historical Park, https://www.nps.gov /tuma/learn/nature/heritage-orchard.htm; "Preserving Historic Orchards at Redwood National and State Parks," National Park Service, https://www .nps.gov/articles/historic-orchards-redwood.htm; "Orchards," Capitol Reef National Park, https://www.nps.gov/care/learn/historyculture/orchards.htm; all sites accessed July 18, 2022.

4. Karskens, "Water Dreams," 136–37.

5. Karskens, 120, 131.

6. Karskens, 138, 145.

7. Soto, "Object Afterlives," 460.

8. Soto, 464.

9. Soto, 462–68; National Park System Advisory Board, *Revisiting Leopold*, 11.

10. Eiler, oral history, December 13, 2021.

11. Eiler, oral histories, November 8 and December 13, 2021.

12. Bureau of Land Management, "BLM, Forest Service and Five Tribes of the Bears Ears Commission Commit to Historic Co-management of Bears Ears National Monument," US Department of the Interior press release, June 21, 2022, accessed June 29, 2022, https://www.doi.gov/pressreleases /blm-forest-service-and-five-tribes-bears-ears-commission-commit-historic-co -management; Joseph R. Biden, Presidential Proclamation 10285, October 8,

2021, Fed. Reg. 86, no. 197 (October 15, 2021), 57321–32, accessed August 1, 2022, https://www.govinfo.gov/content/pkg/FR-2021-10-15/pdf/2021-22672 .pdf; Bureau of Land Management Director to Utah BLM State Director, December 16, 2021, 6, accessed August 1, 2022, https://www.blm.gov/sites /default/files/docs/2021-12/BENM%20Interim%20Guidance%2012-16-21 _Final508.pdf; Eiler, oral history, December 13, 2021.

13. Vazquez, oral history; Eiler, oral histories, November 8 and December 13, 2021.

14. Escobar, *Designs for the Pluriverse*, xvi; Toomey, "Making of a Conservation Landscape"; Subcomandante Marcos, "Fourth Declaration of the Lacandon Jungle," January 1, 1996, 10, accessed January 11, 2022, https:// schoolsforchiapas.org/wp-content/uploads/2014/03/Fourth-Declaration-of -the-Lacandona-Jungle-.pdf.

15. Tsing, *Friction*, 155–70.

16. Toomey, "Making of a Conservation Landscape"; Tsing, *Friction*; Escobar, *Designs for the Pluriverse*.

17. Escobar, *Designs for the Pluriverse*, iv, xv.

18. Wilkerson, *Caste*, ix.

BIBLIOGRAPHY

INTERVIEWS AND ORAL HISTORIES

Cooper, Aaron. Research interview, by phone with Jared Orsi, October 19, 2021.

Eiler, Lorraine Marquez. Oral history, by phone with Jared Orsi and Ariel Schnee, November 8, 2021.

———. Oral history, by phone with Jared Orsi and Ariel Schnee, December 13, 2021.

———. Research interview, by phone with Jared Orsi and Ariel Schnee, August 16, 2021.

Jose, Verlon. Oral history, Ajo, Arizona, with Jared Orsi and Ariel Schnee, March 11, 2022.

Kingston, Lauren. Research interview, by phone with Jared Orsi, October 18, 2021.

Moräwe, Rijk. Research interview, by phone with Jared Orsi, October 25, 2021.

Vazquez, Marlene. Oral history, by phone with Jared Orsi, November 10, 2021.

———. Research interview, by phone with Jared Orsi and Ariel Schnee, October 18, 2021.

———. Research interview, by phone with Jared Orsi, July 26, 2022.

SOURCES

"Activists to Protest U.S.-Mexico Border Wall at Organ Pipe Cactus National Monument." Associated Press, November 8, 2019. https://www.azcentral.com/story/news/politics/border-issues/2019/11/08/activists-protest-border-wall-arizona-organ-pipe-cactus-national-monument/2532812001/.

"Ajo History Points of Interest." *Ajo Copper News.* Accessed September 27, 2010. http://cunews.info/ajohistory.html.

Alanen, Arnold R., and Robert Z. Melnick, eds. *Preserving Cultural Landscapes in America.* Baltimore: Johns Hopkins University Press, 2000.

Aldhous, Peter. "Ecosystems under Threat from Drug Trafficking." *New Zealand Herald* (Auckland), August 31, 2006.

Allen, Paul L. "Hia-C'ed O'odham Thought to Be Extinct." *Tucson Citizen*, October 15, 1996. http://tucsoncitizen.com/morgue2/1996/10/15/65888-hia-ced-o-odham-thought-to-be-extinct/.

Altschul, Jeffrey H., and Adrianne Rankin. *Fragile Patterns: The Archaeology of the Western Papaguería*. Tucson: SRI Press, 2008.

Anderson, David G., and J. Christopher Gillam. "Paleoindian Colonization of the Americas: Implications from an Examination of Physiography, Demography, and Artifact Distribution." *American Antiquity* 65, no. 1 (2000): 43–66.

Anderson, Joan B., and James Gerber. *Fifty Years of Change on the U.S.-Mexico Border: Growth, Change, and Quality of Life*. Austin: University of Texas Press, 2008.

Anderson, Keith M., Fillman Bell, and Yvonne G. Stewart. "Quitobaquito: A Sand Papago Cemetery." *Kiva* 47 (Summer 1982): 215–37.

Anderson, T. W., and R. L. Laney. *Reconnaissance of Ground-Water Conditions in Quitobaquito Springs and La Abra Plain Area, Organ Pipe Cactus National Monument, Arizona*. Tucson: US Geological Survey, 1978.

Anderson, T. W., and N. D. White. *Possible Effects of Ground-Water Withdrawals in Mexico on Ground-Water Conditions in the Sonoyta Valley, Organ Pipe Cactus National Monument*. Tucson: US Geological Survey, 1978.

Andreas, Peter. *Border Games: Policing the U.S.-Mexico Divide*. 2nd ed. Ithaca, NY: Cornell University Press, 2009.

Andrews, Christina. Letter to the editor. "Hia-Ced O'odham Viewpoint." *Ajo Copper News*, September 8, 2020. http://ajo.stparchive.com/Archive/AJO/AJO09082020P002.php?tags=hia-ced|o%27odham|viewpoint.

Andrews, Thomas G. *Coyote Valley: Deep History in the High Rockies*. Cambridge, MA: Harvard University Press, 2015.

Annerino, John. *Dead in Their Tracks: Crossing America's Desert Borderlands*. New York: Four Walls Eight Windows, 1999.

Appleman, Roy Edgar. *Blankenship Ranch: Historic Structures Report, Parts I & II, Organ Pipe Cactus National Monument*. Washington, DC: Office of Archeology and Historic Preservation, 1969.

Arreola, Daniel D. *Postcards from the Sonora Border: Visualizing Place through a Popular Lens, 1900s–1950s*. Tucson: University of Arizona Press, 2017.

Austin, Megan S. "A Culture Divided by the United States–Mexico Border: The Tohono O'odham Claim for Border Crossing Rights." *Arizona Journal of International and Comparative Law* 8, no. 2 (Fall 1991): 97–116.

Bahr, Donald, ed. *O'odham Creation and Related Events: As Told to Ruth Benedict in 1927 in Prose, Oratory, and Song by the Pimas William Blackwater, Thomas Vanyiko, Clara Ahiel, William Stevens, Oliver Wellington, and Kisto*. Tucson: University of Arizona Press, 2001.

Bahr, Donald M. "Pima and Papago Social Organization." In *Handbook of North American Indians*, edited by Alfonso Ortiz, 10:178–92. Washington, DC: Smithsonian Institution, 1983.

———. "Who Were the Hohokam: The Evidence from Pima-Papago Myths." *Ethnohistory* 18, no. 3 (Summer 1971): 245–66.

Bahr, Donald, Juan Smith, William Smith Allison, and Julian Hayden. *The Short, Swift Time of Gods on Earth: The Hohokam Chronicles*. Berkeley: University of California Press, 1994.

Bahre, Conrad J. "Human Ecology of the Sonoran Desert." *Yearbook of the Association of Pacific Coast Geographers* 60 (1998): 50–74. https://www.jstor.org/stable /24041463.

Bailey, L. R., ed. *The A. B. Gray Report*. Los Angeles: Westernlore Press, 1963.

Baird, Spencer F., and Charles Girard. "Descriptions of New Species of Fishes Collected by Mr. John H. Clark, on the U.S. and Mexican Boundary Survey, under Lt. Col. Jas. D. Graham." *Proceedings of the Academy of Natural Sciences of Philadelphia* 6 (1852–1853): 387–90.

Baiza, Lee, Julie Rodriguez, and Frank Quimby. "Interior and Homeland Security Collaborate on Border Protection, Resource Conservation along US/Mexico Border." US Department of the Interior press release, March 13, 2010. http://www .doi.gov/news/pressreleases/2010_03_13_release.cfm.

Banks, Leo. "Border Fence Benefits the Environment." *Daily Caller* (Washington, DC), October 4, 2010. http://dailycaller.com/2010/10/04/border-fence-benefits -the-environment/.

Barton, Huw. "The Thin Film of Human Action: Linterpretations of Arid Zone Archaeology." *Australian Archaeology*, no. 57 (2003): 32–41.

"Baskets and Pottery Are Featured at Organ Pipe." *Ajo Copper News*, March 24, 2010. http://ajo.stparchive.com/Archive/AJO/AJO03242010p004.php?tags=baskets |and|pottery|are|featured|at|organ|pipe.

Bassett, Carol Ann, and Michael Hyatt. *Organ Pipe: Life on the Edge*. Tucson: University of Arizona Press, 2004.

Becket, Stefan. "Construction Begins on 30-Foot Border Wall in Fragile Arizona Desert." CBS News, August 29, 2019. https://www.cbsnews.com/news/trump-border -wall-construction-begins-on-30-foot-barrier-in-organ-pipe-cactus-national -monument-in-arizona/.

Bell, Fillman, Keith M. Anderson, and Yvonne G. Stewart. *The Quitobaquito Cemetery and Its History*. Tucson: Western Archeological Center, National Park Service, December 1980. http://npshistory.com/series/anthropology/wacc/quitobaquito /report.pdf.

Bennett, P. S., and M. R. Kunzmann. *Organ Pipe Cactus National Monument Biosphere Reserve Sensitive Ecosystems Program*. Special report. Tucson: Cooperative National Park Resources Studies Unit, University of Arizona, 1987.

Bennett, Peter S., Raymond Roy Johnson, and Michael M. McCarthy. *Assessment of Scientific Information and Activities at Organ Pipe Cactus National Monument Biosphere Reserve*. Tucson: Cooperative National Park Resources Studies Unit, University of Arizona, 1990.

Bennett, Peter S., and Michael R. Kunzmann. *A History of the Quitobaquito Resource Management Area, Organ Pipe Cactus National Monument, Arizona*. Tucson: Cooperative National Park Resources Studies Unit, University of Arizona, 1989.

Bess, Jennifer. "The Tohono O'odham 'Attack' on El Plomo: A Study in Sovereignty, Survivance, Security, and National Identity at the Dawn of the American Century." *Western Historical Quarterly* 51 (Summer 2020): 137–60. https://doi.org/10 .1093/whq/whaa002.

Bezy, John V., Gordon Haxel, and James T. Gutmann. *A Guide to the Geology of Organ Pipe Cactus National Monument and the Pinacate Biosphere Reserve*. Tucson: Arizona Geological Survey, 2000.

"Bird Watching at Quitobaquito." *Sunset*, April 1972.

Blansett, Kent. *A Journey to Freedom: Richard Oakes, Alcatraz, and the Red Power Movement*. New Haven, CT: Yale University Press, 2018.

Bloomquist, Dick. "Quitobaquito." *Arizona Highways*, April 1978.

Blyth, Lance R. *Chiricahua and Janos: Communities of Violence in the Southwestern Borderlands, 1680–1880*. Lincoln: University of Nebraska Press, 2012.

Bock, Carl E., and Jane H. Bock. *Sonoita Plain: Views from a Southwestern Grassland*. Tucson: University of Arizona Press, 2005.

Bolton, Herbert E. *Kino's Historical Memoir of Pimería Alta*. Berkeley: University of California Press, 1948.

———. *Rim of Christendom: A Bibliography of Eusebio Francisco Kino, Pacific Coast Pioneer*. New York: Macmillan, 1936.

Booth, William. "In the Desert, a Drink of Mercy, Protest; Water to Migrants Questioned." *Washington Post*, June 11, 2001.

"Border Blunder: Security Fence Causes Flooding." Associated Press / MSNBC, n.d.

"Border Wall Construction Begins in Southern Arizona." KOLD, Tucson, September 25, 2019.

Bowen, Thomas. "Seri Basketry: A Comparative View." *Kiva* 38, no. 3/4 (1973): 141–72. https://www.jstor.org/stable/30245894.

Bowers, Faye. "Shadow Wolves' Track Drug Smugglers the Native American Way." *Christian Science Monitor*, July 5, 2007.

Bowers, J. E. "Flora of Organ Pipe Cactus National Monument." *Journal of the Arizona-Nevada Academy of Science* 15 (1980): 33–47.

Bradt, George M. "Quitobaquito: Past and Present." *Desert Magazine*, February 1980.

Brean, Henry. "Conservation Groups Seek Injunction to Stop Border Wall Construction in 3 Arizona Preserves." *Arizona Daily Star* (Tucson), August 7, 2019.

Breternitz, David. "A Brief Archaeological Survey of the Lower Gila River." *Kiva* 22, no. 2/3 (1957): 1–12. https://www.jstor.org/stable/30246970.

Briggs, John M., Katherine A. Spielmann, Hoski Schaafsma, Keith M. Kintigh, Melissa Kruse, Kari Morehouse, and Karen Schollmeyer. "Why Ecology Needs Archaeologists and Archaeology Needs Ecologists." *Frontiers in Ecology and Environment* 4, no. 4 (2006): 180–88.

Brocious, Ariana. "Grijalva Asks Feds to 'Respect Tribal Lands' during Border Construction." Arizona Public Media, January 9, 2020. https://news.azpm.org/p/news -splash/2020/1/9/164133-grijalva-asks-feds-to-respect-tribal-lands-during-border -construction/.

———. "More Concern, Outrage over Border Wall's Impact on Sensitive Desert Lands." Arizona Public Media, January 30, 2020. https://news.azpm.org/p/news -splash/2020/1/30/165195-more-concern-outrage-over-border-walls-impact-on -sensitive-desert-lands/.

Brockington, Dan, and Rosaleen Duffy, eds. *Capitalism and Conservation*. Malden, MA: Wiley-Blackwell, 2011.

Brown, Bruce. *Land Use Trends Surrounding Organ Pipe Cactus National Monument*. Tucson: Cooperative National Park Resources Studies Unit, University of Arizona, July 1991.

————. *Tendencias del uso de la tierra alrededor de Organ Pipe Cactus National Monument*. Tucson: Cooperative National Park Resources Studies Unit, University of Arizona, February 1992.

Brown, Bryan T., Lupe P. Hendrickson, R. Roy Johnson, and William Werrell. *An Inventory of Surface Water Resources at Organ Pipe Cactus National Monument, Arizona*. Tucson: Cooperative National Park Resources Studies Unit, University of Arizona, January 1993.

Brown, Bryan T., and R. Roy Johnson. "The Distribution of Bedrock Depressions (Tinajas) as Sources of Surface Water in Organ Pipe Cactus National Monument, Arizona." *Journal of the Arizona-Nevada Academy of Science* 18, no. 2 (1983): 61–68.

Brown, Bryan T., and Peter L. Warren. *A Descriptive Analysis of Woody Riparian Vegetation and Quitobaquito Springs Oasis, Organ Pipe Cactus National Monument, Arizona*. Tucson: Cooperative National Park Resources Studies Unit, University of Arizona, August 1986.

Broyles, Bill. "Desert Archaeology: An Interview with Paul Ezell, 1913–1988." *Journal of the Southwest* 30, no. 3 (1988): 398–449. https://www.jstor.org/stable/40169590.

————. "Natural History." In *Last Water on the Devil's Highway: A Cultural and Natural History of Tinajas Altas*, edited by Bill Broyles, Gayle Harrison Hartmann, Thomas E. Sheridan, Gary Paul Nabhan, and Mary Charlotte Thurtle, 179–89. Tucson: University of Arizona Press, 2012.

Broyles, Bill, Fillman C. Bell, and Oscar Bell. "Accidental Anthropologists: Thomas Childs, Jr., and His Daughter Fillman Childs Bell." *Journal of the Southwest* 59, no. 3/4 (2017): 617–90.

Broyles, Bill, Richard S. Felger, Gary Paul Nabhan, and Luke Evans. "Our Grand Desert: A Gazetteer for Northwestern Sonora, Southwestern Arizona, and Northeastern Baja California." *Journal of the Southwest* 39, no. 3/4 (Autumn–Winter 1997): 703–856.

Broyles, Bill, and Gayle Harrison Hartmann. "Surveyors to Campers: 1854 to the Present." In *Last Water on the Devil's Highway: A Cultural and Natural History of Tinajas Altas*, edited by Bill Broyles, Gayle Harrison Hartmann, Thomas E. Sheridan, Gary Paul Nabhan, and Mary Charlotte Thurtle, 115–77. Tucson: University of Arizona Press, 2012.

Broyles, Bill, Gayle Harrison Hartmann, and Thomas E. Sheridan. "Desert Water." In *Last Water on the Devil's Highway: A Cultural and Natural History of Tinajas Altas*, edited by Bill Broyles, Gayle Harrison Hartmann, Thomas E. Sheridan, Gary Paul Nabhan, and Mary Charlotte Thurtle, 9–41. Tucson: University of Arizona Press, 2012.

Broyles, Bill, Gayle Harrison Hartmann, Thomas E. Sheridan, Gary Paul Nabhan, and Charlotte Thurtle, eds. *Last Water on the Devil's Highway: A Cultural and Natural History of Tinajas Altas*. Tucson: University of Arizona Press, 2012.

Broyles, Bill, and George H. Huey. *Organ Pipe Cactus National Monument: Where Edges Meet*. New York: Southwest Parks and Monument Association, 1997.

Brunet-Jailly, Emmanuel. *Borderlands: Comparing Border Security in North America and Europe*. Ottawa: University of Ottawa Press, 2007.

Bryan, Kirk. *The Papago Country*. Washington, DC: Department of the Interior, US Geological Survey, 1925.

———. *Routes to Desert Watering Places in the Papago Country*. Washington, DC: Department of the Interior, US Geological Survey, 1922.

Bryan, P. W. "Geography and Landscape: Address to the Geographical Association." *Geography* 43, no. 1 (1958): 1–9. http://www.jstor.org/stable/40564113.

Burnett, John. "Border Wall Rising in Arizona, Raises Concerns among Conservationists, Native Tribes." National Public Radio, October 13, 2019. https://www.npr.org/2019/10/13/769444262/border-wall-rising-in-arizona-raises-concerns-among-conservationists-native-trib.

———. "Security Worries Overshadow U.S.-Mexico Park Plan." National Public Radio, June 16, 2010. http://www.npr.org/templates/story/story.php?storyId=127874281.

Burnham, Phillip. *Indian Country, God's Country: American Indians and National Parks*. Washington, DC: Island Press, 2000.

Búrquez, Alberto, and Angelina Martínez-Yrizar. "Conservation and Landscape Transformation in Sonora, Mexico." *Journal of the Southwest* 39 (Autumn–Winter 1997): 371–98.

Burro. "Border-Crossings Impact Fragile Desert Environments." Indybay/San Francisco Bay Area Independent Media Center, March 31, 2006. https://www.indybay.org/newsitems/2006/03/31/18125471.php.

Burrus, Ernest J. *Kino and Manje, Explorers of Sonora and Arizona: Their Vision of the Future, a Study of Their Expeditions and Plans*. Rome: Jesuit Historical Society, 1971.

Bustamante, Enriquena, and Alberto Búrquez. "Effects of Plant Size and Weather on the Flowering Phenology of the Organ Pipe Cactus (*Stenocereus thurberi*)." *Annals of Botany* 102, no. 6 (2008): 1019–30.

Bytnar, Bruce W. *A Park Ranger's Life: Thirty-Two Years Protecting Our National Parks*. Tucson: Wheatmark, 2009.

"Cactus, Ghost Towns and History." *New York Times*, January 11, 2008.

Cadava, Geraldo L. "Borderlands of Modernity and Abandonment: The Lines within Ambos Nogales and the Tohono O'odham Nation." *Journal of American History* 98, no. 2 (September 2011): 362–83. https://doi.org/https://doi.org/10.1093/jahist/jar209.

———. *Standing on Common Ground: The Making of a Sunbelt Borderland*. Cambridge, MA: Harvard University Press, 2013.

Callicott, J. Baird. "The Wilderness Idea Revisited: The Sustainable Development Alternative." *Environmental Professional* 13 (n.d.): 235–47.

Calverton, George E., ed. *U.S.-Mexico and Southwest Border Violence: Spillover Threats and Issues*. New York: Nova Science, 2010.

Cantu, Francisco. "I Was a Border Patrol Agent. Our Walls Need to Be Torn Down." *New York Times*, December 5, 2019.

Carr, Ethan. *Wilderness by Design: Landscape Architecture and the National Park Service*. Lincoln: University of Nebraska Press, 1998.

Carruth, R. L. "Hydrogeology of the Quitobaquito Springs and La Abra Plain Area, Organ Pipe Cactus National Monument, Arizona, and Sonora, Mexico." Tucson: US Department of the Interior, 1996.

Castetter, Edward F., and Willis H. Bell. *Pima and Papago Indian Agriculture*. Albuquerque: University of New Mexico Press, 1942.

Castetter, Edward Franklin, and Ruth Murray Underhill. "The Ethnobiology of the Papago Indians." *University of New Mexico Bulletin Biological Series* 4, no. 3 (1935).

Celaya, Alberto, Paul H. Ezell, and Henry F. Dobyns. "An Interview with Alberto Celaya, 1952." *Journal of the Southwest* 49, no. 3 (Autumn 2007): 422–87.

Chadwick, Douglas H. "Songs of the Sonoran." *National Geographic* 210, no. 3 (September 2006): 124–52.

Chavez, Karen, and Trevor Hughes. "Trump: Park Rangers Will Patrol Mexican Border, Arrest Migrants." *USA Today*, December 10, 2019.

Chester, Charles C. *Conservation across Borders: Biodiversity in an Interdependent World*. Washington, DC: Island Press, 2006.

Childs, Tom. "Sketch of the 'Sand Indians.'" *Kiva* 19, no. 2/4 (Spring 1954): 27–39.

Clay, Willard. "Organ Pipe Cactus National Monument." *National Parks* 74 (April 2000): 36–38.

Clotts, H. C. *Report on Nomadic Papago Surveys*. Tucson: Arizona State Museum, 1915.

Clynes, Tom. "Arizona Park 'Most Dangerous' in U.S." *National Geographic News*, February 2003.

Cockrum, E. Lendell. *Bat Populations and Habitats at the Organ Pipe Cactus National Monument*. Tucson: Cooperative National Park Resources Studies Unit, University of Arizona, 1981.

Cohn, Jeffery P. "Sonoran Desert Conservation." *BioScience* 51 (August 2001): 606–10.

Cole, Gerald A., and Melbourne C. Whiteside. "An Ecological Reconnaissance of Quitobaquito Spring, Arizona." *Journal of the Arizona Academy of Science* 3 (April 1965): 159–63.

Coleman, Tyler, Lauren Kingston, and Rijk Moräwe. *Quitobaquito Cottonwood Tree Removal, Pond Retention Dam Repair, Organ Pipe Cactus National Monument*. Organ Pipe Cactus National Monument, August 2016.

Corbett, Jessica. "Critics Decry 'Publicity Stunt with Genuine Consequences' as Trump Deploys 'Surge' of Park Rangers to Patrol Southern Border." Common Dreams, December 3, 2019. https://www.commondreams.org/news/2019/12/03/critics -decry-publicity-stunt-genuine-consequences-trump-deploys-surge-park-rangers.

Coues, Elliot, ed. and trans. *On the Trail of a Spanish Pioneer: The Diary and Itinerary of Francisco Garcés in His Travels through Sonora, Arizona, and California, 1775–1776*. 2 vols. New York: Francis P. Harper, 1900.

Cox, Thomas Joseph. "A Behavioral and Ecological Study of the Desert Pupfish (*Cyprinodon macularius*) in Quitobaquito Springs, Organ Pipe Cactus National Monument." PhD diss., University of Arizona, 1966.

Crosswhite, Frank. "The Annual Saguaro Harvest and Crop Cycle of the Papago." *Desert Plants Journal* 2 (Spring 1980): 3–61.

Dean, Jeffrey. "Thoughts on Hohokam Chronology." In *Exploring the Hohokam: Prehistoric Desert Peoples of the American Southwest*, edited by George J. Gumerman, 61–149. Albuquerque: University of New Mexico Press, 1991.

Dear, Michael. "Monuments, Manifest Destiny, and Mexico, Part 2." *Prologue* 37, no. 2 (Summer 2005). https://www.archives.gov/publications/prologue/2005 /summer/mexico-2.

DeBuys, William. *A Great Aridness: Climate Change and the Future of the American Southwest.* New York: Oxford University Press, 2011.

De León, Jason. "'Better to Be Hot Than Caught': Excavating the Conflicting Roles of Migrant Material Culture." *American Anthropologist* 114, no. 3 (2012): 477–95.

Delgado, Grace Peña. "At Exclusion's Southern Gate: Changing Categories of Race and Class among Chinese Fronterizos, 1882–1904." In *Continental Crossroads: Re-Mapping U.S.-Mexico Borderlands History.* Durham, NC: Duke University Press, 2004.

Dellios, Hugh. "Desert Park Victimized by Illegal Immigration; Designated a National Treasure in 1937, Organ Pipe Park in Arizona Is No Jewel These Days." *Philadelphia Inquirer*, December 19, 2003.

Devereaux, Ryan. "The Border Patrol Invited the Press to Watch It Blow Up a National Monument." *Intercept*, February 27, 2020. https://theintercept.com/2020/02/27/border-wall-construction-organ-pipe-explosion.

———. "Trump Is Blowing Up a National Monument in Arizona to Make Way for the Border Wall." *Intercept*, February 6, 2020. https://theintercept.com/2020/02/06/border-wall-construction-organ-pipe/.

———. "'We Are Still Here': Native Activists in Arizona Resist Trump's Border Wall." *Intercept*, November 24, 2019. https://theintercept.com/2019/11/24/arizona-border-wall-native-activists/.

Dillehay, Tom D. "Probing Deeper into First American Studies." *Proceedings of the National Academy of Sciences of the United States of America* 106, no. 4 (2009): 971–78.

Dilsaver, Lary M. *America's National Park System: The Critical Documents.* 2nd ed. Lanham, MD: Rowman and Littlefield, 2016.

———. *Preserving the Desert: A History of Joshua Tree National Monument.* Staunton, VA: George F. Thompson, 2016.

Dimmitt, Mark A. "Biomes and Communities of the Sonoran Desert Region." In *A Natural History of the Sonoran Desert*, edited by Steven J. Phillips and Patricia Wentworth Comus, 3–18. Tucson: Arizona-Sonora Desert Museum Press, 2000.

Dinan, Stephan. "Environmental Laws Put Gaps in Mexico Border Security." *Washington Times*, November 16, 2009.

———. "Interior Agency's Agenda Can Top Security; Laws Hinder Illegals Pursuit." *Washington Times*, November 16, 2009.

Di Peso, Charles C. "Prehistory: O'otam." In *Handbook of North American Indians*, edited by Alfonso Ortiz, 9:91–99. Washington, DC: Smithsonian Institution, 1979.

Di Silvestro, Roger. "No Safe Refuge." *National Wildlife*, January 2006.

Dowie, Mark. *Conservation Refugees: The Hundred-Year Conflict between Global Conservation and Native Peoples.* Cambridge, MA: MIT Press, 2009.

Downing, Renee. "Border Patrol? What We See Here Is Anything But." *Washington Post*, May 1, 2005.

Drezner, Taly. "Branch Direction in *Carnegiea gigantea* (Cactaceae): Regional Patterns and the Effect of Nurse Plants." *Journal of Vegetation Science* 14 (December 2003): 907–10.

Eaton, R. *Protecting Quitobaquito: A Summary of Legal Tools and Strategies.* Albuquerque: University of New Mexico Press, 1988.

Edwards, Walter M. "Abundant Life in a Desert Land." *National Geographic,* September 1973.

Egan, Timothy. "Wanted: Border Hoppers. And Some Excitement, Too." *New York Times,* April 1, 2005.

Eggle, Bonnie. "The Murder of Kris Eggle: A Remembrance from His Mother." ImmigrationsHumanCost.org. Accessed November 17, 2016. http://www .immigrationshumancost.org/text/eggle.html.

Eiler, Lorraine Marquez, and David E. Doyel. "The Extinct Tribe." In *Fragile Patterns: The Archaeology of the Western Papaguería,* edited by Jeffrey H. Altschul and Adrianne G. Rankin, 605–30. Tucson: SRI Press, 2008.

Eilperin, Juliet, and Nick Miroff. "Border Wall Construction Could Destroy Archaeological Sites, Park Service Finds." *Washington Post,* September 17, 2019.

Erickson, Winston P. *Sharing the Desert: The Tohono O'odham in History.* Tucson: University of Arizona Press, 1994.

Esbach, Michael S., Flora Lu, and Felipe Borman Quenama. "Conservation and Care among the Cofán in the Ecuadorian Amazon." *Conservation and Society* 19, no. 4 (2021): 259–70.

Escobar, Arturo. *Designs for the Pluriverse: Radical Interdependence, Autonomy, and the Making of Worlds.* Durham, NC: Duke University Press, 2018.

Evans, Charles Edward. "An Authentic Narrative of the Crabb Massacre." In *Tough Times in Rough Places: Personal Narratives of Adventure, Death, and Survival on the Western Frontier,* 101–11. Salt Lake City: University of Utah Press, 2001.

Ezell, Paul H. "The Archaeological Delineation of a Cultural Boundary in Papaguería." *American Antiquity* 20, no. 4 (1955): 367–74.

———. "An Archaeological Survey of the Northwestern Papaguería." *Kiva* 19 (Spring 1954): 1–26.

———. "The Areneños (Sand Papago)—Interview with Alberto Celaya (1952)." In *Ethnology of Northwest Mexico: A Sourcebook,* edited by Randall H. McGuire, 400–405.New York: Garland, 1991.

———. "History of the Pima." In *Handbook of North American Indians,* edited by Alfonso Ortiz, 10:149–60. Washington, DC: Smithsonian Institution, 1983.

Fader, Carole. "Fact Check: Trash Lines Many Illegal Immigration Routes." *Florida Times-Union* (Jacksonville), June 17, 2010.

Faler, Brian. "Assaults Increase on Parks' Workers; Incidents with Rangers Rise 900 Percent." *Washington Post,* August 30, 2002.

"Feds Relocate Native Plants at Organ Pipe for Border Wall." KOLD, Tucson, October 11, 2019.

Felger, Richard S. *Non-native Plants of Organ Pipe Cactus National Monument, Arizona.* Tucson: Cooperative National Park Resources Studies Unit, University of Arizona, April 1990.

Felger, Richard S., and Bill Broyles, eds. *Dry Borders: Great Natural Reserves of the Sonoran Desert.* Salt Lake City: University of Utah Press, 2007.

Felger, Richard S., Susan Rutman, Michael F. Wilson, and Kathryn Mauz. "Botanical Diversity of Southwestern Arizona and Northwestern Sonora." In *Dry Borders:*

Great Natural Reserves of the Sonoran Desert, edited by Richard S. Felger and Bill Broyles, 202–71. Salt Lake City: University of Utah Press, 2007.

Felger, Richard S., Peter L. Warren, L. Susan Anderson, and Gary P. Nabhan. "Vascular Plants of a Desert Oasis: Flora and Ethnobotany of Quitobaquito, Organ Pipe Cactus National Monument, Arizona." *Proceedings of the San Diego Society of Natural History* 8 (June 1, 1992): 1–39.

Fewkes, Jesse Walter. "Casa Grande." In *Twenty-Eighth Annual Report of the Bureau of American Ethnology to the Secretary of the Smithsonian Institution, 1906–1907*, 25–179. Washington, DC: US Government Printing Office, 1912. https://babel .hathitrust.org/cgi/pt?id=mdp.39015029772103&view=1up&seq=7.

Fialka, John J. "In the Wild: A Ranger's Death Shows the New Hazards of a Venerable Job." *Wall Street Journal*, January 22, 2003.

Fish, Larry. "Creating a Monument in the Arizona Desert." *Philadelphia Inquirer*, March 9, 2001.

Fisher, Stuart G. *Hydrologic and Limnologic Features of Quitobaquito Pond and Springs, Organ Pipe Cactus National Monument*. Tucson: Cooperative National Park Resources Studies Unit, University of Arizona, June 1989.

Flores, Dan. *Coyote America: A Natural and Supernatural History.* New York: Basic Books, 2016.

Font, Pedro. *Diary of an Expedition to Monterey by Way of the Colorado River, 1775–1776*. Vol. 4 of *Anza's California Expeditions*, edited by Herbert Eugene Bolton. New York: Russell and Russell, 1966.

Fontana, Bernard L. "History of the Papago." In *Handbook of North American Indians*, edited by Alfonso Ortiz, 10:125–36. Washington, DC: Smithsonian Institution, 1983.

———. "Pima and Papago: Introduction." In *Handbook of North American Indians*, edited by Alfonso Ortiz, 10:125–36. Washington, DC: Smithsonian Institution, 1983.

Fontana, Bernard L., J. Cameron Greenleaf, and Donnelly D. Cassidy. "A Fortified Arizona Mountain." *Kiva* 25, no. 2 (1959): 41–52.

Forbes, Robert H. *Crabb's Filibustering Expedition into Sonora, 1857.* Tucson: Arizona Silhouettes, 1952.

Funes, Yessenia. "Why Trump's New Border Policy Threatens National Park Visitors Everywhere." Gizmodo, December 3, 2019. https://gizmodo.com/why-trump-s -new-border-policy-threatens-national-park-v-1840173482.

Gaddis, John Lewis. *The Landscape of History: How Historians Map the Past.* New York: Oxford University Press, 2004.

Galindo, Erin. "O'odham Students Rise Up against Border Wall Construction on Indigenous Land." *State Press*, September 22, 2020. https://www.statepress.com /article/2020/09/sppolitics-border-wall-construction-effecting-hia-ced-oodham -students#.

Ganster, Paul, and David E. Lorey. *The U.S.-Mexican Border into the Twenty-First Century.* Lanham, MD: Rowman and Littlefield, 2008.

Garcés, Francisco. *Diary and Itinerary of Francisco Garcés.* Vol. 2 of *On the Trail of a Spanish Pioneer*, edited and translated by Elliott Coues. New York: Francis P. Harper, 1900.

Gibson, Emma. "Hundreds Protest Border Wall Construction through National Monument." Arizona Public Media, November 12, 2019. https://news.azpm.org /p/news-articles/2019/11/12/161553-hundreds-protest-border-wall-construction -through-national-monument/.

———. "Indigenous Group Reaffirms Importance of Quitobaquito Springs amid Border Wall Construction." Arizona Public Media, March 13, 2020. https://news .azpm.org/p/news-topical-nature/2020/3/13/167643-indigenous-group-reaffirms -importance-of-quitobaquito-springs-amid-border-wall-construction/.

Gifford, E. W. "Archaeology in the Punta Peñasco Region, Sonora." *American Antiquity* 11, no. 4 (1946): 215–21.

Gilbert, Samuel. "'National Tragedy': Trump Begins Border Wall Construction in UNESCO Reserve." *Guardian*, September 21, 2019.

Gilger, Lauren. "As Indigenous Protestors Take On Border Wall Construction, National Park Service Closes Road to Sacred Spring." Fronteras, October 1, 2020. https://fronterasdesk.org/content/1623254/indigenous-protesters-take-border -wall-construction-national-park-service-closes.

Goodstein, Laurie. "Church Group Provides Oasis for Illegal Migrants to US." *New York Times*, June 10, 2001.

Gould, C. N. *Geology and Organ Pipe Cactus National Monument*. US Department of the Interior, National Park Service, 1938.

Gray, A. B. *The A. B. Gray Report, and Including the Reminiscences of Peter R. Brady Who Accompanied the Expedition*. Los Angeles: Westernlore Press, 1963.

———. "Report of A.B. Gray upon the Atlantic and Pacific Railway, 1855." In *The A. B. Gray Report*, edited by L. R. Bailey, 7–142. Los Angeles: Westernlore Press, 1963.

Greene, Jerome A. *Historic Resource Study: Organ Pipe Cactus National Monument Arizona*. Denver: Denver Service Center Historic Preservation Division, National Park Service, US Department of the Interior, September 1977.

"Greenway Said to Have New R.R. Funds." *Weekly Journal-Miner* (Prescott, AZ), December 10, 1919.

Grossman, David. "The Border Wall Now Threatens a National Monument." *Popular Mechanics*, September 21, 2019. https://www.popularmechanics.com/science /archaeology/a29110356/organ-pipe-cactus-border-wall/.

Grusin, Richard. *Culture, Technology, and the Creation of America's National Parks*. New York: Cambridge University Press, 2004.

Gumerman, George J., and Emil W. Haury. "Prehistory: Hohokam." In *Handbook of North American Indians*, edited by Alfonso Ortiz, 9:75–90. Washington, DC: Smithsonian Institution, 1979.

Hackenberg, Robert A. "Aboriginal Land Use and Occupancy of the Papago Indians." In *Papago Indians*, edited by David Agee Horr, 1:23–309. New York: Garland, 1974.

———. "Economic Alternatives in Arid Lands: A Case Study of the Pima and Papago Indians." *Ethnology* 1, no. 2 (1962): 186–96. https://www.jstor.org/stable /3772874.

———. "Pima and Papago Ecological Adaptations." In *Handbook of North American Indians*, edited by Alfonso Ortiz, 10:161–77. Washington, DC: Smithsonian Institution, 1983.

Haley, J. Evetts. *Jeff Milton: A Good Man with a Gun.* Norman: University of Oklahoma Press, 1948.

Halvorson, William, Cecil Schwalbe, and Charles Van Riper III. *Southwestern Desert Resources.* Tucson: University of Arizona Press, 2010.

Harman, Danna. "Illegal Migrants Persist despite Fences, Danger; Mexicans Try Many Routes to Get into USA." *USA Today*, March 30, 2006.

———. "South of the Border, Fence Is No Deterrent." *Christian Science Monitor*, March 2006.

Hartmann, Gayle Harrison, and Mary Charlotte Thurtle. "The Archaeology of Tinajas Altas, a Desert Water Hole in Southwestern Arizona." *Kiva* 66, no. 4 (2001): 489–518. https://www.jstor.org/stable/30246374.

Hartmann, Gayle Harrison, Mary Charlotte Thurtle, and Gary Paul Nabhan. "Native Peoples of the Tinajas Altas Region: Prehistoric to Present." In *Last Water on the Devil's Highway: A Cultural and Natural History of Tinajas Altas*, edited by Bill Broyles, Gayle Harrison Hartmann, Thomas E. Sheridan, Gary Paul Nabhan, and Mary Charlotte Thurtle, 43–69. Tucson: University of Arizona Press, 2012.

Hartmann, William K. "Country Enough for Many Years of Conquest: The First European Explorations of the Western Papaguería, 1536–1542." In *Fragile Patterns: The Archaeology of the Western Papaguería*, edited by Jeffrey H. Altschul and Adrianne G. Rankin, 447–68. Tucson: SRI Press, 2008.

Havlick, David G., Marion Hourdequin, and Matthew John. "Examining Restoration Goals at a Former Military Site: Rocky Mountain Arsenal, Colorado." *Nature and Culture* 9, no. 3 (2014): 288–315.

Hawley, Chris. "Drug Smugglers Curtain Scientists' Work." *USA Today*, December 27, 2007.

Hayden, Julian D. "Of Hohokam Origins and Other Matters." *American Antiquity* 35, no. 1 (1970): 87–93.

———. "Pre-altithermal Archaeology in the Sierra Pinacate, Sonora, Mexico." *American Antiquity* 14, no. 3 (July 1976): 274–89.

———. "A Summary History and Pre-history of the Sierra Pinacate, Sonora." *American Antiquities* 32 (1967): 335–44.

———. "The Vikita Ceremony of the Papago." *Journal of the Southwest* 29, no. 3 (1987): 273–324.

Hays, Rachel. "Native Nations Pursue Sovereignty, Fair Trade, and a Clean Environment in the Borderlands." *Race, Poverty, and the Environment* 6/7, no. 4/1 (1996): 42–44. https://www.jstor.org/stable/41495631.

Hays, Samuel P. *Conservation and the Gospel of Efficiency: The Progressive Conservation Movement, 1890–1920.* Cambridge, MA: Harvard University Press, 1959.

Hendrick, Troy. "El Camino del Diablo: The Devil's Highway." *Road Runner Motorcycle Touring and Travel*, April 2004.

Hensley, M. Max. "Ecological Relations of the Breeding Bird Population of the Desert Biome of Arizona." *Ecological Monographs* 24 (April 1954): 185–208.

Hernández, Kelly Lytle. *Migra! A History of the U.S. Border Patrol.* Berkeley: University of California Press, 2010.

"Hia C'ed O'odham Exploring Federal Recognition as Tribe." *Runner*, July 17, 2015.

Hill, J. Brett. *From Huhugam to Hohokam: Heritage and Archaeology in the American Southwest.* Lanham, MD: Lexington Books, 2020.

Hill, J. Brett, Jeffrey J. Clark, William H. Doelle, and Patrick D. Lyons. "Prehistoric Demography in the Southwest: Migration, Coalescence, and Hohokam Population Decline." *American Antiquity* 69, no. 4 (October 2004): 689–716.

Himot, Kate. "America's Ten Most Endangered National Parks." *National Parks*, 2004.

Hinkes, Madeleine J. "Migrant Deaths along the California-Mexico Border: An Anthropological Perspective." *Journal of Forensic Sciences* 53 (January 2008): 16–20.

"History and Culture." Tohono O'odham Nation. Accessed November 17, 2016. http://www.tonation-nsn.gov/history_culture.aspx.

Hoover, J. W. "Generic Descent of the Papago Villages." *American Anthropologist* 37, no. 2 (1935): 257–64. https://www.jstor.org/stable/662261.

Hornaday, William T. *Camp-Fires on Desert and Lava.* New York: Charles Scribner's Sons, 1908.

Howkins, Adrian, Jared Orsi, and Mark Fiege, eds. *National Parks beyond the Nation: Global Perspectives on "America's Best Idea."* Norman: University of Oklahoma Press, 2016.

Hoy, Bill. "Don Tomás and Tomasito: The Childs Family Legacy in Southern Arizona." *Journal of Arizona History* 40 (Spring 1999): 1–28.

———. "Hardscrabble Days at the Ajo Mines: George Kippen's Diary, 1855–1858." *Journal of Arizona History* 36 (Autumn 1985): 233–50.

———. "Sonoyta and Santo Domingo: A Story of Two Sonoran Towns and the River That Went By." *Journal of Arizona History* 31, no. 2 (Summer 1990): 117–40.

———. "War in Papaguería: Manuel Gandara's 1840–41 Papago Expedition." *Journal of Arizona History* 35 (Summer 1994): 141–63.

Hoy, Bill, and Bill Broyles. "Pinacate Campmates." *Journal of the Southwest* 49, no. 3 (2007): 323–55.

Hoy, Willton E. "A Quest for the Meaning of Quitobaquito." *Kiva* 34, no. 4 (April 1969): 213–18.

Hu-DeHart, Evelyn. *Missionaries, Miners, and Indians: Spanish Contact with the Yaqui Nation of New Spain, 1533–1820.* Tucson: University of Arizona Press, 1981.

Hultgren, John. "American Environmentalism, Sovereignty, and the 'Immigration Problem.'" PhD diss., Colorado State University, 2012.

"Illegal Border Traffic Is Wearing Out Preserve." Associated Press, October 23, 2013. http://www.msnbc.msn.com/id/13416072/ns/us_news-environment/t/illegal-border-traffic-wearing-out-preserve/.

Ingram, Mrill. "Desert Storms." In *A Natural History of the Sonoran Desert*, edited by Steven J. Phillips and Patricia Wentworth Comus, 41–50. Tucson: Arizona-Sonora Desert Museum Press, 2000.

International Sonoran Desert Alliance. "Creative Placekeeping." Accessed July 31, 2022. https://www.isdanet.org/creative-placemaking-1.

"ISDA and NPS Presented Ideas on How to Restore Quitobaquito Pond." *Ajo Copper News*, October 13, 2020. http://ajo.stparchive.com/Archive/AJO/AJO10132020P005.php?tags=isda|and|nps|presented|ideas|on|how|to|restore|quitobaquito|pond.

"ISDA Has New Board Members and Officers." *Ajo Copper News*, February 26, 2014. http://ajo.stparchive.com/Archive/AJO/AJO02262014P07.php?tags= isda|has|new|board|members|and|officers.

"ISDA's Annual Meeting Focused on Quitobaquito." *Ajo Copper News*, March 3, 2021. http://ajo.stparchive.com/Archive/AJO/AJO03032021P009.php?tags=isda %27s|annual|meeting|focused|on|quitobaquito.

"ISDA's Annual Meeting Will Be Virtual with Focus on Quitobaquito." *Ajo Copper News*, February 24, 2021. http://ajo.stparchive.com/Archive/AJO/AJO02242021P007 .php?tags=isda%27s|annual|meeting|focused|on|quitobaquito.

Ives, Ronald L. "Alberto Celaya, 1885–1962." *Kiva* 28, no. 3 (April 1963): 21–22.

———. "Desert Floods in the Sonoyta Valley." *American Journal of Science*, 5th ser., 32 (1936): 349–60.

———. "The Origin of the Sonoyta Townsite, Sonora, Mexico." *American Antiquity* 7, no. 1 (July 1941): 20–28.

———. "A Trinchera near Quitovaquita, Sonora." *American Anthropologist* 38 (1936): 257–59.

———. "Ygnacio C. Quiroz, 1886–1962." *Kiva* 28, no. 3 (February 1963): 33–34.

Jackson, John Brinckerhoff. *Discovering the Vernacular Landscape*. New Haven, CT: Yale University Press, 1984.

———. *Sense of Place, Sense of Time*. New Haven, CT: Yale University Press, 1994.

Jacoby, Karl. *Crimes against Nature Squatters, Poachers, Thieves, and the Hidden History of American Conservation*. Berkeley: University of California Press, 2001.

———. *Shadows at Dawn: A Borderlands Massacre and the Violence of History*. New York: Penguin Press, 2008.

Johnson, R. Roy, Bryan T. Brown, and Sharon Goldwasser. *Avian Use of Quitobaquito Springs Oasis, Organ Pipe National Monument, Arizona*. Tucson: Cooperative National Park Resources Studies Unit, University of Arizona, December 1983.

Jordahl, Laiken. "Hundreds Expected Saturday at Tucson Border Wall Protest with Rep. Grijalva." Center for Biological Diversity, December 5, 2019. https:// biologicaldiversity.org/w/news/press-releases/hundreds-expected-saturday-tucson -border-wall-protest-rep-grijalva-2019-12-05/.

———. "Wednesday Border Wall Action Planned at Arizona's Organ Pipe National Monument." Center for Biological Diversity press release, February 25, 2020. https://biologicaldiversity.org/w/news/press-releases/wednesday-border-wall -action-planned-at-arizonas-organ-pipe-national-monument-2020-02-25/.

Joseph, Alice, Rosamond B. Spicer, and Jane Chesky. *The Desert People: A Study of the Papago Indians*. Chicago: University of Chicago Press, 1949.

Kanno-Youngs, Zolan. "Park Service Says Archaeological Sites Are Imperiled by Border Wall." *New York Times*, September 17, 2019. https://www.nytimes.com/2019 /09/17/us/politics/archaeological-sites-border-wall.html.

Karskens, Grace. "Water Dreams, Earthen Histories: Exploring Urban Environmental History at the Penrith Lakes Scheme and Castlereagh, Sydney." *Environment and History* 13, no. 2 (2007): 115–54.

Keller, Robert H., and Michael F. Turek. *American Indians and National Parks*. Tucson: University of Arizona Press, 1998.

Kenworthy, Tom. "New Outlaws Plague Arizona Desert Refuges; Park Rangers Take on Extra Duties as Scenic Lands Become Illegal Gateways to USA." *USA Today*, August 23, 2006.

Kidd, D. E., and W. E. Wade. "Algae of Quitobaquito: A Spring-Fed Impoundment in Organ Pipe Cactus National Monument." *Southwestern Naturalist* 10 (1965): 227–33.

Kingsley, Kenneth J. *Invertebrates of Organ Pipe Cactus National Monument, Arizona*. Tucson: Cooperative National Park Resources Studies Unit, University of Arizona, December 1998.

Kingsley, Kenneth J., and Richard Bailowitz. *Grasshoppers and Butterflies of the Quitobaquito Management Area, Organ Pipe Cactus National Monument, Arizona*. Tucson: Cooperative National Park Resources Studies Unit, University of Arizona, July 1987.

Kingsley, Kenneth J., Richard A. Bailowitz, and Robert L. Smith. *A Preliminary Investigation of the Arthropod Fauna of Quitobaquito Springs Area, Organ Pipe Cactus National Monument, Arizona*. Technical report. Tucson: Cooperative National Park Resources Studies Unit, University of Arizona, July 1987.

Kino, Eusebio. "Relación Diaria." In *Father Kino in Arizona*, edited by Fay Jackson Smith, John L. Kessell, and Francis J. Fox, 8–34. Phoenix: Arizona Historical Foundation, 1966.

Kino, Eusebio Francisco. *Kino's Historical Memoir of Pimería Alta: An Account of the Beginnings of California, Sonora, and Arizona*. Translated by Herbert Eugene Bolton. Cleveland: Arthur Clark, 1919.

Klein, K. L. "Frontier Products: Tourism, Consumerism, and the Southwestern Public Lands, 1890–1990." *Pacific Historical Review*, February 1993, 39–71.

Knight, Jasper. "Development of Palimpsest Landscapes." Vignettes, January 13, 2022. https://serc.carleton.edu/vignettes/collection/67822.html.

Kresan, Peter L. "A Geologic Tour of the Dry Borders Region." In *Dry Borders: Great Natural Reserves of the Sonoran Desert*, edited by Richard S. Felger and Bill Broyles, 31–45. Salt Lake City: University of Utah Press, 2007.

Kynard, B., and R. Garret. "Reproductive Ecology of the Quitobaquito Pupfish from Organ Pipe Cactus National Monument, Arizona." *Proceedings of the First Conference on Scientific Research in National Parks* 82 (1979): 625–29.

Kynard, Boyd E. *Preliminary Study of the Desert Pupfish and Their Habitat at Quitobaquito Springs, Arizona*. Technical report. Tucson: Cooperative National Park Resources Studies Unit, University of Arizona, September 1976.

Ladefoged, Thegn N., and Michael W. Graves. "Variable Development of Dryland Agriculture in Hawai'i: A Fine-Grained Chronology from the Kohala Field System, Hawai'i Island." *Current Anthropology* 49, no. 5 (2008): 771–802. https://doi.org/10.1086/591424.

Laird, Wendy, Joaquin Murrieta-Saldivar, and John Shepard. "Cooperation across Borders: A Brief History of Biosphere Reserves in the Sonoran Desert." *Journal of the Southwest* 39, no. 3/4 (Autumn/Winter 1997): 307–13.

Langston, Nancy. "Resource Management as a Democratic Process: Adaptive Management on Federal Lands." In *Communities and Forests: Where People Meet the Land,* edited by Robert G. Lee and Donald R. Field, 52–76. Corvallis: Oregon State University Press, 2005.

———. *Where Land and Water Meet: A Western Landscape Transformed.* Seattle: University of Washington Press, 2003.

Learning, George F. *The Economic Impact of Organ Pipe Cactus National Monument.* Tucson: University of Arizona, Division of Economic and Business Research, 1970.

Lee, Erika. *At America's Gates: Chinese Immigration during the Exclusion Era, 1882–1943.* Chapel Hill: University of North Carolina Press, 2003.

Lee, Ronald F. *The Antiquities Act of 1906.* Washington, DC: Office of History and Historic Architecture, Eastern Service Center, 1970.

Legner, E. F., R. A. Medved, and W. J. Hauser. "Predation by Desert Pupfish, *Cyprinodon macularius* on *Culex* Mosquitoes and Benthic Chironomid Midges." *Entomophaga* 20, no. 1 (1975): 23–30.

Leskiw, Tom. "A Region of Wounds Severing the U.S.-Mexico Borderlands." *Terrain* 24 (Fall/Winter 2009). https://www.terrain.org/articles/24/leskiw.htm.

Leza, Christina. *Divided Peoples: Policy, Activism, and Indigenous Identities on the U.S.-Mexico Border.* Tucson: University of Arizona Press, 2019.

Lissoway, Brenna Lauren. "An Administrative History of Organ Pipe Cactus National Monument: The First Thirty Years, 1937–1967." Master's thesis, Arizona State University, 2004.

Lister, Robert H. *Those Who Came Before: Southwestern Archaeology in the National Park System.* Albuquerque: Southwest Parks and Monuments Association, 1993.

Longstreth, Richard, ed. *Cultural Landscapes: Balancing Nature and Heritage in Preservation Practice.* Minneapolis: University of Minnesota Press, 2008.

Lopez-Hoffman, Laura. *Conservation of Shared Environments: Learning from the United States and Mexico.* Tucson: University of Arizona Press, 2009.

Lowe, C. H., and W. G. Heath. "Behavioral and Physiological Responses to Temperature in the Desert Pupfish, *Cyprinodon macularius.*" *Physiological Zoology* 42 (1969): 53–59.

Lumholtz, Carl. *New Trails in Mexico: An Account of One Year's Exploration in North-Western Sonora, Mexico, and South-Western Arizona, 1909–1910.* New York: Charles Scribner's Sons, 1912.

Lumholtz, Carl, and I. N. Dracopoli. "The Sonora Desert, Mexico." *Geographical Journal* 40, no. 5 (November 1912): 503–18.

MacDougal, D. T. "Across Papaguería." *Bulletin of the American Geographical Society* 40, no. 12 (1908): 705–25.

Madsen, Kenneth Dean. "A Basis for Bordering: Land, Migration, and Inter-Tohono O'odham Distinction along the U.S.-Mexico Line." In *Making the Border in Everyday Life*, edited by Reece Jones and Corey Johnson, 93–116. London: Ashgate, 2014.

———. "A Nation across Nations: The Tohono O'odham and the United States–Mexico Border." PhD diss., Arizona State University, 2005.

Magaña, Rocío. "Desolation Bound: The Enforcement of the Border on Migrant Bodies in the Arizona-Mexico Desert Regions." PhD diss., University of Chicago, 2008.

Magrane, Eric, and Christopher Cokinos, eds. *The Sonoran Desert: A Literary Field Guide.* Tucson: University of Arizona Press, 2016.

Maier, Charles S. "Consigning the Twentieth Century to History: Alternative Narratives for the Modern Era." *American Historical Review* 105 (June 2000): 807–31.

Main, Douglas. "Sacred Arizona Spring Drying Up as Border Wall Construction Continues." *National Geographic,* July 20, 2020. https://www.nationalgeographic.com/science/2020/07/quitobaquito-springs-arizona-drying-up-border-wall/.

Malakoff, David. "A Hohokam Hybrid?" *American Archaeology* 14 (Summer 2010): 27–33.

Manje, Juan Mateo. *Luz de Tierra Incógnita: Unknown Arizona and Sonora.* Translated by Harry J. Karns. Tucson: Arizona Silhouettes, 1954.

Marak, Andrae M., and Laura Tuennerman. *At the Border of Empires: The Tohono O'odham, Gender, and Assimilation, 1880–1934.* Tucson: University of Arizona Press, 2013.

Martínez, David. "Hiding in the Shadows of History: Revitalizing Hia-Ced O'odham Peoplehood." *Journal of the Southwest* 55, no. 2 (2013): 131–73.

Mason, J. Alden. "The Papago Migration Legend." *Journal of American Folklore* 34, no. 133 (September 1921): 254–68.

McAuliffe, J. R. "Herbivore-Limited Establishment of a Sonoran Desert Tree, *Cercidium microphyllum.*" *Ecology* 67 (February 1986): 276–80.

McBride, Kelly. "Inadequate Funds, Pollution Cited as National Park Woes; Advocacy Group Names 10 Most Endangered Sites." *Washington Post,* January 14, 2004.

McCarthy, James. *A Papago Traveler: The Memories of James McCarthy.* Tucson: University of Arizona Press, 1985.

McCarty, Kieran, ed. *A Frontier Documentary: Tucson and Sonora, 1821–1848.* Tucson: University of Arizona Press, 1997.

McCombs, Brady. "6 More Bodies Found in Desert; Fiscal-Year Total: 164." AZStar.net. Accessed November 17, 2016. http://azstarnet.com/news/local/border/article_ce6b0b72-557f-5368-b727-59971ffee658.html.

McEvoy, Arthur F. "Toward an Interactive Theory of Nature and Culture: Ecology, Production, and Cognition in the California Fishing Industry." *Environmental Review* 11 (Winter 1987): 289–305.

McGee, W. J. "The Old Yuma Trail." *National Geographic,* April 1901.

———. "Papaguería." *National Geographic,* 1898.

McGivney, Annette. "The Wildest Park in America." *Backpacker,* April 2003.

McGuire, Randall H. *Ethnology of Northwest Mexico: A Sourcebook.* New York: Garland, 1991.

McIntyre-Tamwoy, Susan, and Rodney Harrison. "Monuments to Colonialism? Stone Arrangements, Tourist Cairns and Turtle Magic at Evans Bay, Cape York." *Australian Archaeology,* no. 59 (2004): 31–42.

McNamee, Gregory. "Broken Borders: At Organ Pipe Cactus National Monument, Wildlife Suffers." *Advocacy for Animals* (blog), April 2009. http://advocacy.britannica.com/blog/advocacy/2009/04/broken-borders-at-organ-pipe.

Mearns, E. A. "Preliminary Diagnoses of New Mammals from the Mexican Border of the United States." *Proceedings of the United States National Museum* 18, no. 1103 (1896): 1–3.

Mearns, Edgar Alexander. *Mammals of the Mexican Boundary of the United States.* Smithsonian Institution United States National Museum Bulletin 56. Washington DC: US Government Printing Office, 1907.

Meeks, Eric V. *Border Citizens: The Making of Indians, Mexicans, and Anglos in Arizona.* Austin: University of Texas Press, 2007.

Meltzer, D. J. *First Peoples in a New World: Colonizing Ice Age America.* Berkeley: University of California Press, 2009.

Merrill, William L., Robert J. Hard, Jonathan B. Mabry, Gayle J. Fritz, Karen R. Adams, and John R. Roney. "The Diffusion of Maize to the Southwestern United States and Its Impact." *Proceedings of the National Academy of Sciences* 106, no. 50 (December 15, 2009): 21019–26.

Miller, Joshua Rhett. "Five Federal Lands in Arizona Have Travel Warnings in Place." *Fox News*, June 18, 2010.

Miller, Robert Rush. "Man and the Changing Fish Fauna of the American Southwest." *Papers of the Michigan Academy of Science and Arts* 46 (1961): 365–404.

Miller, Robert Rush, and Lee A. Fuiman. "Description and Conservation Status of *Cyprinodon macularius eremus*, a New Subspecies of Pupfish from Organ Pipe Cactus National Monument, Arizona." *Copeia* 3 (August 1987): 593–609.

———. *Status of* Cyprinodon macularius eremus*, a New Subspecies of Pupfish from Organ Pipe Cactus National Monument, Arizona.* Technical report. Tucson: Cooperative National Park Resources Studies Unit, University of Arizona, 1987.

Minard, Anne. "The Changing of the Guard." *National Parks*, Fall 2006.

Minckley, W. L. *Fishes of Arizona.* Phoenix: Arizona Game and Fish Department, 1973.

Mingura, Mark. "Border Wall Protesters Gather at Organ Pipe National Monument over Weekend." KVOA, Tucson, November 10, 2019. https://www.kvoa.com /archive/border-wall-protesters-gather-at-organ-pipe-national-monument-over -weekend/article_8b7dbd25-6c6f-5d2c-9bc2-9c26c8baee86.html.

Minteer, Ben A., and Stephen Pyne. "Restoring the Narrative of American Environmentalism." *Restoration Ecology* 21 (January 2013): 6–11.

"Most Endangered National Parks Named by NPCA." GovPro/American City and County, February 17, 2004. https://www.americancityandcounty.com/2004/02 /17/most-endangered-national-parks-named-by-npca/.

Mulvihill, Keith. "A Road Trip on the Edge of America." *New York Times*, January 11, 2008.

Nabhan, Gary Paul. "Camel Whisperers: Desert Nomads Crossing Paths." *Journal of Arizona History* 49, no. 2 (2008): 95–118.

———. *The Desert Smells Like Rain: A Naturalist in O'odham Country.* Tucson: University of Arizona Press, 1982.

———. "Destruction of an Ancient Indigenous Cultural Landscape: An Epitaph from Organ Pipe Cactus National Monument." *Ecological Restoration* 21, no. 4 (2003): 290–95.

———. "Papago Indian Desert Agriculture and Water Control in the Sonoran Desert, 1697–1934." *Applied Geography* 6 (January 1986): 43–59.

———. "Welcome to the Sonoran Desert." In *A Natural History of the Sonoran Desert*, edited by Steven J. Phillips and Patricia Wentworth Comus, 1–2. Tucson: Arizona-Sonora Desert Museum Press, 2000.

Nabhan, Gary, Wendy Hodgson, and Frances Fellows. "A Meager Living on Lava and Sand? Hia Ced O'odham Food Resources and Habitat Diversity in Oral and Documentary Histories." *Journal of the Southwest* 31, no. 4 (1989): 508–33. https://www.jstor.org/stable/40169623.

Nabhan, Gary, Amadeo M. Rea, Karen L. Reichardt, Eric Mellink, and Charles F. Hutchinson. "Papago Influences on Habitat and Biotic Diversity: Quitovac Oasis Ethnoecology." *Journal of Ethnobiology* 2, no. 2 (December 1982): 124–43.

Nagel, Carlos. "Report on Treaties, Agreements and Accords Affecting Natural Resource Management at Organ Pipe Cactus National Monument, Arizona." Tucson: Cooperative National Park Resources Studies Unit, University of Arizona, 1988.

National Park Service. *Cultural Landscapes Inventory: Quitobaquito, Organ Pipe Cactus National Monument.* 1998, revised 2002. Accessed October 24, 2013. http://npshistory.com/publications/orpi/cli-quitobaquito.pdf.

———. "Interpretation and Education." Accessed September 30, 2010. http://www.nps.gov/learn/.

———. "History and Culture." Organ Pipe Cactus National Monument. Accessed October 1, 2010. http://www.nps.gov/orpi/historyculture/.

———. Organ Pipe Cactus National Monument. Accessed October 1, 2010. http://www.nps.gov/orpi/.

———. *Organ Pipe Cactus National Monument, Arizona.* Washington, DC, 1964.

———. *Organ Pipe Cactus National Monument, Arizona: Official Map and Guide, 1985.* Washington, DC, 1985.

———. *Organ Pipe Cactus National Monument, Arizona: Supplement to the Draft General Management Plan, Development Concept Plans, Environmental Impact Statement.* Ajo, AZ: US Department of the Interior, National Park Service, 1996.

———. *Organ Pipe Cactus National Monument, Arizona: Wilderness Study.* Denver: US Department of the Interior, National Park Service, Denver Service Center, 1973.

———. *Organ Pipe Cactus National Monument: Final General Management Plan, Development Concept Plans, Environmental Impact Statement.* National Park Service. Accessed November 3, 2016. http://www.nps.gov/orpi/learn/management/upload/fingmp.pdf.

———. *Organ Pipe Cactus National Monument: Foundation for Planning and Management.* Accessed October 25, 2013. http://www.nps.gov/orpi/naturescience/upload/ORPIFoundation514.pdf.

———. *Vascular Plant and Vertebrate Inventory of Organ Pipe Cactus National Monument.* Tucson, 2007.

National Park Service Advisory Board, Science Committee. *Revisiting Leopold: Resource Stewardship in the National Parks.* Accessed November 3, 2016. https://www.nps.gov/calltoaction/PDF/LeopoldReport_2012.pdf.

Nelson, Kent. *Language in the Blood.* Salt Lake City: Peregrine Smith Books, 1991.

Neumann, Roderick P. *Imposing Wilderness: Struggles over Livelihood and Nature Preservation in Africa.* Berkeley: University of California Press, 1998.

Nichols, Tad, and Bill Broyles. "Afield with Desert Scientists." *Journal of the Southwest* 39 (1997): 353–70.

Nicla, Andrew. "Feds to Delay Parts of Arizona Border Wall Construction until October." *Arizona Republic* (Phoenix), August 14, 2019.

Nielsen, Chris. "Illegal Immigrants Bring Problems to Border Parks." Our National Parks, May 5, 2008. http://www.ournationalparks.us/index.php/site/story_issues/illegal_immigrants_bring_problems_to_border_parks/.

Niering, W. A., R. H. Whittaker, and C. H. Lowe. "The Saguaro: A Population in Relation to Environment." *Science*, n.s., 142 (October 4, 1963): 15–23.

"Night Sky Is Focus of Desert Evening." *Ajo Copper News*, September 8, 2010. http://ajo.stparchive.com/Archive/AJO/AJO09082010p04.php?tags=night|sky|is|focus|of|desert|evening.

Nijhuis, Steffen. "Mapping the Evolution of Designed Landscapes with GIS." In *Mapping Landscapes in Transformation*, edited by Thomas Coomans, Bieke Cattoor, and Krista De Jonge, 95–130. Leuven, Belgium: Leuven University Press, 2019.

"The NPS Has Prepared an Environmental Assessment to Address the Environmental Impacts of Proposed Restoration." *Ajo Copper News*, March 19, 2014. http://ajo.stparchive.com/Archive/AJO/AJO03192014P11.php?tags=the|nps|has|prepared|an|environmental|assessment|to|address|impacts|of|proposed|restoration.

Nuñez-Neto, Blas. "Border Security: The Role of the U.S. Border Patrol." Congressional Research Services, 2008. https://ecommons.cornell.edu/handle/1813/77884.

Olson Stevenson, Martha. "The Lure of a Lush Desert." *New York Times*, April 23, 2000.

"The Only Desert Laboratory in the World." *New York Times*, July 15, 1906.

"Organ Pipe Cactus Biosphere Reserve, United States of America." UNESCO. Accessed January 9, 2023. https://en.unesco.org/biosphere/eu-na/organ-pipe-cactus.

Organ Pipe Cactus National Monument. *Biological Assessment: Emergency Actions to Stabilize Quitobaquito Pond Part II: Renovating the Southeast Corner*. ESA Emergency Consultation, October 2009.

———. *Border-Related Impacts to Sonoran Desert Wilderness in SW Arizona: A Presentation Developed by the Resource Management Staff of Organ Pipe Cactus National Monument, Arizona*. n.d.

———. *Emergency Actions to Stabilize Quitobaquito Pond, and Related Activities: Final Project Report and Revised Biological Assessment*. ESA Emergency Consultation, July 2008.

———. "International Border Vehicle Barrier." https://www.nps.gov/orpi/planyourvisit/barrier.htm.

———. *Minimum Requirements Decision Guide Workbook: Quitobaquito Pond Restoration*. 2016.

———. *Natural and Cultural Resources Management Plan, Organ Pipe Cactus National Monument*. December 1994.

———. *Project Summary: Quitobaquito Pond—Cottonwood Sealing*. October 2010.

———. *Repair Quitobaquito Pond, Organ Pipe Cactus National Monument*. ESA Emergency Consultation, August 2016.

———. *Superintendent's 2010 Report on Natural Resource Vital Signs*. Ajo, AZ: National Park Service, 2011.

———. *Water Resources Management Plan.* US Department of the Interior, 1992.

"Organ Pipe Cactus National Monument Damaged by Border Wall Flood Obstruction." Center for Biological Diversity press release, August 15, 2008. http://www.biologicaldiversity.org/news/press_releases/2008/border-wall-08-15-2008.html.

"Organ Pipe Is Holding Programs in Ajo and Why This Season." *Ajo Copper News,* January 26, 2011. http://ajo.stparchive.com/Archive/AJO/AJO01262011p003.php?tags=organ|pipe|is|holding|programs|in|ajo|and|why|this|season.

Orsi, Jared. "Construction and Contestation: Toward a Unifying Methodology for Borderlands History." *History Compass* 12, no. 5 (May 2014): 433–43.

Outka-Perkins, Lisa, Theron Miller, and Jon Driessen. *Personal Safety of Federal Land-Management Field Employees Working along the Mexican Border.* US Forest Service, January 2006.

Parker, Kathleen C. "Site-Related Demographic Patterns of Organ Pipe Cactus Populations in Southern Arizona." *Bulletin of the Torrey Botanical Club* 114, no. 2 (1987): 149–55.

Pate, Ami. *Organ Pipe Cactus National Monument, Ecological Monitoring Program, Annual Report 1996.* Ajo, AZ: National Park Service, Organ Pipe Cactus National Monument, 1999.

Pearson, Gina, and Charles W. Conner. "The Quitobaquito Desert Pupfish, an Endangered Species within Organ Pipe Cactus National Monument: Historical Significance and Management Challenges." *Natural Resources Journal* 40, no. 2 (Spring 2000): 379–410.

Pennisi, Elizabeth. "Living in a Land of Extremes." *National Wildlife* 27, no. 3 (April 1989): 14–21.

Peterson, Jodi. "After 11 Years, Organ Pipe Cactus National Monument Reopens." *High Country News,* September 17, 2014.

Petryszyn, Yar, and E. Lendell Cockrum. *Mammals of the Quitobaquito Management Area, Organ Pipe Cactus National Monument, Arizona.* Tucson: Cooperative National Park Resources Studies Unit, University of Arizona, 1990.

Pfefferkorn, Ignaz. *Sonora: A Description of the Province.* Translated by Theodore E. Treutlein. Tucson: University of Arizona Press, 1989.

Phillips, Steven J., and Patricia Wentworth Comus, eds. *A Natural History of the Sonoran Desert.* Tucson: Arizona-Sonora Desert Museum Press, 2000.

Phippen, J. Weston. "Like 'Building a 30-Foot Wall through Arlington Cemetery': Tribal Leaders in Arizona Are Worried Trump's Border Wall Will Decimate Sacred Sites and Leave Smugglers No Choice but to Cut through Native Land." *Business Insider,* May 17, 2020. https://www.businessinsider.com/trump-border-wall-through-organ-pipe-sacred-tohono-oodham-land-2020-5.

Piekielek, Jessica. "Creating a Park, Building a Border: The Establishment of Organ Pipe Cactus National Monument and the Solidification of the U.S.-Mexico Border." *Journal of the Southwest* 58, no. 1 (2013): 1–27.

———. "Public Wildlands at the U.S. Mexico Border: Where Conservation, Migration, and Border Enforcement Collide." PhD diss., University of Arizona, 2009.

Pierson, Elizabeth, and Raymond M. Turner. "An 85-Year Study of Saguaro (*Carnegiea gigantea*) Demography." *Ecology* 79 (1998): 2676–793.

Pinto, Robin. *The History of Ranching at Organ Pipe Cactus National Monument.* September 8, 2008. Tucson: Desert Southwest Cooperative Ecosystem Studies Unit, University of Arizona.

Plagens, Michael J. "Sonoran Desert Naturalist." Arizonensis.org. Accessed November 17, 2016. http://www.arizonensis.org/sonoran/index.html.

"Plaza Will See Living History Show This Thursday." *Ajo Copper News*, February 22, 2012. http://ajo.stparchive.com/Archive/AJO/AJO02222012p01.php?tags=plaza |will|see|living|history|show|this|thursday.

"Poachers Plague Cactus Reserve in Organ Pipe National Monument." *Washington Post*, November 18, 1980.

Pomfret, John. "Fence Meets Wall of Skepticism; Critics Doubt a 700-Mile Barrier Would Stem Migrant Tide." *Washington Post*, October 10, 2006.

Prendergast, Curt. "Ancient Watering Hole in Southern Arizona at Risk from Border Wall Construction." *Arizona Daily Star* (Tucson), September 8, 2019.

———. "Border Patrol Offers View of Blasting for Wall on Organ Pipe National Monument." *Arizona Daily Star* (Tucson), February 27, 2020. https://tucson.com /news/local/border-patrol-offers-view-of-blasting-for-wall-on-organ-pipe-national -monument/article_c334fa35-1d4a-547b-9cac-e12efc9d5d10.html.

———. "Feds Move Some Saguaros, Destroy Others for Border Wall near Lukeville." *Arizona Daily Star* (Tucson), August 12, 2019. https://tucson.com/news/local /feds-move-some-saguaros-destroy-others-for-border-wall-near-lukeville/article _55b96d3f-2caf-5314-9b8a-87ae400103ce.html.

———. "Trump's Border Wall Rises near Yuma." *Arizona Daily Star* (Tucson), August 10, 2019. https://tucson.com/news/local/trumps-border-wall-rises-near -yuma/article_6507cee9-59f4-5836-ba23-10fbc23e9c14.html.

"Protesters Plan on Gathering in Tucson to Oppose Border Wall." Associated Press, December 12, 2019.

Purdy, P. "A Deadly, Fragile Desert." *Denver Post*, June 4, 2002.

Ramon-Sauberan, Jacelle. "Extinct No More: Hia C'ed O'odham Officially Join Tohono O'odham Nation." *Indian Country Today*, June 30, 2012.

———. "Tohono O'odham Vote Saturday on Dissolving Troubled District." *Indian Country Today*, April 24, 2015.

Rankin, Adrianne G. *Archeological Survey at Organ Pipe Cactus National Monument, Southwestern Arizona: 1989–1991.* Tucson: Western Archeological and Conservation Center, National Park Service, 1995.

Rankin, Adrianne G., Lorraine M. Eiler, and Joseph T. Joaquin. "Water and the Human Spirit: Traditional Sacred Natural Surface Waters." In *Fragile Patterns: The Archaeology of the Western Papaguería*, edited by Jeffrey H. Altschul and Adrianne G. Rankin, 595–604. Tucson: SRI Press, 2008.

Ray, Sarah Jaquette. "The Ecological Other: Indians, Invalids, and Immigrants in U.S. Environmental Thought and Literature." University of Oregon Scholars' Bank, 2009. https://scholarsbank.uoregon.edu/xmlui/handle/1794/10352.

Regan, Margaret. *The Death of Josseline: Immigration Stories from the Arizona Borderlands.* Boston: Beacon Press, 2010.

Reinke, Robin S. "Naming the Dead: Identification and Ambiguity along the U.S.-Mexico Border." PhD diss., University of Arizona, 2016.

Rensink, Brendan W. *Native but Foreign*. College Station: Texas A&M University Press, 2018.

Repanshek, Kurt. "Border Patrol Turns to Explosives to Build Wall in Organ Pipe Cactus National Monument." National Parks Traveler, February 7, 2020. https://www.nationalparkstraveler.org/2020/02/border-patrol-turns-explosives-build-wall-organ-pipe-cactus-national-monument.

———. "Concerns Voiced That Border Wall Construction Is Damaging Quitobaquito Springs at Organ Pipe." National Parks Traveler, August 2, 2020. https://www.nationalparkstraveler.org/2020/08/concerns-voiced-border-wall-construction-damaging-quitobaquito-springs-organ-pipe.

———. "New Director in National Park Service's Intermountain Region Looking Forward to Challenges." National Parks Traveler, 2010. http://www.nationalparkstraveler.com/2010/10/new-director-national-park-services-intermountain-region-looking-forward-challenges7009.

Reznick, Alisa. "Indigenous Activists Arrested in Demonstration against Border Wall Construction near Quitobaquito Springs." Arizona Public Media, September 10, 2020. https://news.azpm.org/s/80016-indigenous-activists-arrested-in-demonstration-against-border-wall-construction-near-quitobaquito-springs/.

———. "In Southern Arizona's Organ Pipe Cactus National Monument, a Race to Save a Tiny Desert Oasis." Fronteras, May 9, 2022. https://fronterasdesk.org/content/1777833/southern-arizonas-organ-pipe-cactus-national-monument-race-save-tiny-desert-oasis.

———. "NPS Closes Route to Quitobaquito Springs." Arizona Public Media, September 29, 2020. https://news.azpm.org/p/news-topical-arts/2020/9/29/180978-nps-closes-route-to-quitobaquito-springs/.

———. "Scientists: Border Wall Construction Wreaking Havoc at Quitobaquito Springs." Arizona Public Media, July 30, 2020. https://news.azpm.org/p/news-splash/2020/7/30/177510-scientists-border-wall-construction-wreaking-havoc-at-quitobaquito-springs/.

———. "Stand Off with Border Patrol, National Park Service Ends in Scuffle with Indigenous-Led Demonstrators." Arizona Public Media, September 23, 2020. https://news.azpm.org/s/80304-stand-off-with-border-patrol-national-park-service-ends-in-scuffle-with-indigenous-led-demonstrators/.

Rickard, Forrest R. "The Copper Ores of Ajo, Arizona, Discovery to World War II." In *History of Mining in Arizona*, vol. 3, edited by J. Michael Canty, H. Mason Coggin, and Michael N. Greeley, 1–13. Tucson: Mining Foundation of the Southwest, 1999.

Ring, Bay. "Border out of Control: National Security Runs Roughshod over the Arizona Wild." *High Country News*, June 9, 2014, 12–19.

Robbins, Jim. "In the Sonoran Desert, Bizarre Is the Rule!" *New York Times*, March 4, 1990.

Rogers, Malcolm J. "San Dieguito Implements from the Terraces of the Rincon-Patano and Rillito Drainage Systems." *Kiva*, 1958, 1–23.

Rolston, Holmes, III. "The Wilderness Idea Reaffirmed." *Environmental Professional*, 1991, 370–77.

Romero, Simon. "Tribal Nation Condemns 'Desecration' to Build Border Wall." *New York Times*, February 26, 2020. https://www.nytimes.com/2020/02/26/us/border -wall-cactuses-arizona.html.

Roosevelt, Margot. "Busted!" *Time*, August 4, 2003.

Rose, Dan. *The Ancient Mines of Ajo*. Tucson: Mission, 1936.

Rosen, Philip C. *Population Decline of Sonoran Mud Turtles at Quitobaquito Springs: Final Report*. February 19, 1986. http://www.nativefishlab.net/library/textpdf/21070.pdf.

Rosen, Philip C., and Charles H. Lowe. *Ecology of the Amphibians and Reptiles at Organ Pipe Cactus National Monument, Arizona*. Technical report. Tucson: Cooperative National Park Resources Studies Unit, University of Arizona, April 1996.

———. *Population Ecology of the Sonoran Desert Mud Turtle* (Kinosternon sonoriense) *at Quitobaquito Springs, Organ Pipe Cactus National Monument, Arizona*. March 27, 1996. https://www.researchgate.net/publication/262911895_Population_ecology _of_the_Sonoran_Mud_Turtle_Kinosternon_sonoriense_at_Quitobaquito _Springs_Organ_Pipe_Cactus_National_Monument_Arizona.

Rosen, Philip Clark, Christina Melendez, J. Daren Riedle, Ami C. Pate, and Erin Fernandez. "Ecology and Conservation in the Sonoyta Valley, Arizona and Sonora." October 2010. https://www.researchgate.net/publication/257343742_ecology _and_conservation_in_the_sonoyta_valley_arizona_and_sonora.

Ross, C. P. *The Lower Gila Region, Arizona: A Geographic, Geologic and Hydrologic Reconnaissance with a Guide to Desert Watering Places*. US Geological Survey Water-Supply Paper. Washington, DC: US Government Printing Office, 1923.

Rothman, Hal. *America's National Monuments: The Politics of Preservation*. Lawrence: University Press of Kansas, 1994.

———. "Forged by One Man's Will: Frank Pinkley and the Administration of the Southwestern National Monuments, 1923–1932." *Public Historian* 8, no. 2 (1986): 83–100.

———. *Preserving Different Pasts: The American National Monuments*. Chicago: University of Illinois Press, 1989.

Rozenberg, Hernan. "Tohono O'odham Push for Hearing on Citizenship Bill." *Arizona Republic* (Phoenix), April 7, 2002.

"Saguaro Harvest Is Next in Series of Desert Evenings." *Ajo Copper News*, June 22, 2011. http://ajo.stparchive.com/Archive/AJO/AJO06222011p06.php?tags= saguaro|harvest|is|next|in|series|of|desert|evenings.

Sanchez, G. "Human (Clovis)-Gomphothere (*Cuvieronius* sp.) Association ~ 13,390 Calibrated YBP in Sonora, Mexico." *Proceedings of the National Academy of Sciences* 111, no. 30 (July 29, 2014): 10972–77.

Sanchez, Sandra. "Member of Hia C'ed O'odham Says Border Wall Is 'Desecrating' Tribal Ancestral Remains in Arizona." *Border Report*, September 25, 2019. https:// www.borderreport.com/border-report-tour/member-of-hia-ced-oodham-says -border-wall-is-desecrating-tribal-ancestral-remains-in-arizona/.

Saxton, Dean, and Lucille Saxton. *O'otham Hoho'ok A'agitha: Legends and Lore of the Papago and Pima Indians*. Tucson: University of Arizona Press, 1973.

Sayre, Nathan F. *The Politics of Scale: A History of Rangeland Science*. Chicago: University of Chicago Press, 2017.

Scarborough, Robert. "The Geologic Origins of the Sonoran Desert." In *A Natural History of the Sonoran Desert*, edited by Steven J. Phillips and Patricia Wentworth Comus, 71–85. Tucson: Arizona-Sonora Desert Museum Press, 2000.

Schamess, Lisa. "Toward Placekeeping: How Design + Dialogue Can Make Cities Better for Everyone." *Public Square*, November 12, 2019. https://www.cnu.org /publicsquare/2019/11/12/toward-placekeeping-how-design-dialogue-can-make -cities-better-everyone.

Schermerhorn, Seth. *Walking to Magdalena: Personhood and Place in Tohono O'odham Songs, Sticks, and Stories.* Lincoln: University of Nebraska Press, 2019.

Schmid, M. K., and G. F. Rogers. "Trends in Fire Occurrence in the Arizona Upland Subdivision of the Sonoran Desert, 1955 to 1983." *Southwestern Naturalist* 33, no. 4 (1988): 437–44.

Schmidt, Cecelia A., Brian F. Powell, and William L. Halvorson. "Plant and Vertebrate Inventory of Organ Pipe Cactus National Monument." Tucson: US Geological Survey Southwest Biological Science Center, 2007.

Schmidt, Jeremy. "Visit the Desert in the Spring before Things Heat Up." *Dallas Morning News*, March 7, 1999.

Schonewald-Cox, C. M., and J. W. Bayless. "The Boundary Model: A Geographical Analysis of Design and Conservation of Nature Reserves." *Biological Conservation* 38 (1986): 305–22.

Schulze, Jeffrey. *Are We Not Foreigners Here? Indigenous Nationalism in the U.S.-Mexico Borderlands.* Chapel Hill: University of North Carolina Press, 2018.

Schwartzman, Amy. *Cultural Placekeeping Guide: How to Create a Network for Local Emergency Action.* CERF+ and South Arts, 2017. https://www.americansforthearts .org/sites/default/files/Cultural-Placekeeping-Guide.pdf.

Scott, Lesli P., Doug Scott, Anita Judson, and Rod Baxter. *Organ Pipe Cactus National Monument Visitor Survey: Data Entry and Analysis.* Denver: National Park Service Denver Service Center, 1989.

"Season of Tradition Ends at Organ Pipe This Weekend." *Ajo Copper News*, March 23, 2011. http://ajo.stparchive.com/Archive/AJO/AJO03232011p003.php?tags= season|of|tradition|ends|at|organ|pipe|this|weekend.

"Security without Walls: The Organ Pipe Experience." Defenders of Wildlife, n.d. Accessed January 25, 2023. https://defenders.org/sites/default/files/publications /security_without_walls.pdf.

Sedelmayr, Jacobo. *Jacobo Sedelmayr: Missionary, Frontiersman, Explorer in Arizona and Sonora, Four Original Manuscript Narratives, 1744–1751.* Translated by Peter Masten Dunne. Tucson: Arizona Pioneers' Historical Society, 1955.

Sellars, Richard West. *Preserving Nature in the National Parks: A History.* New Haven, CT: Yale University Press, 1997.

Sellers, W. D., and R. H. Hill. *Arizona Climate, 1931–1972.* 2nd ed. Tucson: University of Arizona Press, 1974.

Seper, Jerry. "140 Agents Will Be Sent to Border: Security Chief Cites Crackdown on Terrorism, Smuggling, Illegal Immigration." *Washington Times*, March 20, 2003.

———. "Desert Beacons Lead to Illegals." *Washington Times*, March 15, 2007.

Severe, Don. "Community Columnist: Park Rangers' Changing Role Is Deadly." *Green Valley (AZ) News and Sun*, August 17, 2010.

Sheridan, Thomas E. *The Border and Its Bodies: The Embodiment of Risk along the U.S.-Mexico Line*. Tucson: University of Arizona Press, 2019.

———. "Human Ecology of the Sonoran Desert." Arizona-Sonora Desert Museum. Accessed November 17, 2016. http://www.desertmuseum.org/books/nhsd_human_ecology.php.

———. Introduction to *Last Water on the Devil's Highway: A Cultural and Natural History of Tinajas Altas*, edited by Bill Broyles, Gayle Harrison Hartmann, Thomas E. Sheridan, Gary Paul Nabhan, and Mary Charlotte Thurtle, 3–7. Tucson: University of Arizona Press, 2012.

———. *Landscapes of Fraud: Mission Tumacácori, the Baca Float, and the Betrayal of the O'odham*. Tucson: University of Arizona Press, 2006.

Sheridan, Thomas E., and Bill Broyles. "First Europeans to Forty-Niners: 1540–1854." In *Last Water on the Devil's Highway: A Cultural and Natural History of Tinajas Altas*, edited by Bill Broyles, Gayle Harrison Hartmann, Thomas E. Sheridan, Gary Paul Nabhan, and Mary Charlotte Thurtle, 71–113. Tucson: University of Arizona Press, 2012.

Shreve, Forrest. "The Plant Life of the Sonoran Desert." *Scientific Monthly* 42 (March 1936): 195–213.

———. "The Problems of the Desert." *Scientific Monthly* 38 (March 1934): 199–209.

Silver, Robin. "Organ Pipe Cactus National Monument Damaged by Border Wall Flood Obstruction." Center for Biological Diversity press release. Accessed January 25, 2023. https://www.biologicaldiversity.org/news/press_releases/2008/border-wall-08-15-2008.html.

Slattery, Ryan. "Protecting the Parks along the Border." *Washington Post*, April 26, 2004. http://www.latinamericanstudies.org/immigration/parks.htm.

Smith, Ida. "Secret under the Dunes." *Desert Magazine*, November 1967.

Smith, Joel. "The Road West: An Adventure in Arizona's Organ Pipe Cactus National Monument." Cactus Lovers, October 2005. Accessed November 17, 2016. http://cactuslovers.com/organ-pipe-cactus-national-monument.htm.

"Sonoran Desert Celebrated at 4-Day Symposium." *Ajo Copper News*, March 24, 2010. http://ajo.stparchive.com/Archive/AJO/AJO03242010p001.php?tags=sonoran|desert|celebrated|at|4-day|symposium.

Soto, Gabriella. "Object Afterlives and the Burden of History: Between 'Trash' and 'Heritage' in the Steps of Migrants." *American Anthropologist* 120, no. 3 (2018): 460–73. https://anthrosource.onlinelibrary.wiley.com/doi/full/10.1111/aman.13055.

"Southwestern Monuments Monthly Reports." National Park Service. Accessed November 14, 2013. http://npshistory.com/newsletters/sw_mon_rpt/index.htm.

Spellenberg, Richard. *Sonoran Desert Wildflowers: A Field Guide to Common Species of the Sonoran Desert, Including Anza-Borrego Desert State Park, Saguaro National Park, Organ Pipe Cactus National Monument, Ironwood Forest National Monument, and the Sonoran Portion of Joshua Tree National Park*. Guilford, CT: Globe Pequot Press, 2003.

Spence, Mark D. *Dispossessing the Wilderness: Indian Removal and the Making of the National Parks.* New York: Oxford University Press, 1999.

Steenbergh, W. F. *A Report on Recent Ecological Problems at Quitobaquito Springs, Organ Pipe National Monument, Arizona.* National Park Service report to Office of Natural Science Studies. n.d.

Steenbergh, W. F., and P. L. Warren. *Preliminary Ecological Investigation of Natural Community Status and Organ Pipe Cactus National Monument.* Technical report. Tucson: Cooperative National Park Resources Studies Unit, University of Arizona, 1977.

Stegner, Wallace. "The Best Idea We Ever Had: An Overview." *Wilderness*, Spring 1983, 4–13.

Stevens, Stan, ed. *Conservation through Cultural Survival: Indigenous Peoples and Protected Areas.* Washington, DC: Island Press, 1997.

Stewart, Kenneth M. "Southern Papago Salt Pilgrimages." *Masterkey* 39 (1965): 84–91.

St. John, Rachel. *Line in the Sand: A History of the Western U.S.-Mexico Border.* Princeton, NJ: Princeton University Press, 2011.

Stone, Erin. "Video Shows Groundwater Drilling near Sensitive Spring as Border Wall Construction Continues." *Arizona Republic* (Phoenix), December 21, 2019. https://www.azcentral.com/story/news/local/arizona-environment/2019/12/21/groundwater-drilling-border-wall-could-impact-quitobaquito-springs/2710335001/.

Storms, C. Gilbert. *Reconnaissance in Sonora: Charles D. Poston's 1854 Exploration of Mexico and the Gadsden Purchase.* Tucson: University of Arizona Press, 2015.

Suzán, Humberto, Guadalupe Malda, Duncan T. Patten, and Gary P. Nabhan. "Effects of Exploitation and Park Boundaries on Legume Trees in the Sonoran Desert." *Conservation Biology* 6 (December 1999): 1497–1501.

Swantek, Pamela J., William L. Halvorson, and Cecil R. Schwalbe. *GIS Database Development to Analyze Fire History in Southern Arizona and Beyond: An Example from Saguaro National Park.* Technical report. Tucson: Cooperative National Park Resources Studies Unit, University of Arizona, January 1999.

Sykes, Godfrey. "The Camino del Diablo: With Notes on a Journey in 1925." *Geographical Review* 17 (January 1927): 62–74.

Talley, Jenell. "Going, Going, Gone?" *National Parks* 78 (2004): 52–53.

Taylor, Jennifer. "Populus fremontii." In *Fire Effects Information System.* US Department of Agriculture, Forest Service, Rocky Mountain Research Station, Fire Sciences Laboratory. 2000. https://www.fs.usda.gov/database/feis/plants/tree/popfre/all.html.

Teague, Lynn S. "Prehistory and the Traditions of the O'odham and Hopi." *Kiva* 58, no. 4 (1993): 435–54.

Thomas, Robert K. "Papago Land Use West of the Papago Indian Reservation, South of the Gila River and the Problem of Sand Papago Identity." In *Ethnology of Northwest Mexico: A Sourcebook*, edited by Randall H. McGuire, 357–99. New York: Garland, 1991.

Tipton, Ron. "Illegal Marijuana Points to Park Funding." *USA Today*, October 20, 2015.

Toomey, Anne H. "The Making of a Conservation Landscape: Towards a Practice of Interdependence." *Conservation and Society* 18, no. 1 (2020): 25–36.

Truett, Samuel. *Fugitive Landscapes: The Forgotten History of the U.S.-Mexico Borderlands*. New Haven, CT: Yale University Press, 2006.

Truett, Samuel, and Elliott Young. "Making Transnational History: Nations, Regions, and Borderlands." In *Continental Crossroads: Re-Mapping U.S.-Mexico Borderlands History*, edited by Samuel Truett and Elliott Young, 1–32. Durham, NC: Duke University Press, 2004.

"Trump's Border Wall Threatens World Heritage Site: Groups Request 'In Danger' Status for El Pinacate Biosphere Reserve, Border Wall Threatens Protected Sonoran Desert Wildlife." Center for Biological Diversity press release, May 23, 2017. https://www.biologicaldiversity.org/news/press_releases/2017/border-wall-05-23-2017.php.

Tsing, Anna Lowenhaupt. *Friction: An Ethnography of Global Connection*. Princeton, NJ: Princeton University Press, 2005.

Tyrrell, Ian. *Crisis of the Wasteful Nation: Empire and Conservation in Theodore Roosevelt's America*. Chicago: University of Chicago Press, 2015.

Underhill, Ruth M. *Papago Indian Religion*. New York: Columbia University Press, 1946.

———. *Papago Woman: An Intimate Portrait of American Indian Culture*. Long Grove, IL: Waveland Press, 1979.

UNESCO. *Biosphere Reserves: The Seville Strategy and the Statutory Framework of the World Network*. Paris: UNESCO, 1996. http://www.mab.cas.cn/ryswqjh/swqbhq/201411/W020141113678526165131.pdf.

Urrea, Luis Alberto. *The Devil's Highway: A True Story*. New York: Back Bay Books, 2004.

US Congress, House of Representatives. "Honoring the Organ Pipe Cactus National Monument for Being Recognized by the Intermountain Region's Wilderness Stewardship Awards Program." *Congressional Record—Extension of Remarks*, February 25, 2010, E238–39. Accessed January 25, 2023. https://www.govinfo.gov/content/pkg/CREC-2010-02-25/pdf/CREC-2010-02-25-pt1-PgE238-6.pdf.

———. *United States and Mexican Boundary Survey: Report of William H. Emory, Major, First Cavalry and U.S. Commissioner*. 34th Cong., 1st Sess. House Executive Document 135. Washington, DC: Cornelius Wendell, Printer, 1857.

US Congress, House of Representatives, Committee on Government Reform, Subcommittee on Criminal Justice, Drug Policy, and Human Resources. *The Impact of the Drug Trade on Border Security and National Parks: Hearing before the Subcommittee on Criminal Justice, Drug Policy, and Human Resources of the Committee on Government Reform, House of Representatives*. 108th Cong., 1st Sess. (March 10, 2003). Washington, DC: US Government Printing Office, 2003.

US Congress, House of Representatives, Committee on Interior and Insular Affairs, Subcommittee on National Parks and Recreation. *To Prohibit Certain Incompatible Activities within Any Area of the National Park System*. 94th Cong., 1st Sess. (October 6, 1975).

US Congress, Senate. "Organ Pipe Cactus National Monument." Report 108-100. 108th Cong., 1st Sess. (July 11, 2003). https://www.congress.gov/congressional-report/108th-congress/senate-report/100/1.

———. "Report of the Boundary Commission upon the Survey and Re-Marking of the Boundary between the United States and Mexico West of the Rio Grande, 1891 to 1896." Document 247. 55th Cong., 2d Sess. (1898).

———. "Report of the Secretary of the Interior in Compliance with a Resolution of the Senate, of January 22, Communicating a Report and Map of A. B. Gray, Relative to the Mexican Boundary." Senate Executive Document 55. 33d Cong., 2d Sess. (1855).

US Department of the Interior. "Environmental Assessment: Widen North Puerto Blanco Road: Organ Pipe Cactus National Monument, Arizona." Arizona, 2002.

———. "Immigration Fiscal Impact Statement." 2007–2008.

———. "Interior and Homeland Security Collaborate on Border Protection, Resource Conservation along US/Mexico Border." State News Service, 2010.

———. *Organ Pipe Cactus National Monument: Draft General Management Plan, Development Concept Plans, Environmental Impact Statement.* Ajo, AZ, 1995.

US General Accounting Office. *Border Security: Agencies Need to Better Coordinate Their Strategies and Operations on Federal Lands.* June 2004.

US Government Accountability Office. *Illegal Immigration.* August 2006.

Vance, Haynes C., and Bruce B. Huckell. *Murray Springs: A Clovis Site with Multiple Activity Areas in the San Pedro Valley, Arizona.* Tucson: University of Arizona Press, 2007.

Vanderpool, Tim. "Amid Cactuses, a Park's War on Smuggling." *Christian Science Monitor*, June 19, 2001.

———. "Parks Under Siege." *National Parks* 76, no. 9–10 (November/December 2002): 23–27.

Van Devender, T. R., A. M. Rea, and W. E. Hall. "Faunal Analysis of Late Quaternary Vertebrates from Organ Pipe Cactus National Monument, Southwestern Arizona." *Southwestern Naturalist* 36 (1991): 94–106.

Van Devender, Thomas R. "The Deep History of the Sonoran Desert." In *A Natural History of the Sonoran Desert*, edited by Steven J. Phillips and Patricia Wentworth Comus, 61–69. Tucson: Arizona-Sonora Desert Museum Press, 2000.

Van Dyke, John C. *The Desert.* Salt Lake City: Gibbs M. Smith, 1987.

Van Horn, Lawrence F. "A Document and Indigenous Politics." *Practicing Anthropology* 22, no. 3 (Summer 2000): 39–42.

Van Valkenburgh, Richard. "Tom Childs of Ten-Mile Wash." *Desert Magazine*, December 1945.

Veech, Andrew S. *Archaeological Survey of 18.2 Kilometers (11.3 Miles) of the U.S.-Mexican International Border, Organ Pipe Cactus National Monument, Pima Country, Arizona.* July 2019. https://media.azpm.org/master/document/2019/9/20/pdf/orpi2019bdraftreport07252019b_final_redacted_reduced.pdf.

Viele, Egbert L. "The East and West Boundary Line between the United States and Mexico." *Journal of the American Geographical Society of New York* 14 (1882): 259–84.

"Virtual Meeting about Quitobaquito Will Be Held by ISDA on Thursday." *Ajo Copper News*, October 6, 2020. http://ajo.stparchive.com/Archive/AJO/AJO10062020P009.php?tags=virtual|meeting|about|quitobaquito|will|be|held|by|isda|on|thursday.

Waddell, Jack O. *Papago Indians at Work.* Tucson: University of Arizona Press, 1969.

"The Wall to Be Topic of a Town Meeting." *Ajo Copper News*, June 25, 2019. http://ajo
  .stparchive.com/Archive/AJO/AJO06252019P001.php?tags=the|wall|to|be|topic
  |of|a|town|meeting.

Walter, Sue. "Public Access Increases." Organ Pipe Cactus National Monument. September 17, 2014. https://www.nps.gov/orpi/learn/news/public-access-increases
  .htm.

Walters, L. L., and E. F. Legner. "Impact of the Desert Pupfish, *Cyprinodon macularius*
  and *Gambusia affinis* on Fauna in Pond Ecosystems." *Hilcardia* 48, no. 3 (1980):
  1–18.

Warren, Louis. *The Hunter's Game: Poachers and Conservationists in Twentieth-Century
  America*. New Haven, CT: Yale University Press, 1997.

Warren, Peter L. *Vegetation of Organ Pipe Cactus National Monument*. Tucson: Cooperative National Park Resources Studies Unit, University of Arizona, 1981.

Warren, Peter L., and L. Susan Anderson. *Vegetation Recovery Following Livestock
  Removal near Quitobaquito Spring Organ Pipe Cactus National Monument*. Technical report. Tucson: Cooperative National Park Resources Studies Unit, University
  of Arizona, January 1987.

Watson, Traci. "National Parks an Escape for Drug Smugglers." *USA Today*, December
  10, 1999.

Watt, Laura Alice. *The Paradox of Preservation: Wilderness and Working Landscapes at
  Point Reyes National Seashore*. Berkeley: University of California Press, 2017.

Wauer, Roland H. *Birding the Southwestern National Parks*. College Station: Texas
  A&M University Press, 2004.

Weber, David J. *The Spanish Frontier in North America*. New Haven, CT: Yale University Press, 1992.

West, Elliot. *The Contested Plains: Indians, Goldseekers, and the Rush to Colorado*. Lawrence: University Press of Kansas, 1998.

West, Robert C. *Sonora: Its Geographical Personality*. Austin: University of Texas Press,
  1993.

Whisnant, Anne Mitchell, Marla R. Miller, Gary B. Nash, and David Thelen. *Imperiled Promise: The State of History in the National Park Service*. Bloomington, IN:
  Organization of American Historians, 2011. https://www.nps.gov/parkhistory
  /hisnps/imperiled_promise.pdf.

Wigglesworth, Zeke. "Arizona's Giant Desert Plants Are Stars of Its Deserted Parks."
  Toronto Star, December 2, 1995.

Wild, Peter. *John C. Van Dyke: The Desert*. Boise: Boise State University Printing and
  Graphic Services, 1988.

"Wildlife Habitat Supporters Are Nearing Goal." *Ajo Copper News*, December 26,
  2012. http://ajo.stparchive.com/Archive/AJO/AJO12262012P08.php?tags=wild
  life|habitat|supporters|are|nearing|goal.

Wilkerson, Isabel. *Caste: The Origins of Our Discontents*. New York: Random House,
  2020.

Williams, Logan. "The Disappearance of Quitobaquito Springs: Tracking Hydrologic
  Change with Google Earth Engine." Bellingcat, October 1, 2020. https://www
  .bellingcat.com/resources/2020/10/01/the-disappearance-of-quitobaquito-springs
  -tracking-hydrologic-change-with-google-earth-engine/.

Wyckoff, William. *Riding Shotgun with Norman Wallace: Rephotographing the Arizona Landscape.* Tucson: University of Arizona Press, 2020.

Wyllys, R. K. "Henry A. Crabb: A Tragedy of the Sonora Frontier." *Pacific Historical Review* 9 (1940): 183–94.

Zepeda, Ofelia. "The Sand Papago Oral History Project." Oral history. Tucson: Western Archeological and Conservation Center, National Park Service, 1985.

INDEX

A'al Vaipia. *See* Quitobaquito
A'al Waippia. *See* Quitobaquito
Adang, Uma, 141
agriculture, 2, 124, 134–36; Akimel
    O'odham, 23–25, 44; American
    dreams of, 43–44, 49; Apache, 28;
    boarding school labor, 67; origins of,
    20, 22, 24; Quitobaquito, 25, 37–38,
    45–49, 51, 53, 62–63, 70–73, 90,
    122, 141; Sonoyta River, 29, 82, 120;
    Spanish, 26–30, 32; Tohono O'odham,
    23, 27. *See also* Hohokam
Aguajita Wash, 2
Ajo, Ariz., 43, 64, 118; copper mines,
    42, 46, 50, 57, 60, 62, 67, 68, 122,
    127; highway to Sonoyta, 60, 100;
    O'odham inhabitants, 5, 12, 38, 48,
    53, 55, 87; railroad, 50; revitalization,
    127–29; transborder migrants, 106
Ajo Mountain Drive, 99
Ajo Mountains, 19, 24, 25, 27, 41, 62, 64,
    65, 71
ak chin farming, 23
Ak-Chin Indian Community, 119
Akimel O'odham, 29, 88; border
    surveyors' opinions of, 44; name,
    23; relations with other tribes, 24,
    34, 35; storytellers, 16. *See also*
    agriculture
Alamo Canyon, 68
Alcatraz, 116–17, 120
Allison, William, 16
Altar River, 27

Altar (Sonora), 39, 40
American Indian civil rights movement,
    84, 87, 116–17, 120. *See also* American
    Indian Movement; Red Power
    Movement
American Indian Movement, 78
American Indian Religious Freedom Act,
    121
Antiquities Act (1906), 56, 65, 68
Apaches (Ndee), 20, 28, 30, 32–33, 35,
    41–42, 44, 95–96
archaeology, 14, 16, 99, 109, 140;
    Hohokam, 21–22; in Organ Pipe
    Cactus National Monument, 21.
    See also Organ Pipe Cactus National
    Monument; Quitobaquito
Areneños. *See* Hia C'ed O'odham
Arizona, 1, 16, 18, 20–21, 23, 40–46,
    49–54, 58–69, 73–74, 76, 79, 80–90,
    93, 95–96, 98, 100–102, 106–8, 115,
    123, 126–28,134
Arizona Archeological Center, 85
Arizona Highway 85, 100, 106, 137
Arizona Mining and Trading Company,
    50, 60
Arizona Republic, 76, 83, 101
Arizona Small Miners Association, 69
Arizona-Sonora Desert Museum, 80
Arizona State Historic Preservation Office,
    87, 89, 93, 115
Arizona State Museum, 86, 123
Armour Packing Company, 54
Australia, 135

Printed in the USA
CPSIA information can be obtained
at www.ICGtesting.com
LVHW041532151223
766513LV00002B/327